Mary Tudor

DAVID LOADES

AMBERLEY

This edition first published 2012

Amberley Publishing
The Hill, Stroud
Gloucestershire, GL5 4EP

www.amberley-books.com

British Library Cataloguing in Publication Data.
A catalogue record for this book is available from the British Library.

ISBN 978-1-4456-0818-1

Typesetting and Origination by Amberley Publishing.
Printed in Great Britain.

Contents

PREFACE

All the kings and queens of England deserve to be revisited every few years. This is not only because new research reveals further information about their lives and careers, but also because our own perceptions and agendas change. Sir Geoffrey Elton wrote many years ago that to write history backwards – that is, to select historical evidence to suit a contemporary purpose – is the sin against the Holy Ghost. Protestants, Catholics, Whigs, Marxists, feminists, and no doubt others, have all been guilty of this sin in varying degrees, and such 'schools' of historical writing are now rightly regarded with suspicion. I like to think of myself as a neo-pragmatist, but I am also conscious of changing my mind over the years. Sometimes this is because of other people's research, sometimes because of my own, and sometimes simply the result of rethinking the meaning of familiar evidence.

It is now nearly twenty years since I wrote *Mary Tudor: A Life*, and although I have not changed my mind about her in striking ways, I have rethought aspects of her life and reign. I have also learned more about Mary's husband, Philip of Spain, at this crucial early stage of his career. Since I first addressed the subject over forty years ago, I have learned a lot from Michael Graves, the late Jennifer Loach, Glyn Redworth, Mia Rodriguez Salgado, Judith Richards and a number of others. Most particularly, I have benefited recently from collaborations with Charles Knighton and Eamon Duffy, both of whom have – in different ways – applied correctives to my established views.

I should also like to thank those who aided this book to completion: Mark Hawkins-Dady, who commissioned and oversaw the first edition; Jonathan Reeve, who took on the second, and Patricia Hymans, the indexer.

David Loades, October 2010

INTRODUCTION

In terms of her own ideas and purposes, Mary Tudor was a failure, and nothing can conceal that fact. Like Richard III or Edward II she has consequently had a loser's press. For about four hundred years the predominant tenor of English historical writing was Protestant, and to the historians in that tradition she was 'Mary, Mary, quite contrary', flying in the face of what John O'Sullivan would later call (in a different context) 'manifest destiny'. This was a perception magnificently summed up in *1066 and All That* in the words 'since England was bound to be C. of E. anyway, all the burnings were wasted'. It was also Messrs Sellers and Yeatman who called her (with sharp insight) 'Broody Mary'.

It is easy now to mock such a blinkered view, but anyone who was at school in England before about 1980 is likely to have been taught something very like it – unless the period was omitted altogether. More importantly, books written as late as the 1960s (and some more recently still) glossed over the reign as being of small importance. Henry VIII was important because of the break with Rome and the rise of Parliament. Edward VI was important because he was the first Protestant monarch, and because his reign saw much social upheaval. Elizabeth was important because she presided over the English Renaissance and defeated the Armada. But Mary was not important because her reign was a dead end and the only thing she did (apart from burning Protestants, hence 'Bloody Mary') was to lose England's last French possession, Calais.

The early Protestant writers John Foxe and John Strype never made the mistake of thinking that Mary did not matter; but to them (and particularly to Foxe) she was a dire warning of what could happen when a lawful ruler was seduced by the Devil. Foxe's legacy lay less in learned history and more in popular prejudice. Mary herself was not his target, but the Catholic Church was, and centuries of popular anti-Catholicism sprang from Foxe's *Acts and Monuments*. Because of her marriage to the Spanish Habsburg Philip, Mary also became the godmother of the association between popery and arbitrary (foreign) power. For about three hundred years she was a hate figure for liberal Anglicans and evangelicals alike, and when those storms had died down, she found herself dismissed as insignificant. More recently, a tendency towards broadly based social and economic history, and a rejection of 'reign-based' history, have also tended to undervalue the period.

Only historians of religion have not followed that trend, and important new work has been done on the Church of Mary by Tom Mayer, Eamon Duffy, Bill Wizeman, Lucy Wooding and John Edwards. This has been a very welcome development, not least because Catholic historical writing has traditionally been almost as blinkered as Protestant. To near contemporaries such as Nicholas Harpesfield and Robert Persons, Mary's failure in so noble a cause was an inexplicable tragedy. Later historians in the same tradition, such as John Lingard and Philip Hughes, shook their heads sadly, and blamed her bad health or her mistaken marriage. Eamon Duffy is no less saddened by Mary's failure, but his interpretation is both more sophisticated and more open, particularly showing the strength of the continuities that bound the restored Catholic Church to its pre-Reformation roots. The fact that these recent historians of religion in Mary's reign do not agree with one another has created a fruitful discussion.

While contributing somewhat to this discussion, the main concern of this book is with the queen herself. In an era of personal monarchy, the character and personality of the occupant of the throne was necessarily of great importance. No one knew how to deal with a sovereign lady. The world of high politics (or even low politics) was a masculine preserve. No public office above the level of churchwarden was open to a woman – except the crown itself. How did a councillor react to having a creature by custom regarded as weak, vacillating and gullible on the throne? How did a courtier react to having to deal with a privy chamber that was now also a boudoir? The fact that these problems were not openly discussed did not make them any less real. There were examples abroad, but none very close, either in time or circumstances. Isabella of Castile had been a similar sovereign, but it is very unlikely that any of Mary's councillors knew how she had conducted business. Mary of Hungary (regent of the Netherlands) was much closer and more familiar, but she was an agent, not a sovereign; and the queen of Scotland was an adolescent living in France.

At Mary's accession the country was at peace, so there were no military priorities to confuse matters, and her councillors seem to have set out to advise her in the same way they would have done a king. However, they were deceived, for one of the first things that she did was to put her marriage into the hands of her cousin, the Holy Roman Emperor Charles V, because of an emotional dependency going back over many years. Thus the councillors found that the queen had excluded them from the marital decision-making process – something that no king would ever have done. However, they then proceeded to negotiate a treaty that was explicitly designed to protect the realm from the weakness that might result from having a (female) ruler who was also the subordinate partner in a marriage. That process they carried further by legally 'un-gendering' the crown; but in truth nobody knew how the husband/wife partnership would affect the royal prerogative. It is not surprising that some of them sought to return to firm conceptual ground by accepting Philip as a real king rather than a consort. Both Mary and her subjects were confused by an unprecedented constitutional situation. It was easier to resolve the gender problems of the crown in law than it was in practice or perception.

Abroad, in Continental Europe the power relations were reversed. Although in theory Mary shared all her husband's titles, outside of England she had no role. Even in the Low Countries, which any child of the marriage stood to inherit along with England, she was presented simply as a consort, as is made plain by the complex iconography of several windows in Dutch churches.[1]

In terms of personal qualities, Mary was nobody's fool and nobody's puppet. She was intelligent, hard working and in many respects both tough and obstinate. Her hatred of heresy was a consuming passion, and in her strength of will she ignored everyone, including Philip, who tried to persuade her to take a more dispassionate approach. She was, however, extremely conventional in her perception of a woman's limitations. She knew that she was expected to be both indecisive and emotionally dependent, and up to a point she was both. The main reason why she married was certainly to get an heir, but another was to have a partner who could handle those matters that were not by custom deemed 'pertinent to women'. Repeatedly she besought Philip to return to her because the country needed his 'strong hand'. Whether or not she really wanted to marry, we do not know; but marriage, like so many other things, was a duty imposed on her by her status. A less conventional or more independent woman might have found ways of coping with these problems – as Elizabeth subsequently did. Mary's mother had brought her up to be a good Catholic and a good wife, but not a ruler, and many of Mary's problems stemmed from the fact that she found the roles incompatible. Hence, perhaps, that 'sourness of temper' which Gilbert Burnet found in her, and to which he attributed her willingness to follow the edicts of her 'popish clergy'.

These same problems put Philip in an impossible position. It was not unprecedented, however. His great-grandfather, Ferdinand of Aragon, had been in a rather similar situation in respect of Castile, but Ferdinand's wife, Isabella, had been (except in her piety) a very different sort of woman from Mary. Philip must have found Mary a very frustrating consort. Most of the time that he was in England she was convinced that she was pregnant, and consequently was unavailable to him. Once he had left, she was simultaneously begging him to return and refusing to give him either a realistic share in the government, or a coronation, or any reasonable financial support. As the Duke of Alba rightly observed, Philip, although the King of England in name, had no sovereignty in his own realm. He could manage, advise and cajole, but he could not command. However, he could still do business with the English council, and also with at least some of the English nobility, not – as the Count of Feria believed – because he was able to bribe them, but because he was a man and (in spite of language difficulties) they could understand him on that basis.

Philip's attitude towards England is an interesting subject in itself. When the possibility of marriage to Mary was raised, he seems to have been torn between ambition for a prestigious 'crown matrimonial' and a reluctance to link himself to a kinswoman who was significantly older than himself, by eleven years. The country itself was the home of myth. On the one hand it was the mysterious land of Albion, home to the mist-girt castles of Arthur and of romantic chivalry, and on the other hand it was a nest of villainous heretics and schismatics – the land of Anne Boleyn and of the murderers of the papal loyalists John Fisher and Thomas More. Once Philip had allowed his ambition to be a king to overcome his reluctance to accept so limiting a treaty, his own attitude seems to have become pragmatic. He even learned a few words of English: Mary carefully taught him to say 'Good night my lords and ladies', though this was perhaps the limit of his proficiency in the tongue. With Latin-speaking clerics and nobles of lineage he was at home, and he exerted himself seriously to bring the English Church back into the papal fold. What he really thought of his new subjects and their peculiar ways, we do not know. Most of our knowledge of the 'Spanish mission' comes from his courtiers and followers, who came with a full baggage of prejudices that they had no intention of relinquishing.

To a much greater extent than Mary, Philip was image conscious. He knew what magnificence was, and what part it played in royalty. Unfortunately the imagery that he understood was mainly Imperial and religious. He was very good at presenting himself, in paint or stained glass, as Solomon or the son of David. He could also present himself as a Spanish conquistador. But he had not the faintest idea how to be a king of England, and his inability (or unwillingness) to go native, even to a limited degree, meant that there was no lessening of the hostility felt against him. The resulting propaganda concentrated upon his sexual adventures, because it was realised that such tales would cause maximum distress to Mary. Whether he was really as promiscuous as alleged, we do not know, but it is unlikely in view of his rigid piety. On the other hand a man who very seldom saw his wife could well keep a mistress – or a succession of mistresses – without ever feeling called upon to acknowledge the fact.

There is one other contemporary figure in Mary's orbit who has substantially affected what Mary means to us today: her half-sister, successor and nemesis, Elizabeth. Both as a person and as a queen, Mary has always suffered by comparison with Elizabeth – largely because Elizabeth made sure that she would. Recently there has been a tendency to point out that Mary reigned for only five years, where her half-sister reigned for forty-five, so any comparison is invalid. In terms of the achievements of their respective reigns that is probably so, but both were mature women and their personalities can be legitimately contrasted. Mary had something of her father's intelligence, the obstinacy of both her parents, and her mother's compulsive piety. Elizabeth had her father's political instincts, and her mother's wit and feisty sexuality. Mary regarded her sex as a liability; Elizabeth used hers as a weapon. Elizabeth was moody (even violent), indecisive, procrastinating, and always an actress. Nobody really knows to what extent her notorious tendency to change her mind was the result of genuine indecision, or a ploy to keep her councillors on their toes and demonstrate who was in charge. Similarly, we do not really know whether (or when) she decided not to marry, or to what extent her various negotiations were diplomatic devices. What we do know is that her virginity became a symbol of the inviolability of the realm, in total contrast to the popular perception that Mary's Spanish marriage and Catholicism had surrendered national authority to Spanish and Italian priorities. Elizabeth is alleged to have claimed that if she was turned out of the realm in her petticoat, she would 'fare for herself' – and that is a measure of the self-confidence that was her defining characteristic.

By contrast Mary is painfully transparent. Duty to God was her lodestar: it determined her bid for the throne in 1553, her decision to marry Philip, and her ruthless persecution of heretics. There was nothing of the actress in her make-up, and her idea of presenting herself to her subjects was confined to dressing magnificently and surrounding herself with pomp. To Elizabeth there were no 'matters impertinent to women' – in 1588 she even donned armour and proposed to lead her army. To Mary the perceived distinctions of gender formed an intangible but very real barrier that partly determined her relationship with her husband. Altogether Elizabeth was far better equipped by nature to deal with the situation in which she found herself. Both women had passed through difficult and traumatic times as adolescents, but whereas the experience had left Mary in poor health and uncertain of herself, it had left Elizabeth crafty and wary.

Mary's real tragedy is that she was born to be a royal consort, the pious and dutiful wife of a powerful king. Instead she found that God had given her the duty of ruling a realm. What Elizabeth was born to be is anyone's guess, but she coped very successfully with what God threw at her. Considering all these limitations, and the shortness of her time, Mary's reign was, nevertheless, in many respects successful, not least because she set precedents and also made some of the mistakes that Elizabeth was thereby able to avoid. As a person Mary was (as even John Foxe recognised) a tragic figure, but as a queen she was important. In fact there is a lot to be said for looking at England from 1553 to 1603 as the realm of the queens – the time when England came to terms with the challenging fact of a woman on the throne. This is the story of the first of those powerful women.

I

THE CHILD

Mary's story begins nearly thirty years before her birth, when the three-year-old Catherine of Aragon was first proposed as the future wife of Arthur, the eldest son of King Henry VII of England. Catherine was the youngest child of Ferdinand of Aragon and Isabella of Castile, known as the Catholic Kings, who had united the crowns of Spain by their marriage over twenty years before.[1] The Trastamaras were one of the oldest and best established ruling families of Europe, and the Tudors were parvenus, whose dubious claim to the throne of England had been established on the battlefield in the year of Catherine's birth. Henry VII's approach was therefore strictly practical. He was beset by pretenders to the crown, and he needed all the support and recognition that he could get. The pope had already obliged, and if he could persuade the Trastamaras to follow suit, his position would be greatly strengthened.

Young Catherine was a small player in her father's dynastic schemes, and the English alliance seemed attractive enough, so an agreement in principle was reached, and the child grew up to think of herself as the Princess of Wales, the betrothed of Arthur, heir to the crown of England. In fact, the situation was not quite so straightforward. The deaths of Catherine's elder sister Isabella in childbed in 1493, and of her brother the Infante Juan in 1497, threw her father's plans into disarray, and it seemed for a while as though she might have to be married off elsewhere. However, when her sister Juanna bore a healthy

15

son to Philip, the son of the Emperor Maximilian, in 1500, and survived the experience, it seemed safe to allow Catherine to come to England. In 1501, at the age of seventeen, she reached London, to be greeted with the most lavish celebrations of which England was capable, and was wedded to the fifteen-year-old Arthur.[2] That marriage, which lasted barely six months, was to be the source of the crisis that was later to destroy Catherine's life, and to inflict terrible damage upon her daughter Mary.

Arthur died at Ludlow on 2 April 1502. It was said of him, as it had been said of the Infante Juan five years earlier, that premature and excessive sexual activity had proved fatal, but his death is more likely to have been caused by pneumonia. It later became a significant question whether the marriage had ever been consummated at all. Catherine had denied it, but by then she had good reason to claim that she had gone to her second husband as *virgo intacta*. Arthur apparently made adolescent boasts about the subject, but no certainty is possible. At the age of eighteen, Catherine had thus become a widow with uncertain prospects. Neither Henry VII nor Ferdinand wanted to end the connection that the marriage had established, and Henry had no desire to refund a substantial dowry, so there was immediate talk of her remarriage to Arthur's younger brother, Henry. However, Henry was only eleven years old, and the propriety of such a marriage under canon law was uncertain. As a precaution, a dispensation was obtained from Pope Julius II, which, again as a precaution, assumed that the marriage had been consummated, since that would have constituted the greater impediment.[3] This was to cause a great deal of trouble in the future. Catherine's mother, Isabella, was in favour of the marriage, but she died in November 1504, before young Henry had reached the minimum age of co-habitation, and that seriously altered the situation in Spain.

Ferdinand was King of Aragon and had no title to the larger kingdom of Castile. Nor did Isabella give him one. At her death her heir was her elder daughter Juana (known as Joanna to the English), married to Philip of Burgundy and the mother of two sons. However, there were those in Castile who did not want the foreigner Philip as king, and the next heir was the currently unmarried Catherine. Since Ferdinand was also hoping to capitalise upon the anti-Burgundian feeling to secure some title for himself, the last thing he wanted was Catherine back in Spain. Meanwhile, Henry VII had gone off the whole idea of a second marriage, and caused his son to repudiate the agreement when he reached the age of fourteen in 1505. Catherine was left in limbo by these developments, and she consoled herself, with her few remaining Spanish servants, by multiplying her religious devotions. She was twenty-one, lonely and short of money.[4] In Spain, Philip and Juana secured their title, and Ferdinand was forced to retreat to Aragon, but in 1506 Philip died and Juana became (at least temporarily) deranged. This enabled Ferdinand to re-establish himself, and made him more reluctant than ever to welcome Catherine home. By this time she had convinced herself that it was the will of God that she should marry Prince Henry, and this gave her an adequate incentive to wait quietly while the king's health deteriorated. On 21 April 1509 Henry VII died.

Henry VIII was two months short of his eighteenth birthday, but a regency was never suggested. He became king, and one of his first acts was to marry his sister-in-law. Whether he had fancied her for some time, or heeded his father's dying wish (as he claimed), his councillors were astounded and Catherine triumphantly vindicated. All the hypothetical objections – the question of consummation with Arthur ('consanguinity'), his own repudiation of the marriage agreement – were simply swept aside. Ferdinand's assent was taken for granted. They were married in a low-key ceremony at the house of the Franciscan Observant monks at Greenwich in early June, and crowned together on Midsummer's Day. Catherine was twenty-four and, if her portraits are anything to go by, remarkably attractive. It was a time of great joy for her, and for the whole court, and within a few weeks she was pregnant. Henry, meanwhile, was intent on flexing his muscles in a different direction by picking a quarrel with Louis XII of France. The older councillors whom he had inherited from his father were appalled, but there was no gainsaying this magnificent young man, and his wife busied herself resurrecting the old alliance with her father. Not even Henry believed that he could fight the French on his own and Catherine became for a while his chief foreign-policy adviser.

Things then began to go wrong. The Anglo-Spanish treaty was duly signed, but the queen's child was born dead. With hindsight, this is more significant than it looked at the time. Stillbirths were not uncommon, and were not necessarily ominous. By May 1510 Catherine was pregnant again, and on New

Year's Day 1511 delivered an apparently healthy son, who was immediately christened 'Henry'.[5] For a few weeks, as the king continued his preparations for war, his queen enjoyed the luxury of being the mother of the heir to the throne. The war duly proceeded according to plan, but Prince Henry did not. On 21 February he died, almost before the sounds of his splendid christening tournament had faded away. This time the royal couple were devastated, and a shadow fell between them. The conventional wisdom of the time was that infant deaths declared a constitutional weakness in the woman. Catherine redoubled her pious exercises, seeking for an explanation of how she could have offended the God who was afflicting her in this way. Henry went to war and, if court gossip is to be believed, to the beds of other women.

However, their relationship was not seriously damaged. In the summer of 1513, while the king was campaigning in France, his queen acted as regent; and the forces led by the Earl of Surrey on her behalf won a more significant victory over the Scots at Flodden than Henry enjoyed over the French at the capture of Tournai. Nevertheless it was Henry, in a mood of romantic chivalry, who brought the token of his victory to lay at her feet. As the war was coming to an end in the summer of 1514, she conceived again. This time the outcome is less clear, but it appears that in December she suffered another stillbirth, this time of a boy. The omens were now distinctly bad and could not be ignored. There was no heir, and Catherine had failed again. She was nearly thirty, and her time was getting short.

Catherine was also now less influential politically than she had been. Henry did not hold her responsible when her father Ferdinand signed a separate treaty with France in the summer of 1514, but he certainly felt betrayed.[6] He also had his own man, in the person of Thomas Wolsey, rapidly emerging as his closest and most influential adviser. Catherine was wise enough not to resent this openly, but her role as a *de facto* councillor was effectively over. As she was forced to retreat from the council chamber to the boudoir, the queen found herself challenged there as well. Henry probably did not consciously intend to revenge himself for Ferdinand's defection by taking a mistress, but that is effectively what happened. Elizabeth Blount's relationship with the king has a shadowy start, and we cannot be sure that the covert gossip of the time refers to her, but it may well have done. Threatened on all sides in the early part of

1515, and with a husband resting from his martial preoccupations, Catherine had only one weapon. In the late summer she became pregnant again. This time the rejoicings were muted, and anxiety was more obvious than expectation. However, on 18 February 1516, in the palace at Greenwich, a healthy child was born. Unfortunately, it was a girl, where every prophet who had ventured to pronounce had forecast a boy. A few days later she was christened with great pomp – and named Mary.[7]

In spite of their undoubted disappointment, Henry and Catherine put on a great show of rejoicing. Successful procreation had restored their relationship, if not the queen's political influence. A few days before Mary's birth, Catherine's father Ferdinand had died, and that precluded any possibility of her influencing Anglo-Spanish relations. His grandson, Charles of Ghent, succeeded to both crowns at the age of sixteen, nominally ruling Castile jointly with his mother, Juana, although she was now permanently confined as insane, and known as *la loca* ('the mad'). Henry paraded his daughter at court, no doubt to demonstrate that she was a whole and perfect child, and referred to her as 'a token of hope'. That was all very well for him. He was twenty-five and in the full vigour of youth. Catherine was thirty-one; she had endured at least four pregnancies, and her beauty was fading fast. It was the spring of 1518 before she conceived again, and this time expectation was again at fever pitch. Would this be the longed-for prince? On 9 November the queen was delivered again – of another daughter – and the only report we have does not say whether she was stillborn or died immediately after. Either way, the child did not survive, and although Catherine quickly recovered her health, this was to be her last conception. She was now thirty-three, and it is quite possible that she went through the menopause soon after. Nothing, of course, was said, and ostensibly the royal couple continued to hope for a male heir, but as time passed the prospect diminished. From Catherine's point of view the pain of this situation was greatly increased by the fact that in 1519 Elizabeth Blount bore Henry a healthy son, whom the king immediately acknowledged, naming him Henry Fitzroy.

A bastard, however, did not solve the succession problem, and Mary emerged from infancy into childhood still the heir to the throne. She had unwittingly performed her first duty as early as 1518, when the Anglo-French treaty that was embraced within the wider settlement known as the Treaty of London contained a provision for her to marry the dauphin of France, an infant even younger than herself. Neither party took this very seriously. Although the provision depended on Mary being Henry's heir, that was only in default of sons, which Henry at the age of twenty-seven was not really willing to contemplate. The person who did take this entente seriously, however, was Charles of Spain. Although he was a signatory of the Treaty of London, with lands in the Low Countries as well as the Iberian peninsula, he was always likely to need leverage against the French, and that Henry was uniquely placed to provide. When Charles became Holy Roman Emperor on the death of his paternal grandfather Maximilian in 1519, and thus held lands almost encircling France, the likelihood of renewed conflict sharply increased. By the time that Francis I of France and Henry held their planned meeting at the field of Cloth of Gold in 1520, their friendship was already souring, and within a few weeks Wolsey had negotiated on his master's behalf a new treaty with Charles that effectively abrogated the earlier treaty with France, and prepared the way for a new war.[8] Mary now found herself, at the age of four, with a new fiancé in the person of the twenty-year-old Emperor. In 1522, when he visited England, she met him for the first and only time, and played the virginals for his entertainment. In later years she was to remember the solemn young man who might have been her husband with a mixture of affection and awe, while he remembered her as a dainty, pretty child, anxious to please.

MARY'S MARRIAGE TO CHARLES V

A) THE TREATY, 25 AUGUST 1521, BRUGES

Articuli sub beneplacito SDN concepti pro arctiori foedera inter Stm. Caesarem et Regen Angliae et Franciae innuendo ...

[Clause 11] The Pope shall, before the ratification of this league, grant dispensation for the marriage between the Emperor and the King of England's daughter, Mary, notwithstanding the espousals already made between the Emperor and the French King's daughter, and between Mary and the Dauphin.

[*Letters and Papers*, iii, 1508. BL Cotton MS Galba B VII, f 102]

B) RATIFICATION AND PROVISO, 14 SEPTEMBER 1521

Ratification of the treaty of marriage concluded 25th August between Margaret of Savoy* and, John de Bergis on one part and Thomas Wolsey on the other; with a proviso made 26th August touching Mary's marriage portion in the event of a male heir being born to the King of England. In the case of such issue it was agreed that the marriage portion, which had been agreed at 400,000† crowns should be increased to 600, 000. It is by this agreed between the parties that this augmentation, although promised to the Emperor to satisfy his subjects, shall not in reality ever be exacted. Brussels.

[*Letters and Papers ... of the Reign of Henry VIII*, iii, 1571. TNA E30/868.]

* Charles' sister, Regent of the Low Countries.

† French and Imperial crowns were worth 6s 4d sterling.

As befitted her rank, Mary was given her own household from birth. This was a modest establishment of seven women and three men, presided over at first by Elizabeth Denton, and then by Margaret Bryan.[9] Four of the women were described as 'Rockers', which identifies the whole set up as a glorified nursery. There must have been separate provision for service departments, because the overall cost of her establishment was £1,400 a year, but they are not listed and it seems that the child was not expected to spend any length of time apart from her parents. By the time that she was three, however, and espoused to the dauphin, this was not considered adequate. Margaret Pole, Countess of Salisbury, was given the position of 'lady governess'. Mary's chamber, the 'above-stairs' component of her household, now consisted of two men (the treasurer and the chaplain), five gentlewomen and six gentlemen, and to these were added twenty-seven other men, variously described as 'valets', 'grooms of the chamber' and 'grooms of the household'.[10] Perhaps the latter were intended to provide some of the household service when Mary was, as frequently happened by this time, on her own for a while.

The year 1519 clearly marked a stage in her emergence from infancy, and the increase of dignity may have been connected with the appearance on the scene of her illegitimate half-brother Henry Fitzroy. In 1522, when she was six and her schooling was just beginning, politics shook this domestic environment. The Countess of Salisbury was suspected of collusion in the alleged treasons of the Duke of Buckingham, and was removed from her post, although no other action was taken against her. In her place came Sir

Philip Calthorpe as chamberlain, and his wife Jane as governess. A new chaplain was appointed, and fifteen pages were added to the 'below-stairs' establishment.

Whether the chaplain was also expected to act as a tutor is not entirely clear. Catherine seems to have assumed responsibility for her daughter's first steps in literacy herself, although whether on a regular or occasional basis is not clear either.[11] It used to be thought that the distinguished Spanish humanist Juan Luis Vives performed this function for a time, but it is now believed that he confined himself to writing *The Education of a Christian Woman* at Catherine's request and other works such as the *Satellitium sive Symbola*, which contains a dedication to Mary. The *Education* was certainly aimed at the princess, and if his suggested curriculum was followed it would have involved a strong diet of biblical and classical reading – the latter suitably selected to protect her chaste youth. Vives was to some extent ahead of his time in taking the education of a girl seriously at all, but what he suggested was not particularly revolutionary, and certainly not intended to give Mary the impression that she had a masculine intellect.[12] There was much emphasis upon chastity, piety and humility, as befitted a future royal wife, but nothing that might have prepared her for being a ruler herself – except of course a sound grounding in classical Latin, the foundation stone of all learning and much business. If Catherine had given up all hope of bearing a son, that is not apparent in the education that she provided for Mary between 1522 and 1525. Probably, menopause or no menopause, she continued to believe in the power of fervent prayer to deliver what she and the king both so desperately wanted. Although Elizabeth Blount had been succeeded by Mary Boleyn in Henry's favours, much to Catherine's chagrin, there is no suggestion until much later that the royal couple had given up sleeping together – and while there was copulation there was hope.

Henry was proud of his daughter. At first she was shown off to fascinated diplomats as a perfect specimen of childhood, and as soon as she had talents to display they were demonstrated to a similar audience. She does not seem to have been particularly precocious, except in music, but she danced prettily and had, apparently, a beguiling gravity of demeanour. Noting her absence from the festivities at Calais in 1520, Francis sent three of his gentlemen to find out why, under the guise of paying their respects to their future queen. Mary received them at Richmond with 'the most goodly countenance, proper communication and pleasant pastime ... her young and tender age considered'.[13] She was four. Henry insisted, and Catherine made no attempt to demur, that Mary should be brought up as an English princess. As we have seen, her grandmother Isabella – the iron lady of Castile – was not held up as a role model, although it might have been more appropriate if she had been. Catherine had lived in England for over twenty years, and never returned to Spain after 1501. She retained some Spanish servants, but she spoke English perfectly – although it was sometimes convenient to pretend that she did not – and there is no certainty that Mary ever learned her mother's native tongue. Several years later, when both were in disfavour, it was claimed that they exchanged notes in Spanish, to deceive their attendants; and when Mary was queen she seems to have understood her husband's tongue, but to have spoken it very haltingly. It is probably safest to assume that she picked up a little from Catherine's conversations with her confessor and apothecary, without ever being specifically taught it. French she did learn, under the tuition of Giles Duwes, and later she spoke and wrote fluently in that language.

Between 1520 and 1525, Mary can be glimpsed occasionally in the diplomatic correspondence, usually in words of studied flattery. In 1524, in spite of her engagement to Charles, there was talk of her marrying the eight-year-old James V of Scotland. This was favoured by James' mother, Margaret, Henry VIII's sister, but the negotiations came to nothing. More intimately, some of her treasurer's accounts survive, showing her giving and receiving presents, and occasionally giving alms, usually when she was travelling from place to place and was presumably more accessible. However, there is no sign of her ever having had companions of her own age – unless some of the so-called 'ladies' of her privy chamber were really children.

In later years, both her brother Edward and sister Elizabeth were taught in small 'school rooms' of contemporaries, but there is no sign that Mary was schooled in this way. As a child she seems to have been unusually close to both her parents, and her health was cared for as carefully as the knowledge of the time permitted; but of a peer group there is no sign. This may be merely a defect in the records, but a lonely childhood might help to explain the difficulty that she was to have in later life in establishing relationships. 'Cherishing', as the contemporary wisdom ran, 'marreth sons but utterly destroyeth daughters.' It is possible that, until the age of about nine, Mary was cherished, in other words coddled and kept apart from other children.

In 1525 a major change took place in the young princess's circumstances. Henry, it would appear, was beginning to despair of ever having a son by Catherine. She had not conceived for nearly seven years, and it was becoming increasingly obvious, even to her, that her childbearing days were over. He was thirty-four, but she was now forty, and ageing rapidly. Prayer was a great solace, but perhaps she was not worthy of the miracle that would now be necessary. The king had to do something about the succession. As things stood, with Mary betrothed to the Emperor – and now within about three years of the minimum age of cohabitation – if Henry were to die, England would become a part of the burgeoning Habsburg empire, along with Germany, the Low Countries, Spain and most of Italy. Only if Mary were to die while Henry was alive, leaving a son, would England retain her independence. The idea that a ruling queen could marry and maintain the autonomy of her kingdom was one whose time had not yet come. Even the formidable Isabella of Spain had not achieved that. Henry therefore had three options. He could accept the situation as it was, and take whatever steps were possible to secure English interests; he could attempt to legitimate his bastard son, Henry Fitzroy, and settle the succession on him; or he could try to repudiate his wife, Catherine, and start again.

In 1525 Henry had not quite screwed up the courage to face these options, but Cardinal Wolsey, his chancellor since 1515, was urging the need for him to get a stronger grip on the government of Wales and the north, and this suggested a way ahead. There were already royal councils, both in the north and in the marches, but they were moribund and ineffective.[14] Wolsey proposed that each should be reconstituted, with a royal child as its nominal head to establish the monarch's presence, but staffed by efficient servants of his own choosing. On 18 June Henry Fitzroy, aged about six, was created Duke of Richmond, and despatched to Middleham in Yorkshire with a large household and a new council. He was not legitimated, but the choice of title was significant and, in spite of his tender years, he now had status. Catherine, we are told, was outraged. At about the same time Mary, equipped with a similar establishment, was sent to the west to 'bear the face of the king' in Wales and the marches. She was not, however, formally constituted Princess of Wales, which would have confirmed her position as heir to the throne.[15] Henry was keeping his options open, and at the same time separating the child from what he probably saw as the overweening influence of her mother. With hindsight this looks like an ominous move, but at the time it was a sensible precaution. If the queen was also annoyed by this, she was wise enough not to show it.

THE HOUSEHOLD IN WALES 18 August 1525
THE NAMES OF ALL THE LADIES AND GENTLEWOMEN WHO ARE TO ACCOMPANY THE PRINCESS INTO WALES, WITH THE QUANTITY OF THE BLACK VELVET ALLOWED TO EACH
Lady Salisbury; Lady Katherine Grey; Mrs Katherine Montacue, Mrs Elizabeth Poole; Mrs. Constance Poole; Mrs Anne Knevett; Mrs Dannet; Mrs Baker; Mrs Cecill Dabridgecourt; Mrs Frances Elmer; MrsAnne Rede; Mrs Marie Wyncter; Mrs Peter; Mrs Anne Dannet and Mrs Anne Darrell. Mrs Parker and Mrs Geynes are to have black damask. [Memorandum in the margin of the delivery of the velvet to each of the ladies, by Mr. Leg,, J. Scutte, Mr. Wheeler and Ric. Hage. Signed by Wolsey.]
[*Letters and Papers ... of the Reign of Henry VIII*, iv, 1577. TNA SP1/35, pp. 261-2.]

A household and council numbering some 304 individuals was created for Mary in July 1525. The domestic establishment was again headed by the Countess of Salisbury, now restored to favour, and a new schoolmaster was appointed in the person of Dr Richard Fetherstone. Fetherstone was a competent scholar, and his main duty was to work on the princess's Latin style. Separate instructions were also given for her music, diet and physical recreation. The council was headed by John Veysey, Bishop of Exeter (who had held the position earlier), and was equipped with a formidable range of commissions to enable it to function in just about every judicial capacity within the marches.

Mary and her entourage assembled at Wolsey's residence of The More, near Rickmansworth, in early August, and set off from there on the 12th. They appear to have travelled by a circuitous route, via Woburn and Reading, reaching Thornbury Castle in Gloucestershire on or about the 24th. Mary's itinerary over the next year or so can be approximately tracked.[16] The council also moved about a good deal, sometimes being in the same place as the princess, but often not. She seems to have spent most of the latter part of 1525 at Tewkesbury, while the council was at Worcester, Hereford and (probably) Shrewsbury. Her presence was not really necessary for its work, except on major ceremonial occasions. She seems to have inaugurated her regime with a ceremonial entry into Gloucester in September, but did not stay long, and does not appear to have repeated the process in other towns. Although Ludlow was the theoretical base of the council, neither the council nor Mary appear to have spent more than a few days there, in May 1526 – probably owing to the fact that the building work in progress there was still incomplete.

Very little is known about how Mary occupied her time during these peregrinations, although it can be presumed that her strict regime of schoolwork and exercise continued. Her offerings at shrines or religious houses are sometimes recorded, but how she relaxed, and with whom, is not clear. She turned ten in February 1526, and seems to have been treated throughout as a small adult rather than a child. She apparently enjoyed hawking, and it may have been at this time that she developed her taste for small-scale gambling with dice or cards; but of play in any childish sense there is no mention at all. She had sixteen ladies, some of whom may have been close to her in age, under the watchful eye of the Countess of Salisbury, who was old enough to have been her grandmother. All were strictly chaperoned, and it is highly unlikely that Mary ever encountered any boys of even approximately her own age. As a result she grew up deeply suspicious of the men with whom she had to deal, and had a poor understanding of their motivation and psychology. She wrote some formal letters during this period in the Welsh marches, a few of which have survived, but they tell us nothing beyond the fact that she was diligent in her studies, and performed official tasks as requested. After about a year, in September 1526, she was allowed to travel east for a reunion with her parents. Whose idea this was, we do not know, but the suggestion probably came from the lady governess, and the king put himself out to accommodate it. They met at Stony Stratford in Buckinghamshire on about 25 September, and spent some two weeks together there and at Ampthill in Bedfordshire before she returned to Hartlebury, near Worcester, about the middle of October.[17]

Mary's tour of duty as princess was, however, coming to an end. Her entourage was hugely expensive, costing (with the necessary repairs to relevant houses) over £4,500 during the first year, and it was probably not clear to either Wolsey or the king that such a heavy expenditure was justified. At some uncertain date towards the end of 1526 she paid a brief visit to Coventry, and appears to have kept her Christmas at Bewdley, but by the middle of February the decision had been taken to recall her. There is no record of this decision, but she reached Abingdon in Oxfordshire on 17 February, from thence proceeding to Windsor and London. Options were kept open for a while, and a part of her household was kept on somewhere in the marches until 1528 (the accounts for payment do not state where); but it was then stood down and Mary did not go back to Wales.

Expense was not the only reason for bringing this experiment to an end. Henry's involvement in war with France, for which he had signed up with the Emperor in 1521, was something of a fiasco. The campaign of 1523 fizzled out ignominiously, and the king was too short of money to undertake anything significant in 1524. Early in 1525 Charles inflicted a crushing defeat on Francis at the battle of Pavia, and captured him. Henry then had the audacity to suggest a partition of the kingdom of France, with himself receiving a large share for doing precisely nothing. When the king attempted to raise a war fund by means of a forced loan – the so-called Amicable Grant – the result was another fiasco.[18] Charles was not only not interested, he was mortally offended. In 1526 he signed a separate treaty with France and married the Infanta Isabella of Portugal, a lady of more suitable years than his English fiancée.

Henry had been expecting such an outcome for some time, but the temptation to make a grievance out of this repudiation was too good to miss. The result was a hectic round of diplomacy as Wolsey attempted, with French assistance, to put together a coalition against the now over-powerful Emperor. Francis, although he had been constrained to leave his sons in Imperial hands as the price of his own release, had no intention of abiding by the treaty that he had been forced to sign. In May 1526 the League of Cognac came into existence, although England was not at first a member. Anglo-French negotiations continued, and early in 1527 a deal was brokered that would have involved a marriage between Mary, then aged eleven, and Francis himself, aged thirty-three and currently a widower. The King of France did not have a good reputation where women were concerned, and it is reasonable to suppose that Catherine was not consulted over this proposal. In any case, although she had little leverage by this time, such influence as she still had would have been exercised in favour of her nephew Charles. Early in 1527 Francis proposed to send a discreet mission to inspect the princess as his intended bride, and this was perhaps the most important reason for summoning her back from Wales.

Another reason may well have been the deteriorating state of her parents' own marriage. It was allegedly the negotiation for a marriage between Mary and Francis that first raised the vexed question of the princess's status. The French envoys are supposed to have asked for reassurances about Mary's legitimacy in the light of the bar of consanguinity that had existed between her parents at the time of their marriage. Pope Julius II's dispensation of 1503 was known both in England and in France, but its sufficiency was doubted. Whether it was indeed the French envoys who had raised this doubt is uncertain, but it is clear that somebody had, and the king, who in certain moods was extremely superstitious, was becoming convinced that he had made a terrible mistake. In the Book of Leviticus, 20th chapter, it was decreed that if a man took his brother's wife to himself it was an offence against God, and the couple would be childless. Preoccupied with Catherine's misfortunes in childbearing, Henry overlooked the fact that they were not actually childless. Wanting to be convinced, he allowed himself to be persuaded that the original Hebrew had said 'they shall be without sons'.[19]

By early 1527 Henry's state of mind had also been influenced by more practical considerations. Mary was an undergrown scrap of a child. The king was not yet old, and she might very well wed and bear sons in his lifetime, but it was not to be counted upon, and the thought that England might fall into the hands of a foreign dynasty was deeply distasteful, not only to Henry but also to his nobility. Catherine, oblivious to English sensibilities on this subject, simply could not see his problem. On the other hand, legitimating Henry Fitzroy was a highly uncertain proceeding. His mother, Elizabeth Blount, was no longer available even if the king had been disposed to marry her (which he was not). Any other process of legitimation would depend upon a special grace from Rome, and even then would be insecure. If Henry had ever considered his illegitimate son as a candidate for the succession, he had ruled him out by 1527. It was becoming increasingly obvious that Catherine would have to go.

There were apparently only two ways in which this could be accomplished. If the queen were to take herself to a nunnery, the marriage would be effectively terminated, irrespective of its earlier validity. Mary would remain Henry's legitimate heir, but would be superseded by any son born to a subsequent union. Given that Catherine must have been aware that (miracles apart) her childbearing was over, and given her conspicuous piety, this was not an unreasonable option. The alternative was to secure an annulment from the pope on the grounds of consanguinity. Henry unwisely foreclosed the first option (which would have required his wife's cooperation) by brusquely confronting her in July 1527 with the news that they had never been properly married. This was a direct challenge to Catherine's own conviction that God had inspired Henry to wed her in 1509, in answer to years of fervent prayer. Compromise or an amicable arrangement were now alike impossible, and only an annulment offered a way ahead. Unfortunately Henry had just quarrelled violently with the Emperor Charles, who was Catherine's nephew, and Charles had the pope by the throat after his army had inadvertently sacked Rome in May 1527.[20] By June, an amended version of Julius II's brief, making good the alleged deficiencies of the original, had turned up in Spain and was known to Wolsey, who found himself confronted with an impossible task. In the teeth of the Emperor's opposition, and of his unchallengeable ascendancy in Rome, he had to persuade Pope Clement VII (not a robust or courageous man) to overturn his predecessor's edict, and thus to call the whole authority of papal judgements into question. Clement could, of course, have done so, but whether he would was quite a different question.

It was into this developing crisis that Mary returned. She received the French envoys at Greenwich on St George's Day, 23 April, speaking to them both in Latin and in fluent French, also entertaining them, as was her wont, on the virginals. They were impressed by her accomplishments and by her seemly gravity, but they also observed that she was 'so thin, spare and small as to make it impossible to be married for the next three years'.[21] The French king could not afford to wait that long, and the agreement that was eventually reached was for an engagement between the princess and Francis' second son, the Duke of Orléans. Knowledge of this uncongenial arrangement had already reached Catherine when she had her confrontation with her husband in July, and had done nothing to sweeten her mood. She seems to have been ignorant of the fact, but the complex situation that was then developing was made worse by Henry's developing relationship with Anne Boleyn.

Anne was the younger sister of the king's earlier mistress, Mary Boleyn, now happily married off, and seems to have come to his attention at some time during 1526. In spite of the intensity that it later developed, this was not at first a passionate infatuation, and seems to have grown gradually out of a charade of courtly love. In June Anne was ill of the 'sweat' and Henry was worried, but it was not clear at this point to anyone (except perhaps the parties themselves) that Catherine's place in her husband's affections had been usurped by one of her own ladies. However, even if she had known, the queen could hardly have been more obdurate. Realising what Wolsey was now about on the king's behalf, she sent a secret message to Charles, begging him to use all his influence to frustrate the English moves in the curia (the papal court). In the circumstances, he hardly needed any urging.

As she emerged from childhood, Mary was thus caught in a domestic and political firestorm for which she was ill-equipped. Before moving to Wales, she had been urged by her mother to study diligently with Dr Fetherstone, but most of the evidence for her having done so is indirect, in the form of commendations from others – most notably from Erasmus. Almost the only direct evidence is that she translated a prayer of St Thomas Aquinas into English, while the French envoys of 1527 testified to the success of Mary's French tutor, Giles Duwes. As far as her health was concerned, evidence of sickness during her stay in the marches is very scant, although she was moved from time to time to avoid infection. However, of her personality at this stage in her life nothing very much emerges. She seems to have been a biddable child who answered to expectations, diligent but not noticeably bright, and not apparently showing much curiosity about the world around her. Although well known in some quarters by the summer of 1527, the rupture between her parents was not understood outside the court, and Mary seems for some time to have been protected from its implications. It was not until 1529, when she was thirteen, that she found herself in the painful position of having to decide how she was going to react.

2

DISRUPTION

Henry's case for an annulment of his first marriage was not strong, but he did have a case – and in other circumstances it might have been sufficient to persuade the pope to oblige him. Two considerations could have worked in his favour. Firstly, Julius II's dispensation was from consanguinity, in other words it assumed that Arthur and Catherine had consummated their marriage; but if, as Catherine insisted, her marriage to Arthur had never been consummated, that was an irrelevant issue. The impediment of what was called 'public honesty', the marriage ceremony with Arthur itself, remained. This was not a strong argument, but it could have been sufficient. Stronger, but much more controversial, was the argument that Leviticus 20:21, which forbade a man to marry his brother's wife, constituted divine law from which the pope did not have the power to dispense. Not only was this theologically dubious, because the ruling was apparently contradicted by a passage in Deuteronomy (ch. 25), but it also savoured of the Lutheran precept of *sola scriptura* – that the word of scripture must take precedence over any ruling of canon law.[1]

As was observed several years ago, to have succeeded, Henry's case in Rome would have required both good luck and highly skilled management – neither of which it received.[2] Henry himself rendered the public honesty argument inoperative by insisting that Catherine had not come to him as a virgin, and sabotaged any chance of an amicable arrangement by his dogmatic clumsiness.

Wolsey was battling against overwhelming odds, but in 1528 he did secure a legatine commission for himself and Cardinal Lorenzo Campeggio to hear the case in England, with a verbal undertaking that Pope Clement would confirm the finding.

This was the nearest he came to success. Campeggio's mission was doomed from the start, because Henry was so committed to his divine-law opinion that 'an angel from heaven could not dissuade him'.[3] The king was also furiously impatient, because his relationship with Anne Boleyn was coming to the boil, and she was holding out on him. Even more seriously, both cardinals Wolsey and Campeggio were the victims of the pope's duplicity, because, being committed to the Emperor (who was Catherine's nephew), he had not the slightest intention of confirming any finding that they might make in Henry's favour. He was merely buying time in the rather desperate hope that the situation would resolve itself. Although he was unaware of this, Wolsey knew the king well enough to be seriously worried. If Henry did not get his own way, not only would Wolsey's own career be finished, but England might break with the papacy altogether. 'I close my eyes before such horror … I throw myself at the Holy Father's feet', he wrote in December 1528. Perhaps Clement did not take such blusterings seriously; at any rate they made no difference.

When the legatine court at length convened on 18 June 1529, Catherine refused to recognise its competence, and after a futile exchange of arguments, the session was adjourned on the pretext of the Roman vacation. The king was enraged beyond measure, and Wolsey was disgraced, much to the satisfaction of his many enemies, but to no positive gain whatsoever.[4] Henry's bluff had been called, and he had to decide what to do, because dismissing his chancellor made not the slightest difference in Rome. For the time being Catherine had won, and was still the king's lawful wife. However, that had always been likely to happen, given the pope's predicament, and if it was a consolation to her, it was no benefit. While Henry groped around for a new policy, and she retained her status at court, Anne Boleyn moved in and a curious *ménage à trois* developed. Politically Anne and her friends dominated the king's council, but she refused to share the king's bed. Catherine continued to accompany her husband on official occasions, and, as far as we can tell, continued to sleep with him, at least intermittently, for another two years.

Inevitably Henry found himself reproached by both women for this indecisive situation, and caught between their fierce tongues he appears more than a little ridiculous.[5] The tensions must frequently have become intolerable. Mary was now thirteen, and must have been well aware of what was going on, although she was not normally resident at court. For the time being nobody was much interested in her. She remained betrothed to the Duke of Orléans, but nothing much could be expected to happen until he reached the canonical age of cohabitation, which would not be until 1533. Given her lack of physical development, her own puberty may well have been delayed, but such matters were not discussed and her household accounts, which could have been revealing in that respect, do not survive for this period. She seems to have been a frequent and welcome visitor at court, and we know she was there at Christmas 1529, when her father gave her extra pocket money to the tune of £20 'for to disport her with'. She went with both her parents to mass on the Feast of the Circumcision (2 January), but how long she remained after that we do not know. At an age when even a royal princess might have expected something a little more entertaining, she seems to have spent most of her time at her books, relieved only by needlework and music, and mostly on her own.

According to Augustino Scarpellino, who visited the court on behalf of the Duke of Milan in the summer of 1530, Mary was 'always apart, at a distance of ten or fifteen miles, with a suitable establishment ...'[6] Henry sent her regular presents of £10 or £20, perhaps to ease his conscience, and she on one occasion sent him a buck. This suggests that by this time she was relieving the tedium with a little hunting, because the point of such a present would surely be that she had killed it herself. Apart from Scarpellino's comment that she was 'said to be already advanced in wisdom and stature', we get hardly any sight of her – and he was reporting a general opinion, because he never met her himself. She seems to have spent most of her time at Richmond, which would just about meet Scarpellino's description.

There were insubstantial rumours of alternative marriages for Mary – to Francesco Sforza, the Duke of Milan, even to her half brother Henry Fitzroy – but none of these had any substance. The Fitzroy idea, which Eustace Chapuys, the new Imperial ambassador, instinctively attributed to 'the concubine' (Anne Boleyn) because it was so repellent, seems in fact to have originated with an increasingly desperate pope. Clement was simultaneously suggesting bigamy to Henry, so the holy father was doing himself no favours.[7] At Christmas 1530 Mary was again at court, and again received £20. Although she was fifteen in February 1531, the early part of that year really marked the end of her childhood – the calm before the real storms of adolescence began. She spent almost the whole of March with her mother, and in June her father came to Richmond and 'made great cheer' in her company.

However, in early April Mary fell ill from what Scarpellino described as 'hysteria', and was still not fully recovered three weeks later. This was clearly a menstrual disorder of some severity, and may well have represented the delayed and somewhat irregular onset of puberty. She was attended by the king's physicians, and by a certain Dr Bartelot, who was probably the Tudor equivalent of a consultant gynaecologist. As he was paid £20 for his attendance, he was clearly a specialist of some standing.[8] The stress of her parents' deteriorating relationship may also have been a factor in this illness. In May, Henry and Catherine fell out bitterly over their respective relations with their daughter, and that may well have been a factor in the final breakdown, which came at the end of June. Henry dismissed his wife from the court, with the furious words that he never wished to see her again. She was ordered to retire to The More (in the king's hands since the death of Wolsey in November 1530), while Mary was to remain at Richmond. They were ordered never to see each other again.

This was not quite as final as it sounded, because Catherine was at Windsor in July, and Mary spent some time with her there. It did, however, represent a serious intention, and the queen was at The More by the end of August. Thereafter contact between mother and daughter was by way of written messages.[9] In some respects Henry's bark was worse than his bite. He had threatened to reduce Catherine's household drastically, but did not in fact do so, and she had over 200 servants at The More, including a chamber staff of 50, which was a full complement for a queen consort. In some ways Mary was harder hit than her mother. Her material circumstances remained unchanged, but her mother's occasional company had been a great comfort to her as she faced the daunting challenge of growing up. Now she was on her own apart from the frequent company of Margaret Pole, the Countess of Salisbury, whose own adolescence was so far in the past that she may not have been much help. Christmas 1531 was miserable. Mary received her usual £20, but was not at court, probably by her own choice. Communication with Catherine was prohibited, and Anne Boleyn, in spite of her political ascendancy, was in no position to take over Catherine's role.

Moreover the news from Rome was as bad as it could be. Henry had obstinately persisted with his representations there, long after it should have been obvious that they were futile. His last throw had been to claim a partial exemption from certain aspects of papal jurisdiction (such as matrimony) on the basis of the ancient liberties of England. Now he learned that that bid had also failed, and that it was only a matter of time before a definitive sentence was pronounced against him.[10]

In theory, Mary's relations with her father remained unchanged, but in practice her sympathies were entirely with her mother. Henry was fond of his daughter, but he was too prone to treat her as a dynastic chess piece – too obviously in control – for her to regard him with much human warmth. The prohibition on communication was a challenge that mother and daughter conspired to evade, and the king's security arrangements were distinctly porous, perhaps by design. Chapuys was convinced, probably correctly, that Anne Boleyn was the real problem. Not only was her very presence an insult to Mary, Catherine and their sympathisers, but she had good reason to fear a girl who represented an alternative vision of the future to any that she could offer. Catherine had been defeated, but Mary's relationship with her father was of a different order, and might prove more difficult to unravel. According to Chapuys, who was well informed but by no means impartial, Anne hated her 'as much as the queen, or more so because she sees the king has some affection for her'.[11]

In November 1531 Mary's matrimonial prospects again evaporated when Francis decided to marry his son to the pope's niece, Catherine de'Medici. This time Henry decided not to take offence, because a strengthening of French influence in Rome might conceivably work in his favour as he struggled against the consequences of Habsburg dominance. The Duke of Cleves immediately expressed an interest, but nothing came of it and the princess was once again available. Whether she was even aware of these developments is uncertain.

They certainly made no difference to her normal routine, but she was now of full age to marry, and she would have been less than human if she had not been interested in her own prospects. She was, according to a contemporary observer, pretty and well proportioned, although not very tall. Her father continued to demonstrate his affection rather clumsily with lavish provision for her household and a generous New Year gift, but Anne was his main preoccupation, and he did not want to take the risk of bringing them together.

1532 was to be a decisive year. Even before it had begun, Imperialist cardinals and diplomats were fearing that Henry was about to do something desperate. They spoke of the need to get Catherine and Mary out of his clutches, and the pope prepared a solemn excommunication – just in case. Since 1530 the king had been trying intermittently to blackmail the curia by bullying the English Church with charges of *praemunire* – the crime of exercising ecclesiastical jurisdiction without the king's consent. The clergy had bought these charges off, but the threat remained.[12]

There was at the time an anti-clerical element in the House of Commons, and Thomas Cromwell, the king's secretary, who was the formulator although not the inspirer of royal policy at this juncture, sensed an opportunity. In the summer of 1532 he persuaded his allies to present to Parliament a 'Supplication against the Ordinaries', which he probably drafted himself. This was a complaint, along the lines of the previous *praemunire* proceedings, that the Church courts were not subject to the royal prerogative. Stephen Gardiner, the Bishop of Winchester, as spokesman for the clergy, walked straight into what looks very much like a trap. He responded to the supplication with a thumping defence of ecclesiastical independence. Henry was seriously angry, and Cromwell was able to push through an act compelling the bishops to accept a royal veto on any new canons. On 16 May, immediately following the passage of the act, Sir Thomas More resigned as lord chancellor. A way ahead in the king's 'Great Matter' was now opening up.[13]

On 23 August the Archbishop of Canterbury, William Warham, died, and it began to look as though Imperial suspicions would be confirmed. The king would seek a solution from his own bishops, without reference to the pope. In September he created Anne Boleyn Marquis of Pembroke in her own right, with land worth £1,000 a year. As a declaration of intent, this was unambiguous.

There was nothing that Catherine could do about this. She had many and strong sympathisers in England (particularly among aristocratic women) and almost unanimous support in Europe, but her defences, although intact, were about to be outflanked. Much against her will, she was compelled to hand over her jewels to a woman whom she described as 'the scandal of Christendom'. For several obvious reasons Anne and her supporters were strongly pro-French, but when she accompanied Henry to Calais for a meeting with Francis in October 1532, her presence presented the French king with a dilemma. He could hardly refuse to meet her without causing offence to Henry, and she was in any case acting as hostess. So he compromised, allowing himself to be entertained by her, but keeping his own queen carefully out of the way, in order to avoid disputes over protocol, as well as respecting Eleanor's opinion of Anne's morals. He had, in any case, his own agenda in Rome. Pressure was applied on Mary to take part in what was, in effect, the triumph of her mother's rival, but she was not present and her inclusion in the published propaganda account was a fiction.[14] Meanwhile, the queen continued her rearguard action. Her case had not yet been officially heard in Rome, because Clement was an inveterate believer in delay. Catherine did her best to cajole the Emperor into forcing the issue, but he had no desire to make a definitive break with Henry, and was beginning to find his aunt an embarrassment.

It was events in England which brought a solution. Before Christmas the king had decided that his next archbishop would be Thomas Cranmer. Cranmer, an erstwhile Cambridge academic and a committed supporter of the king's cause, was presently on a diplomatic mission to the Emperor, in the course of which he had (secretly) married and picked up various unorthodox religious opinions.[15] In January 1533 Anne, who had probably surrendered at last to the king's sexual yearnings during their stay in Calais, was found to be pregnant. Cranmer's appointment was made public and the pope (who knew his track record but was still trying to avoid a showdown) duly confirmed him. By the time that this happened Henry and Anne had married in a secret ceremony, and on 23 May Cranmer, using his own authority and jurisdiction, declared that marriage valid, and the earlier contract between Henry and Catherine null and void. On Saturday 30 May a visibly pregnant Anne was duly crowned as queen.[16]

The news was received across Europe with shudders of revulsion, and the Emperor was urged to make war upon England 'with the aid of the people'. Chapuys was convinced that there would be a great rising in Catherine's support, but Charles' council advised him more soberly that Henry's matrimonial tangles were a private matter, and that the King of England had given him no pretext to intervene. In July 1533 Catherine was visited by a powerful delegation of Henry's council, which demanded that she renounce the title of queen and accept that of Princess Dowager of Wales. She refused. Henry thereupon reduced her household to the level deemed appropriate for a princess dowager, and removed her to the manor of Buckden in Huntingdonshire, where she effectively remained under house arrest. In spite of Chapuys' shrill and horrified protests, the house was commodious and in good repair, and the financial allowance generous.[17] Her friends came and went freely – except Mary, who was strictly forbidden to go to Buckden.

There had been various comings and goings in Mary's household since 1528. Lord Hussey had become her chamberlain at some point before the autumn of 1530. Her treasurer, the long-serving Richard Sydnor, had retired, and Richard Wollman had replaced Fetherstone as her tutor. However, by 1533 she was seventeen, and the days of regimented schoolwork were probably over. Both in 1532 and 1533 there were renewed rumours of a marriage with the King of Scots, and a rather wilder report of a negotiation with Transylvania.

All this was gossip, but it was linked to a significant new development. Some of the Emperor's servants (although not Charles himself) were eyeing the possibility of using her as an agent against her father. Catherine was useless from that point of view. Even if she had been willing (which she was not), she had no claim to the throne of England – but Mary had. In the summer of 1533 it was being reported in France and Italy that the Scots had invaded, backed by the Emperor and the Danes, and that the English were rising in her favour because she was so popular. An exotic alternative was that the knight errant coming to Mary's aid was Dom Luis of Portugal, and that the Scots were being supported by a Genoese fleet in the service of the Emperor.[18]

The only substance behind all this was that Mary was now politically more important than her mother, a fact of which Henry was perfectly well aware. In spite of this, and much to Anne's chagrin, the ban on communication between mother and daughter, which had theoretically been in place since 1531, was not only being regularly evaded but was occasionally specifically relaxed. Mary was ill again both in March and June 1533. The first time the king's physicians attended her, but the second time she asked for her mother's servants, 'which the king was well pleased to grant'. At that time messengers were passing freely between them, with the king's knowledge and indulgence. Visits, however, remained prohibited. Anne apparently fumed against the younger woman, vowing that she would reduce her to a servant or marry her to a varlet, but she was powerless to put any of these threats into effect.[19]

Henry, meanwhile, was hesitating over what to do about his daughter. In the light of Cranmer's decision regarding the validity of her mother's marriage, Mary was now illegitimate. However, the king seems to have hoped that by proceeding gently and showing her favour, he would persuade her to accept the new situation without a fuss. The only warning was that Lord Hussey was instructed to inventory her jewels, an exercise that was frustrated by the intransigence of the Countess of Salisbury. It is unlikely that Mary herself even knew about it.

On 7 September Anne Boleyn was delivered of a daughter, who was named Elizabeth, and this event focused everyone's mind. The royal couple were bitterly disappointed, and the hostile courts of Europe could hardly contain their mirth.

Henry had moved heaven and earth to beget a legitimate son – and this was the result. Clearly God had a sense of humour. More importantly, it now became critical to distinguish between the legitimate and illegitimate daughters. By the laws of the Catholic Church Mary was legitimate and Elizabeth a bastard, but by the laws of England the reverse was the case. There must be no mistake over which was to prevail. Within a week Mary was informed that she was no longer princess but rather 'the Lady Mary, the King's daughter' (and therefore outranked by her illegitimate half-brother, the Duke of Richmond), that her household would be reduced, and that her servants were henceforth to wear the king's livery rather than hers. She refused to receive these tidings in any form other than a letter from the king, but Henry seems to have believed that she had submitted. On 1 October he authorised a new household for her, to number 162 persons and still headed by Lord Hussey and the Countess of Salisbury.[20]

Chapuys made his habitual protest, but the reduction was probably no more than 25 per cent, and would have reduced the cost from almost £3,000 per annum to about £2,500. It soon became apparent, however, that such generosity was contingent upon her unequivocal acceptance of her new status. On 30 September she was visited by a commission headed by the Earl of Oxford, which required her, on pain of the king's displeasure and punishment by law, to stop using the title of princess. This she adamantly refused to do, and followed up her refusal on 2 October with a letter of self-righteous reproach to her father, worthy of her mother at her most outspoken. She could not believe that he would act with such manifest injustice – and so on.[21]

The king now had two recalcitrant female consciences to deal with, and he was not pleased. Moreover, in view of the plotting that was going on, both within England and abroad, his daughter's defiance might well turn into serious danger. Henry pretended to believe that her mother and her servants were really responsible for this defiance, but the punishment could only be inflicted upon Mary herself. In early November, about a month after her refusal, Mary's entire establishment was dissolved, and she herself, with some half dozen personal servants, was placed within the household then being created for Princess Elizabeth. Chapuys was speechless with indignation, blaming everything on the malice of Anne, 'the concubine'. If he was right, it was an act of justifiable self-defence in view of the symbolic position that Mary now occupied. From Buckden Catherine wrote to her daughter with a kind of gloomy exaltation: 'Almighty God will prove you, and I am very glad of it, for I trust he doth handle you with a good love.' They were now companions in martyrdom as well as misfortune.[22] Theoretically the new household was for both the king's daughters, but of course Elizabeth as the legitimate princess took precedence in everything, and 'the Lady Mary' was under house arrest, in much less comfortable circumstances than her mother. It was not until 16 December that the decisions about the provision for Mary and Elizabeth were put into effect, so the former had had over a month to get used to the idea of her impending suffering. This makes her own protests on the day, and those of the Countess of Salisbury, appear distinctly theatrical, especially as a sympathetic crowd seems to have been assembled to witness the distressing scene. In spite of Cromwell's diligence, Henry was not doing well in the battle for hearts and minds.[23]

CHAPUYS' LETTER TO CHARLES V 16 December 1533

According to the determination come to by the king about the treatment of the Princess and the bastard,* of which I wrote in my last, the said bastard was taken three days ago to a house seventeen miles from here; and although there was a shorter and a better road, yet for greater solemnity and to insinuate to the people that she is the true Princess, she was taken through this town with the company which I wrote in my last; and next day the Duke of Norfolk went to the Princess to tell her that her father desired her to go to the court and service of the said bastard, whom he named Princess. The Princess answered that the title belonged to herself and to no other; making many very wise remonstrances that what had been proposed to her was strange and dishonourable. To which the Duke could not reply. After much talk he said that he had not come there to dispute, but to accomplish the king's will; and the Princess, seeing that it was needless excusing herself, demanded half an hour's respite to go to her chamber, where she remained about that time, to make, as I know, a protestation which I had sent her, in order that, if compelled by force or fraud to renounce her rights, or enter a nunnery, it might not be to her prejudice. On returning from her chamber she said to the Duke that since the king her father was so pleased, she would not disobey him, begging him to intercede with the king for the recompense of her servants, that they might have at least a year's wages. She then asked what company she should bring. The Duke said it was not necessary to bring much, for she would find plenty where she was going; and so she parted with a very small suite. Her gouvernante, daughter of the late Duke of Clarence and near kinswoman to the king,† a lady of virtue and honour, if there be one in England, has offered to follow and serve her at her own expense, with an honourable train. But it was out of the question that this would be accepted; for in that case they would have no power over the Princess, whom it is to be feared they mean to kill, either with grief or otherwise, to make her renounce her right, or marry basely, or make her stain her honour, to have grounds for disinheriting her, since notwithstanding the remonstrances I have hitherto made touching the Princess, to which I have had no reply, the king has proceeded to such excesses; and considering that my words served only to irritate him, and make him more fierce and obstinate, I have resolved not again to address to him a single word, except he oblige me, without a command from the Queen. In order that the mother may have no occasion to envy her daughter

41

being visited on the part of the king, certain persons, as I wrote to you, have gone to resolicit the Queen to ratify the sentence of Canterbury, and revoke the interdict which the Pope has so injuriously fulminated against the king and his kingdom. And to do this they threaten her punishment, and by degrees will cut off her train and her household.

You cannot imagine the grief of all the people at this abominable government. They are so transported with indignation at what passes, that they complain that your majesty takes no steps in it; and I am told by many respectable people that they would be glad to see a fleet come hither in your name to ra ise the people; and if they had any chief among themselves who dared raise his head, they would require no more ...

[*Letters and Papers ... of the Reign of Henry VIII*, VI, 1528.

The original, in French, is in the Vienna Staatsarchiv]

* Elizabeth.

† Margaret Pole, Countess of Salisbury.

3

TRAUMA

Over the next two years, Mary became an affliction to herself, and to everyone who had to deal with her. In February 1534, claiming that she was 'nearly destitute of clothes', she sent a gentleman of the household directly to the king, but since he was instructed not to receive anything unless she was addressed as princess, this was clearly a demonstration rather than a real request. At the end of March in the same year, when the household made a routine move to another residence, Mary refused to budge until she was properly addressed, so that the exasperated Lady Anne Shelton, who was in charge of the female side of the establishment, had her bodily dumped in a litter and carted off – shrilly protesting. This must have had its funny side, but no one at the time was amused.[1] In September 1535, when the Bishop of Tarbes paid a formal visit to Elizabeth on behalf of the King of France, Mary had to be physically restrained from confronting him on the grounds that she was the only princess present, and his business should have been with her. Another furious row with Lady Shelton resulted. When Queen Anne came to visit her daughter, which she did quite frequently, Mary (unless she was kept out of the way) put herself about to behave as insultingly as possible, so that if Anne ever had it in mind to seek a reconciliation with this abrasive young woman – and there are some signs that she did – she was effectively deterred.[2] Chapuys, while ostensibly praising such virtuous behaviour, became in fact more than a little anxious. After the

Act of Succession in 1534, designating Anne's offspring as the royal heirs, Mary was technically guilty of high treason, and so were any of the servants who subscribed to her point of view, publicly or privately. Henry might still be fond of his difficult child, but his patience was notoriously erratic and Thomas Cromwell, himself under threat, could not afford to be squeamish.

Apart from the occasions when she deliberately provoked her minders, Mary was not treated brutally, or even unsympathetically. Her health was fragile, due no doubt to the impact of stress upon an already unstable menstrual cycle, and frequent visits by the royal physicians are recorded, together with significant expenditure on medication. In March 1535, when she was recovering from 'her usual ailment', it was reported that:

> ... the Lady Mary, the King's daughter, after she was restored to health of her
> late infirmity, being in her own house, was much desirous to have her meat
> immediately after she was ready in the morning, or else she should be in danger
> eftsoons to return to her said infirmity ...[5]

On medical advice, she was taking her main meal between nine and ten o'clock in the morning, which was not in keeping with the practice of the rest of the household. Nevertheless her preference was indulged, at an additional cost of £26 to the 'diets'.

Except for those comparatively brief periods when some outburst had left her confined to quarters by her irate father, Mary seems to have taken regular exercise, riding or walking in the extensive parks that surrounded most of the royal residences. She was never, of course, unaccompanied, but this was less for restraint than to ensure that she was not removed by sympathisers who might have taken her overseas, where she would have been an even greater threat. Like her mother, she was extremely nervous of poison, but in that respect they both of them did the king a major injustice. Had Henry been willing to employ such methods, he could have saved himself a lot of trouble, but he was not. More serious perhaps (and this was something which worried Catherine a lot) was the risk of 'contamination'. It would have been relatively easy for Cromwell to have involved her in a scandal with some male member of the household, and immensely damaging to her reputation. Her own scrupulousness would not necessarily have protected her, and it can be reasonably assumed that it was the king, rather than the harassed Lady Shelton, who protected her from any such attempt.

Much of what we know about Mary during the two and a half years that she spent in this joint household is derived either from the accounts or from Chapuys' despatches. Consequently we know about her 'rheums', her 'usual ailment' and sundry neuralgias and other afflictions for which medicines were provided. We also know that the Imperial ambassador provided her and her mother with everything from 'books of consolation' to political advice. He was constantly in touch with Mary, and made endless and tediously repetitive representations to the council on her behalf.[4]

Chapuys was indulged because he represented a powerful master. Henry was again hankering after improving his relations with the Emperor, and only twice was goaded into telling the ambassador that his master should be encouraged to mind his own business. Most specifically, in September 1534 he instructed his own ambassador to tell Charles '… we think it not meet that any person should prescribe unto us how we should order our own daughter, we being her natural father'. Had the king really been aware of the extent and nature of Chapuys' activities, he could not have failed to demand his recall. The ambassador was deeply involved with the English malcontents, and in September 1534 was actually discussing the possibilities of a rising in England, particularly with Lord Darcy and Lord Hussey – Mary's former chamberlain.[5] He did his level best to persuade Charles that this was a realistic prospect, and that 'all good people' in England would support it. The Emperor was unconvinced, but he did discuss with his council the possibility of supporting the Kildare revolt in Ireland, 'considering the offers made by divers princes there to remain under the Emperor's authority, and hold the country of the Queen and Princess'. Quite what this would have meant in practice is not clear, but for a couple of months at least intervention seems to have been a real possibility. However, it did not happen, partly because the rebels were not doing well enough for a mere token gesture to suffice. If the Irish were really going to overthrow Henry's rule, then a serious commitment of troops would be called for, and that was quite sufficient to deter Charles from taking any action. Nor did anything happen in England, which is no doubt why Chapuys' machinations went undetected. Catherine, in any case, had made it clear that she would be no party to insurrection. However good her cause, it was not to be defended in that way.

Mary was more biddable. She was keenly aware of the immense debt that she owed to the ambassador for his moral and practical support, and expressed herself in the warmest terms to Charles – her one-time fiancé. He was, she is alleged to have said, her real father, and she would never consider marrying without his advice and consent.[6] In October 1535 she went further, writing (by way of Chapuys) to Gattinara, the Emperor's chief minister, that 'the affairs of this kingdom will go to total ruin if his majesty does not, for the service of God ... take brief order and apply a remedy'. This was treason, as even the ambassador must have known, and indicates that had there been any equivalent of the Kildare rebellion in England, Mary would have been deeply involved, and if it had failed she would have lost her head.

The Emperor was in a cleft stick. Because of his permanently bad relations with France, and the threat from the Ottomans, to say nothing of the developing religious tensions in Germany, he needed English support, as he frankly admitted. On the other hand he could not contemplate doing anything prejudicial to the cause of 'the Queen and Princess'. A bit of pressure in Ireland would have been acceptable, and if the English themselves (by whatever means) could have persuaded Henry to give up Anne and return to Catherine, he would have been delighted. But he had no desire to see Henry overthrown, nor England reduced to the kind of turmoil that would have rendered it useless as an ally in an emergency.

In May 1534 the Rota, the supreme ecclesiastical court in Rome, finally adjudicated Catherine's appeal in her favour. This made not the slightest difference to the situation in England, but Catherine became more self-righteous than ever in correspondence with her nephew. She explained at great length the horrendous sins of the English in general and of Henry in particular; both she and her daughter, she complained, were suffering the pains of purgatory. 'I am as Job,' she wrote, 'waiting for the day when I must go sue for alms for the love of God.' As she was sitting at the centre of a household that was costing her iniquitous husband nearly £3,000 a year, this was pure fiction.[7]

What both women did, partly out of genuine conviction and partly because it was politically convenient, was to blame Anne Boleyn for their troubles. Chapuys assiduously promoted the same view, partly because it gave a pretext for Charles to maintain diplomatic relations with Henry, and partly because he knew perfectly well that her political influence was pro-French. In truth Anne seems to have been largely indifferent to Catherine, whom she probably regarded as a spent force. Mary she both feared and disliked, but her influence over the king in that direction was limited. She may well have persuaded Henry to curtail his daughter's liberty when she had been particularly obnoxious, but such restraints were always short lived, and the king's anger with Mary was not because she had upset his queen so much as because her behaviour was making it impossible for him to treat her with the affection that he still felt.

Given the trouble that they were causing him, Henry behaved towards both women with considerable restraint. When the Act of Succession became law on 30 March 1534, it became high treason to refuse to accept Elizabeth as the king's lawful daughter and heir.[8] Henry knew perfectly well that both Catherine and Mary would refuse such an oath, so, in spite of some graphic threats, he would not allow it to be administered to them. Their servants were compelled to swear, and did so, much to Catherine's disgust. She complained that that made them 'rather gaolers than servants', but it seems to have made no difference either to their diligence or to their loyalty to her. In her anger, Catherine was less than fair, and never showed any appreciation of the king's forbearance towards her own person. There was also, of course, an element of self-interest in his attitude, because if he had proceeded to extremes against either of them, then even the deaths of Thomas More and Bishop John Fisher (who had both refused to accept Henry as supreme head of the Church) would have paled into insignificance beside the scandal that would have been created.

In 1535 Mary was nineteen, and in normal circumstances would have been married and preoccupied with the running of a great household. As it was, her scope was extremely limited. She had no responsibilities, public or private, and the physical exercise that she craved was inevitably restricted. As she was no great scholar, boredom was probably a serious problem. There is no evidence that she was receiving any systematic instruction, and no reference to exceptional piety or devotional exercises. Several years later, one of the ladies who had served her at this difficult time testified that it had been works of classical literature – *literae humaniores* – that had been her solace on sleepless nights, rather than books of spiritual guidance, but the lady's memory was selective in other respects and we cannot be sure.[9] Mary was under constant surveillance, but that was not for the purpose of monitoring her daily routine. Letters to and from Chapuys must have been privileged, because some of the things that she is alleged to have told him would have got her into serious trouble. His messages were carried by his own servants, and although Cromwell occasionally prohibited such visits, the bans were never of long duration. Correspondence with Catherine, which was surreptitious by necessity, may have escaped scrutiny, or may simply have been regarded as innocuous. Those letters that survive are full of affection and encouragement, but have no political significance. Letters from her mother's friends and allies were, however, rather different, and there was a fuss in September 1534 over an exchange with Sir Nicholas and Lady Carew, which Anne Shelton was ordered to investigate.[10]

Following the final decision of his court in Catherine's favour, Clement had ordered Henry to take her back upon pain of excommunication. When his ultimatum was ignored, the ban came into effect, although it was never fully promulgated, and neither Charles nor Francis broke off diplomatic relations. In December 1535 Catherine became seriously ill, and on 6 January she died at the age of fifty. In spite of all pleas, the king would not allow his daughter to visit her mother in her last illness, perhaps because he did not take the crisis seriously until it was too late. Inevitably there were rumours of poison, and it was briefly believed in Brussels that Mary was *in extremis* for the same reason; however, the real reason for Catherine's death appears to have been coronary thrombosis. Mary was deeply distressed, particularly because she had been unable to say goodbye, but, contrary to what was believed in some quarters, Henry's attitude (and possibly Anne's as well) became more indulgent towards her. This was less for humane reasons than because they had both persuaded themselves that the old queen had been responsible for her daughter's defiant attitude. The threat of the succession oath, which had been allowed to hang in the air since the summer of 1534, was now tacitly withdrawn, and the king sent her a substantial financial gift. All this was wasted upon Mary, sunk in grief at her mother's death; she probably did not notice, and certainly did not care, that rather different signals were now emanating from the court.

Henry is alleged to have 'worn yellow for mourning' when the news of Catherine's death reached him, and to have publicly rejoiced that the threat of war was now lifted.[11] In fact he is unlikely to have been so simple minded. The pope's edict was now overtaken by events, but in other respects Henry's circumstances were unchanged. Anne had still not borne him a son, but she had miscarried, probably of another daughter, in July 1534. There was no estrangement between them, but Henry's sexual drive was almost certainly erratic. There were other problems. The behaviour that the king had found so fascinating in the young woman he was pursuing had become aggravating in a wife. The emotional scenes and passionate reconciliations were becoming tedious and unnecessary, and the pushy political schemer was becoming a liability. Anne was simply unable to adjust to the changed expectations of the man who was now her husband, and their relationship suffered consequent strains. There was nothing particularly serious in all this, but the queen had many enemies, and the king's constant favour meant more to her than the chance of procreation.

However, during the summer progress of 1535 Anne was found to be pregnant again, and the shadows (if there really were any) retreated. It was during this progress that the royal couple visited Wolf Hall near Marlborough, the home of Sir John Seymour and his substantial brood. It was subsequently alleged that during this visit Henry's fancy lighted upon Sir John's daughter Jane, and that an intrigue resulted that was eventually to be fatal to the queen.[12] In fact, Jane was already at court, and the king must have known her by sight for some time – nor is there any certainty that she was at Wolf Hall at the time of the royal visit – so the story is probably apocryphal. Relations between Henry and Anne were if anything better in the latter part of 1535 than they had been a year before, and that would not have been the case if the queen's sharp eyes had detected a rival in the undergrowth. However, the policies that Anne's ascendancy represented remained unpopular, and while the court was in Hampshire there was disobedience at Greenwich that landed Lady Mary Howard and Lady Jane Rochford (the queen's sister-in-law) in the Tower.

Catherine's death not only simplified matters for the king; it did the same for Mary's supporters. Anne might now be the undisputed queen, but she was also more exposed. Should she fail again to produce a prince, there was nothing to prevent the king from trying some other lady. As well as being a nuisance, Catherine had also been a shield.

In January 1536 Henry was in high spirits, and making much of Elizabeth, as though to point to his queen's very obvious condition. And then disaster struck. Although he was now over forty, the king still indulged in his favourite pastime of jousting, but he was no longer as agile or as skilful as he had once been, and on 24 January he took a heavy fall. He was unconscious for over two hours, and if ever he had needed a reminder of the uncertainty of mortality, this was it. Henry recovered, apparently none the worse apart from a few bruises, but five days later Anne was delivered of a stillborn son.[13] She claimed that it had been the shock of Henry's accident that had brought this about, but there had been earlier signs of difficulty, and it is likely that the true cause was quite different. Shaken as he was, the king again became a prey to superstitious fears. Had he now done something else to offend a God who was proving so unsympathetic? Many years later Nicholas Sanders, who was a bitter enemy of everything that Anne represented, told a story to the effect that the foetus had been deformed, and that Henry convinced himself that he could not have been the begetter.[14] This was plausible in the sense that it represented a view widely held at the time that deformity in a child was the consequence of unlawful procreation; but there is no contemporary evidence either of deformity or of such a reaction on Henry's part. What is true, however, is that like many passionate relationships, the king's second marriage had become unstable. He was not 'tired' of Anne, nor had he given up hope of a son, but he was in a volatile emotional state in February and March 1536.

This was sufficient to give the queen's enemies an opening. Mary's friends were still numerous about the court – not least because she was now a grown woman and Elizabeth still a child. Elizabeth's position, moreover, depended entirely upon what many privately regarded as the king's eccentric behaviour – in other words it had been artificially created and could soon be changed by the same means. Mary may well have seemed a better long-term bet. More critically, however, Thomas Cromwell changed sides. He had for several years been turning Henry's aspirations into political facts by deft jurisdictional engineering, and as long as Catherine had been alive an alliance with the Boleyns had been necessary. Now it was not, and the queen's Francophilia was becoming a serious embarrassment to his preferred foreign policy. No one knew the fragility of Henry's mind better than Cromwell, and at some point during April he or his agents managed to sow in the king's mind the idea that Anne was guilty of adultery.[15]

Exactly how this was done we do not know, and there has been (and still is) much debate about faction and conspiracy. The queen's own behaviour did not help. She had a feisty, flirtatious element in her makeup that was probably quite harmless, and which Henry had frequently indulged in the past, but now it suddenly became significant, and in his eyes sinister. An incident with Sir Henry Norris at a joust on 30 April bounced him over the edge into overt suspicion, and a 'confession' extracted (probably under torture) from a court musician named Mark Smeaton converted suspicion into irrational certainty.[16] Quite suddenly, no story of Anne's misconduct became too implausible to be believed. She was arrested, and under extreme pressure became hysterical. She had been guilty of adultery with a hundred men, including her own brother; she had mocked the king's sexual prowess; even Elizabeth's legitimacy became suspect. Henry is alleged to have confided to some unnamed person that she was really a witch, and that explained the years of ascendancy that she had enjoyed over him.

With the king in a state of maudlin self-pity, and self-interested enemies ready to exploit any charge against Anne, there was no chance that either the queen or her alleged accomplices would receive a fair trial. The latter were arraigned by a special common law commission ('oyer et terminer', in legal French terminology) on 9 May, and the queen and her brother, Lord Rochford, by their peers on the 15th. Although the charge of witchcraft was not mentioned, all were found guilty of treasonable adultery and sentenced to death. On 19 May Anne was beheaded at the Tower.[17]

Although some doubts remain, most of the historians who have studied these events in detail believe that she was ruthlessly framed by people who understood both her own weaknesses and the king's, and that the motivation that drove most of them was a desire to see Mary restored to her rightful place.[18] However, there has from the time of the tragedy itself been an alternative explanation of Henry's motivation. Less than a fortnight after Anne's execution, the king was quietly married to Jane Seymour, and some contemporaries believed that the whole plot had no other end than to enable the king to dispose of a wife who no longer interested him, and obtain a replacement. Cromwell may indeed have had such a thought in mind, because he was not particularly committed to Mary, but was very aware that the king still needed a son. The miscarriage of 29 January may have had a bigger influence on his mind than is usually admitted. Anne was around thirty-five (her exact age is unknown), and had been married to Henry for three years. In that time she had borne one daughter (who had been conceived before the marriage) and one stillborn son. Catherine had last conceived at thirty-three. There was a very strong case for arguing that the king needed a new wife, if only his affection for Anne could be overcome. The method was ruthless, but she was far too skilful a politician to be shunted aside, unlike Henry's next wife but one, Anne of Cleves. As was later to be said of the similarly formidable Earl of Strafford, 'stone dead hath no fellow'.

Not content with executing his wife, Henry decided now to repudiate the union altogether, and the marriage that had cost him so dearly only three years before was declared null and void. This could not be done on grounds of adultery, real or alleged, and the impediment that was used was probably consanguinity – the blood relationship established between them by Henry's previous sexual intercourse with Anne's sister Mary. We cannot be sure because the trial papers have disappeared. This had been well known to Cranmer all along, and if he claimed to have 'discovered' it at this stage, then his claim was disingenuous, which reflects no credit on any of the parties involved.[19] The effect, of course, was to bastardise Elizabeth – something that Eustace Chapuys had been claiming all along – and therefore ostensibly to clear the way for Mary's rehabilitation in a way that Anne's execution alone could not have done. However, that did not happen, and it is at this point that the divergence in aim between Cromwell and his conservative allies becomes clear. Whether Henry had really taken a fancy to Jane Seymour early in the year – or even in the previous year – is not relevant. The chances are that the flirtation that was observed and commented upon was no more than a convention of courtly love, and was understood as such by all those who were close to it. However,

Henry did take Jane as his wife with remarkable (some thought indecent) speed as soon as he was free to do so. Jane was twenty-seven, and the fact that she was unmarried may have had more to do with Sir John's inability to find an adequate dowry than with any physical unattractiveness. To the modern observer she looks plain and dumpy,[20] but she had one big thing in her favour: she came of a proven breeding stock. Sir John had a quiverful of both sons and daughters – hence his inability to provide for them all – and although Jane's own fecundity was a matter of speculation, the omens were good. Cromwell's intention seems to have been to persuade the king to sweep the past aside and to start again. This was aided by the death in July of the Duke of Richmond. Henry was genuinely distressed by the loss of his only son, but it removed one more complicating factor. He now had no son, illegitimate or otherwise, and two illegitimate daughters, so he was free to make whatever arrangement seemed best to him.

It soon became apparent that this did not include a reconciliation with the pope. Jane and her brothers were religious conservatives at this point – indeed Mary's supporters thought of them as potential allies – but the one achievement of the last five years that the king was not prepared to abandon was the royal supremacy over the Church. With Catherine and Anne both dead, he could in theory simply have returned to the position of 1529, and Pope Paul III apparently expected him to do no less, but neither Henry nor Cromwell had any such intention. If Mary were to be returned to her father's favour, it would be on his own terms, and not because her legitimacy had been restored by some wider settlement. The indicators were already there for those that could see them. A few days before the crisis broke over Anne's alleged misdemeanours (but not necessarily before the king was aware of them), he told Chapuys in response to another of the ambassador's endlessly repeated petitions:

> As to the legitimation of our daughter Mary … if she would submit to our grace, without wrestling against the determination of our laws, we would acknowledge her and use her as our daughter; but we would not be directed or pressed herein.[21]

Anne's execution made no difference to this determination. Later in May Chapuys wrote that the council, the common people, even Jane Seymour, were urging Mary's unconditional restoration, but he admitted that the king had given no sign of agreeing to it. Everyone waited and hoped. The pope suspended Henry's excommunication in the hope of a negotiation; Charles hopefully suggested a marriage with the Infanta of Portugal; and Mary's old servants began to turn up at her residence at Hunsdon in the hope of being re-employed. This last was particularly tricky, because with Elizabeth's bastardisation the household lacked any specific status. It was easy to assume that Mary was now the senior partner, but unsafe to do so until the king declared his mind. Chapuys advised Lady Shelton not to take on anyone without the king's explicit authorisation.[22]

Mary herself was either disarmingly innocent or deeply guileful; and most indications suggest that she was innocent. In spite of a sophisticated education, she had an instinctive tendency to see the world in terms of black and white. When her parents had fallen out, Catherine was white and Henry was black. When the nature of Anne Boleyn's influence became clear, it was she who became black, and Henry (sort of) white. Consequently, when Anne ended on the scaffold, Mary not only felt totally vindicated, but also expected her father to revert automatically to being the loving indulgent parent she remembered from her early childhood. Without giving any thought to what else had happened in the meantime, she awaited the summons to return to court and to favour. In the latter part of May she was receiving congratulations from everyone except the person who really mattered. No word came from Henry. Realising after a while that she was expected to make the first move, on the 26th she wrote to Cromwell, asking for his intercession, now that 'that woman' who had alienated her from her father was gone. The secretary replied, promptly and correctly, informing her that obedience was expected as a condition of reinstatement.[23] Surprising as it may seem, Mary did not apparently see what he was driving at. On the 30th she wrote again, asking to see her father, and undertaking to be 'as obedient to the king's grace as you can reasonably require of me'. It seems that she really believed that the issue that had so fundamentally divided them for the last three years had been no more than the product of Anne Boleyn's malice. If that was so, then she probably thought that the royal supremacy was equally insubstantial, and would simply go away in the sunshine of a new age.

The disillusionment that followed was cruel, but not the result of any hardening of Henry's heart. His position remained exactly what it had been. If she would accept her own illegitimacy, and his authority over the Church, he would receive her back into his favour – and if not, not. It was not quite clear what that favour would mean, because a position in the succession was not on offer at this stage; however, an independent household, a place at court and renewed marriage negotiations can reasonably be assumed. Without waiting for a reply to her second epistle to Cromwell, on 1 June Mary wrote directly to the king. She congratulated him upon his (very) recent marriage, and asked leave to wait upon the new queen. She acknowledged her offences in general terms, and begged his blessing and forgiveness 'in as humble and lowly a manner as is possible'. Unfortunately the effect of this dutiful abasement was marred by an unacceptable reservation. She would obey her father in all things 'next to God'. She humbly besought 'your highness to consider that I am but a woman and your child, who hath committed her soul only to God, and her body to be ordered in this world as it shall stand with your pleasure'.[24] Since this reservation covered both the points at issue between them, she was conceding nothing in spite of her humble tone, and Henry did not even bother to reply. Instead, he caused to be drawn up a set of articles of submission to be presented to her, articles that allowed no room for either evasion or equivocation.

Chapuys, who had remained sceptical about the king's good intentions, was by early June seriously alarmed. Cromwell showed him a draft of the articles, ostensibly to invite his cooperation, but really in the hope that the knowledge of them would be communicated to Mary and that she would wake up to the gravity of her situation. Chapuys may not have succeeded, or his cautiously worded warning may have been misunderstood, because on 7 June Mary wrote again to Cromwell, clearly thinking that the problem between herself and her father had been resolved. She expressed her joy at the news that he had 'withdrawn his displeasure', and asked for some token before she would come to court. Three days later she also wrote to the king, copying the letter to Cromwell with a covering note begging not to be pressed in submission further than her conscience would bear.[25]

Mary's state of mind at this point is hard to reconstruct, because she seems to have realised that she had not satisfied her father, but believed that her reservation had been accepted. Given what he knew, Chapuys can hardly have given her that impression, so it may have been derived from some unidentified (and unreliable) courtier. No reply was sent to either of these letters, and on or about 15 June the inevitable happened. The Duke of Norfolk, the Earl of Sussex and the Bishop of Chichester arrived at Hunsdon, bearing the king's commission. Mary was to be asked two questions. Would she repudiate the 'Bishop of Rome' and accept her father's ecclesiastical supremacy? And would she accept the nullity of her mother's marriage? In a stormy and emotional confrontation she rejected both demands.

This was a crisis of the first importance, because the king's daughter was now guilty of treason on at least two counts, and the judges whom Henry consulted recommended that she should be proceeded against by law.[26] This was not Cromwell's doing, because right up to the last minute he had been in correspondence with Mary trying to find an acceptable formula – and believed that he had succeeded. Norfolk's mission blew any such possibility out of the water, and a few days later Cromwell penned a furious letter of reproach, castigating her for obstinacy, and lamenting his own folly in attempting to help her. It was probably never sent, but was a fair reflection of his frustration at the time. The council immediately went into emergency session. Meanwhile, setting his anger aside, the secretary worked furiously to find some solution. Mary's execution for treason formed no part of his plans, and although it would have deprived the conservative malcontents of their figurehead, it would also have given them a martyr, and ruined any hope that he may have had of a *rapprochement* with the Emperor. Only if she could be forced into submission could the malcontents be sidelined and a volatile political situation stabilised. Mary's known sympathisers, such as the Marquis of Exeter and Sir William Fitzwilliam, were excluded from the council during these emergency debates. Other friends – Sir Anthony Browne, Sir Francis Bryan and Lady Hussey – were arrested and interrogated. Apart from the last, who had openly referred to her as 'princess', their only offence seems to have been to speculate on what a splendid heir Mary would be – if she would only submit. The crisis lasted about a week.

It was solved eventually by a mixture of chicanery and psychological torture. Cromwell succeeded in convincing both Chapuys and Mary herself that she was within a whisker of arraignment and execution. Given Henry's long record of hesitancy and emotional confusion in his dealing with his daughter, it is by no means certain that this was the case, but the secretary was making the most frightening noises of which he was capable – and it worked. When it came to the point, Mary did not have her mother's steely resolve – but then Catherine had never been threatened with the axe. It was probably Chapuys who mediated the deal. Once he was convinced that Henry was serious about proceeding to extremes, he began to urge Mary to submit in order to save her life. A martyred princess might make a potent symbol, but a live one (even if slightly tarnished) was more useful. For several days the unfortunate young woman suffered from insomnia, neuralgia, toothache and other stress-related symptoms. Finally, on 22 June, she surrendered. The ever thoughtful Cromwell had apparently provided a comprehensive set of articles of submission, which she signed, and a covering letter, remitting her whole life and estate to the king's discretion, absolutely and without condition. Chapuys believed, or pretended to believe, that she had signed these documents without reading them, but in view of the effusive letter of thanks that she wrote to Cromwell a few days later, it is clear that she was perfectly well aware of the contents.[27] Her gratitude was rather pathetic, given that all he had done was to persuade her into an unconditional surrender – but she believed that he had saved her life, and he was certainly not going to disabuse her.

MARY'S SUBMISSION

Undated, but probably 22 June 1536

The confession of me, the Lady Mary, made upon certain points and articles underwritten, in the which, as I do now plainly and with all mine heart confess and declare mine inward sentence, belief and judgement, with a due conformity of obedience to the laws of the realm; so minding forever to persist and continue in this determination, without change, alteration, or variance, I do most humbly beseech the King's Highness, my father, whom I have obstinately and inobediently offended in the denial of the same heretofore, to forgive mine offence therein, and to take me to his most gracious mercy.

[*Letters and Papers* ..., x, 1137, taken from Thomas Hearne, *Sylloge Epistolarum* (Oxford, 1716). The original does not survive.]

The great crisis therefore ended with a whimper rather than a bang, and Mary's state of mind is hard to assess. According to Chapuys, she was prostrated with grief and remorse at having betrayed both her principles and her mother, but he was bound to say that, if only to obscure his own role in the proceedings. His object now was to preserve some credibility for her, both with the Emperor and among her own supporters, so he asked Charles to obtain a special dispensation from Rome to ease her conscience. Significantly, he did not represent her as having dissimulated her submission. This may have been for fear lest his despatches should be intercepted, but he had made far more damaging revelations in the past and, in view of his generally pro-Imperial stance, Cromwell would not have authorised such interference. He presumably knew that such a statement would have been untrue. In later life, Mary was to be deeply ashamed of her actions at this time, but in July 1536 the overwhelming impression is one of relief.

On 6 July Henry and Jane visited Hunsdon and stayed for two days. Mary was much closer in age to the new queen than she was to her own sister, or Anne Shelton, or her faithful Margaret Pole, and the two young women quickly became friends. Jane seems to have been a peaceful soul, who had a calming influence on everyone around her, and that included Mary, who was much in need of tranquillity after the trauma of the past three years.

The news of Mary's return to favour spread like wildfire, and far outweighed any tidings of how that state of affairs had been achieved. In Rome it was thought that she would be restored to the succession, and that the English schism was about to come to an end. Elsewhere it was believed that she would be created Duchess of York, and it was reported that great crowds had greeted the Countess of Salisbury when she visited the court, on the assumption that Mary would be with her. In fact nothing dramatic happened at all, but her rehabilitation was steadily put in place. Within a few days, and before Henry's visit, she had been invited to suggest appointments to her restored chamber, and she named three women who had been in her service before, including Susan Tonge, better known as Clarencius.[28] By mid-August her new establishment was in place, headed by four gentlewomen, and numbering a total of twenty-nine. There was no chamberlain, and no lady governess. In fact it was not an independent household at all. What happened was that the joint household, which had existed in principle since 1533, was reconstructed to reflect the equal status of its two mistresses. At the same time that Mary was restored, the provision for Elizabeth was reduced, and Sir John Shelton, the controller, reported on 16 August that it was now 'served on two sides'. He estimated that the cost of this *ménage* would be in the region of £4,000 a year.[29] The great advantage of such a set up from Mary's point of view was that her chamber was 'detachable', and that if she wanted to go to court, or to another royal residence on her own, she could do so. In the latter event, she would have taken a proportion of the 'below-stairs' servants with her, but they would have continued to be paid by Shelton, who also both hired and dismissed them as circumstances required. Mary had no control over the service departments – and, more importantly, no land or money of her own. Her whole allowance came from the privy purse, and although she was scrupulously consulted over her chamber appointments, she did not make those either.

Another sign of rehabilitation was renewed talk of marriage. Early in August the Emperor sent a special envoy to suggest a match with Dom Luis, the younger brother of the King of Portugal, who had featured in earlier speculations. Chapuys, a little put out by this intervention, did not believe that Henry would allow his daughter to marry outside the realm, but would rather provide her with a suitable husband himself in order to enhance his control. No doubt aiming to frustrate such a development, he persuaded her to renew her pledge to him not to marry without the Emperor's consent. She was, he reported, not inclined to matrimony at all, 'save for some great advantage to the peace of Christendom'.[30] The ambassador was probably wrong in his assessment of the king's attitude. As far as Henry was concerned, his daughter was now free again to be deployed in whatever way he thought fit. On 12 September he wrote to his 'brother of France', suggesting a match with the young Duke of Angoulême. Henry would legitimate his daughter, and include her in the succession – in default of male heirs – in return for Angoulême's residence in England. How seriously this was intended we do not know. Nothing came of the suggestion, but it indicates that Mary was now back on the European marriage market, and that her status was negotiable.

Meanwhile Chapuys' suggestion of a secret dispensation had been greeted with contempt in Rome. It was pointed out that even if secrecy were permissible in such a matter (which it was not), Henry would be bound to find out, and if he became convinced that his daughter had deceived him, her last state would be worse than her first. For his part, the ambassador made no further mention of conscientious scruples, but reported in early October that Mary had written both to the Emperor and to Mary of Hungary, his regent in the Low Countries, professing to have been enlightened by the Holy Spirit. She now realised that her mother's marriage had been unlawful, and that the pope's power was usurped. Of course Chapuys claimed that she had been forced to write these letters by her father, and the letters themselves do not survive, so there must be an element of uncertainty. The ambassador was writing to explain away the arrival of these unexpected (and unwelcome) epistles, putting the best gloss that he could upon the situation. If we abandon hindsight, and look only at the evidence from the autumn of 1536, it looks very much as though Mary had undergone a genuine conversion to her father's point of view. The effect of extreme psychological pressure is often called brainwashing, and it may be either temporary or permanent. In this case it was not permanent, because years later, as queen, Mary was to use her public policies to reverse and undo most of what her father had done, including the repudiation of her mother. However, for the rest of his life, and well into her brother Edward's reign, Mary gave not the slightest hint of dissent from Henry's proceedings, and given the number of people on the look out for such signs, we must conclude that, for the time being at least, her conversion was genuine.

4

RESTITUTION

During August and September 1536, Mary remained at Hunsdon, exchanging friendly notes with Jane Seymour. Her father sent her £20, Cromwell the gift of a horse. She wrote to Henry commending her 'sister Elizabeth' – 'such a child toward as I doubt not but your highness shall have cause to rejoice of in time coming'. This was little short of a revolution. She had never had a good word to say about the 'little bastard' before, and had never acknowledged her as a sister.[1] There is no sign that this letter was either forced or constrained, and it seems that Chapuys' fretting about her bruised conscience had more to do with his agenda than hers. In October she visited the court, and Cardinal Du Bellay reported that she was 'first after the Queen' in precedence. While revolts against Henry's religious policies in Lincolnshire and the north (the latter known as the Pilgrimage of Grace) were taking her name in vain, demanding her reinstatement in the succession, she made not the slightest move that could be interpreted as encouragement. As Henry and Cromwell were struggling with the biggest protest movement of the reign, she was pottering about at Hunsdon or Richmond as though nothing was happening, and not even Chapuys pretended otherwise.[2] Before Christmas she was sufficiently sure of herself to ask for an increase in her allowance, and she spent the festival itself at court, apparently quite at ease with Jane, her father and herself.

At the end of 1536 Chapuys was withdrawn. This had nothing to do with any deterioration in Anglo-Imperial relations, which were better than they had been for some time. He was simply deployed elsewhere; but the removal of his special brand of inquisitiveness and partisanship diminishes our ability to follow Mary over the following years. Early in 1537 Charles was pressing the Portuguese to make a further proposal for her hand on behalf of Dom Luis. This seems to have been primarily a negative move on his part, designed to block any attempt by the French to woo her, or any temptation on Henry's part to diminish her status with a domestic marriage. The Emperor seems not to have been much interested in her legitimacy, but we do not know enough about the negotiation to be sure whether the Portuguese were equally indifferent. A bid was made, but collapsed during the summer.

Diego de Mendoza, who replaced Chapuys as Imperial ambassador in March 1537, came armed with ambiguous instructions, because on the one hand he was to maintain 'amity', while on the other hand pursue the possibility of a marriage between Mary and her strongly Catholic cousin, Reginald Pole. Had Henry known about this he would certainly have regarded it as hostile, because Pole had denounced the king as a schismatic and been condemned as a traitor.[3] Pole had also been in northern Europe with the intention of persuading Charles to support the Pilgrimage of Grace. By March 1537 the Pilgrimage had long since collapsed, but Henry's feelings towards Pole had not changed – and were not likely to change. From the Emperor's point of view it would have been a suitable match. Pole was an Englishman of royal blood, being a younger son of the Countess of Salisbury and a great-nephew of King Edward IV. Moreover, although he was a cardinal, he was only in deacon's orders, and therefore not beyond the reach of a dispensation to marry. He was sixteen years older than Mary, and if they had ever met neither remembered the fact. Mendoza soon appreciated that such a suggestion would be extremely undiplomatic, and the matter was never raised in public. It remained in the back of the Emperor's mind for a number of years, but there is no sign at this stage that Mary was aware of it. Chapuys had once claimed that Pole was the only man that she was interested in, and his statement may have caused the idea to germinate, but in truth what Mary felt was irrelevant.

More interestingly, Henry was apparently becoming aware of the new ways in which the power of statute could be applied. The second succession Act, of 1536, had not added to the Act of 1534, rather it had repealed it. Whereas it had been possible (with a little creative imagination) to believe that all the Reformation statutes down to 1535 had been simply declaring the law of God, it was no longer possible to say that when one of them had been repealed. (Nor could it logically be argued that the repeal was '*ultra vires*', that is, beyond the power of Parliament if the original statute had been accepted.) Consequently it might be possible to arrange the succession to the throne without reference to the technical legitimacy of the candidates – a totally new concept, which if it had been around in 1460 might have prevented the Wars of the Roses.[4] The king had apparently terminated his negotiation with the Emperor by declaring that the argument that Mary might be legitimate because she had been born *in bona fide parentum* – that is while her parents were ignorant of the bar between them – did not apply because the bar was part of the law of God. He had also suggested that this issue could be resolved by having any treaty ratified by Parliament which was altogether too bizarre a concept for the very conventional Charles. The whole idea of a 'constitutional' solution to the succession issue was so strange to contemporaries that a similar negotiation which was being pursued with the French at the same time collapsed when Francis realised that the way things had gone in England left Mary's rights at the mercy of the estates of the realm, so that any son of his who might marry her could have no certain prospect of the crown matrimonial.[5]

In late 1536 and early 1537 Mary seems to have spent more time in her father's company than she had since her childhood. After Christmas she was in and out of the court, visiting Hatfield and New Hall as well as Greenwich and Westminster. Most of the early summer she was at Greenwich, before moving round the royal residences in the Home Counties during July and August. A modest 'service establishment' must have travelled with her, although it seems clear from the way in which the money was deployed that this remained a part of Sir John Shelton's responsibility. Her wanderlust must have added significantly to the cost. This money all came from the treasury of the chamber, much to the occasional discomfort of the treasurer (Sir Brian Tuke); but Mary was also receiving about £450 a year in 'spending money' from the privy purse. This she deployed mainly on rewards to her own servants, and on gifts to the numerous servants of other noblemen, ladies and courtiers, who sent her presents.[6] She kept a band of minstrels, and her long serving jester 'Jane the Fool' first appears at this point. Her privy-purse expenses give the impression of a full and varied life, but there are also some surprises. Pious offerings appear only at Easter and Candlemas; there are hardly any references to hunting, or to her own musical instruments, and no mention at all of books or scholarship. It is possible that such expenses were passing through other accounts, but the impression given is that of a friendly, outgoing young woman, well liked by all who came in contact with her, but lacking any desire for either self-improvement or political influence. In spite of her acknowledged status, Mary had no clientage, no body of dependents, and seems instead to have come to a *modus vivendi* with Thomas Cromwell, whereby he catered for her whims and controlled appointments to her staff. Apart from one episode in June 1537, there are no further references to her sickness, and although she employed her mother's former physician and apothecary (both Spaniards), neither appears to have lived in her household, and they were summoned only occasionally, usually (it would appear) to one or other of the servants rather than to Mary herself.

Shortly after Mendoza's arrival, Mary informed him that she had written again to the Emperor, re-emphasising the point that she had made the previous autumn, that she would not allow herself to be used in any way against her father. The ambassador, at whom this warning was clearly aimed, discreetly praised her wisdom, and tactfully let the matter drop.[7]

In the summer of 1537 Queen Jane was visibly pregnant, and the coronation that had been proposed for her was postponed. For the same reason there was no royal progress that summer, and as the autumn came on the king became increasingly edgy. Unlike Anne, Jane's behaviour had given him no cause for either irritation or anxiety. In assuring the Duke of Norfolk that it was his own decision not to travel to the north that summer, and that Jane had not pressed him, he claimed that she:

> … was in every condition of that loving inclination and reverend conformity that she can in all things well content satisfy and quiet herself with that thing which we shall think expedient and determine.[8]

Even such a paragon, however, was subject to the vagaries of nature, and Jane seems to have been uncertain when her own time was due. It was late September when she withdrew into the customary seclusion at Hampton Court, which suggests that she expected to give birth towards the end of October. However, she went into labour on the 9th.

After an easy pregnancy, the birth was hard and bitter. Special prayers and intercessions were made in London, and Henry was deeply worried. Finally, after two days and three nights, on 12 October, a son was born, who was named Edward and christened with great splendour on the 15th, with Mary standing as godmother. The whole realm rejoiced, in a way that it had not done since the early days of 1511, and on the 18th the new prince was proclaimed Prince of Wales, Duke of Cornwall and Earl of Caernarvon. The whole court held its breath, but the child seemed healthy. Unfortunately the same could not be said of his mother. The long struggle had exhausted her, and by the 18th she had developed puerperal fever, also known as childbed fever, a contagious disease often spread by the poor hygiene of attendants and physicians. After the christening she had been well enough to sit in her chamber and receive congratulations, but by the 23rd septicaemia had developed, and she died late on the 25th. Henry had greeted the deaths of both Catherine and Anne with relief, but this time he was genuinely distressed. Jane had not only given him his longed-for son, she had been such a gentle and loveable creature. The chronicler Edward Hall recorded of her death: 'of none in the realm was it more heavily taken than of the King's Majesty himself'. The king immediately moved to Westminster, 'where he mourned and kept himself close and secret a great while'.[9] Henry had described Jane as his only true wife, and it was to be over two years before he married again.

These events affected Mary in a number of ways. Jane had been a good friend to her, and she was too distressed to attend the first stage of her funeral rites, which took place on 30 October. Mary was also no longer the heir to the throne by any English reckoning. Strictly by canon law, Edward's birth made no difference, because Henry and Jane had been married while the realm was in schism, and no marriage conducted in those circumstances was valid. However, the total invalidity of all weddings since 1535, and the consequent bastardisation of all children under two years old, was not something that could be contemplated, let alone insisted upon. For all practical purposes Edward was his father's heir, and was recognised as such. A splendid household was established for him, even more magnificent than that which Mary had enjoyed in the marches of Wales. Unless or until her father married again, Mary was the first lady of the kingdom, but she was a long step further from the centre of events. By 12 November she was sufficiently recovered to take her place at Jane's actual interment, but the Christmas was spent in mourning, so there were no splendid festivities to preside over – which was probably a relief.

By March 1538 the Sheltons had ceased to preside over the joint household of Mary and Elizabeth, but it is not known exactly when they were replaced. Anne Shelton was succeeded by Lady Mary Kingston, the wife of Sir William, who probably acted as controller before moving on to the king's household in 1539.[10] In April 1539, when Sir William was promoted, the Kingstons were replaced by Sir Edward and Lady Baynton. None of this seems to have made much difference to the domestic arrangements, and Mary's chamber staff showed a remarkable stability throughout this period. The same servants, Susan Clarencius, Richard Baldwin, Randall Dodd, Beatrice ap Rice and others are constantly referred to.

As long as Henry remained unmarried – that is from October 1537 to January 1540 – there was a great deal of flexibility between the households. In March 1538, for example, Henry was at Hampton Court, Edward and Elizabeth about three miles off and Mary at Richmond, but this did not mean that Edward and Elizabeth were sharing a household, or that Mary was now independent. It would no doubt have been more convenient to have the two children (six months and four and half years) together, but protocol dictated otherwise. Mary attended her father's fourth wedding, but does not seem to have spent much time at court during Anne of Cleves' brief and problematic reign.[11] Anne was a mistake. The wedding came about because Cromwell wanted some leverage against the Emperor, and Cleves Julich was a significant cluster of territories with reformist Catholic tendencies to Henry's taste. Anne, who was the young Duke William's sister, was reputedly beautiful and virtuous. Holbein was sent across to paint her portrait, Henry was convinced, an agreement was signed, and the new bride arrived in January 1540. Unfortunately her descriptions (and Holbein) had flattered to deceive. Anne may well have been virtuous – indeed she was a total innocent – but she was not beautiful and had neither education nor any courtly accomplishments. Henry was profoundly disappointed, and went through with the ceremony only because he could find no immediate way out. He professed himself quite unable to consummate the union, and the couple shared the same bed for only a few nights, with polite frustration on his side and ignorant bewilderment on hers. The marriage was dissolved on grounds of non-consummation in July 1540, but Anne remained in England with a generous settlement. Later Mary seems to have developed a soft spot for this cast-off queen, who was otherwise neglected by all, but there is little evidence of that from the early part of 1540.

Nor is it known how Mary reacted to the fall of Thomas Cromwell, which occurred at almost exactly the same time. The two events are customarily linked, because it is claimed that Cromwell was responsible for subjecting his master to a disagreeable and humiliating ordeal. In fact this seems not to have been the case, because the marriage had been Henry's decision, and Cromwell was fully prepared to provide the annulment later secured by others. He rather seems to have been undermined by a coalition of enemies (of which he had many), who succeeded in convincing Henry that he was destabilising the religious settlement by patronising heretics. Once that conviction had lodged in the king's mind, everything that had gone wrong recently – including Anne of Cleves – suddenly became Cromwell's fault. On 10 June he was arrested, condemned by Act of Attainder, and executed on 28 July.

Mary had no known connection with any of this, and what she may have thought we do not know. For a time, in the winter of 1536–7, she and Cromwell had been on friendly, almost convivial terms, but as Mary's relations with her father stabilised, he disappears from the picture. Intensely busy about all manner of things, the lord privy seal (as Cromwell now was) seems to have confined himself to occasional friendly gestures. In 1538 he was occupied countermining some of those to whom Mary had been closest, but who now found themselves incriminated by the activities of Reginald Pole. Pole's brother, Lord Montague, and Henry Courtenay, Marquis of Exeter, were arraigned and executed, while his mother Margaret, Mary's long-time mentor, was consigned to the Tower.[12] Reginald was certainly committed to the idea that Edward was a bastard, and that Mary remained the king's only legitimate child. It is quite possible that those with whom he was in touch in England shared that view, which was the king's conviction and the reason why he was prepared to allow Cromwell to act. He seems to have been convinced that the conspirators intended to kill Prince Edward, a charge for which the evidence was purely hearsay. However, her own priority in the succession was a position that Mary herself had ostentatiously abandoned, and she remained in the king's favour, untouched by the so-called 'Exeter conspiracy'. Whether she was in any way shielded by Cromwell, or simply never under suspicion, we do not know. She is bound to have viewed the fall of her erstwhile friends with sorrow, and that may have distanced her from the lord privy seal, but there is no sign of the kind of emotional crisis that followed her mother's death. Cromwell's own fall was also brought about by those who were in some sense Mary's friends, but she was not implicated in their intrigues, and his removal did not affect her position in any discernible way.

After Henry married his fifth wife Catherine Howard in July 1540, Mary appears to have spent an increasing amount of time at court, and to have been living 'on the Queen's side' at the time of Catherine's fall. This was not because of any great affection between them. They were too similar in age and too different in temperament. Catherine, as it subsequently transpired, had a great deal of sexual experience, and a considerable appetite. Mary had no experience at all, and although her appetite remains a matter of speculation, ostensibly she regarded the whole business with distaste. Mary's presence at court must have been by Henry's wish, although the reason is uncertain. He may have hoped that the two women who were now closest to him would grow to like each other, or he may have wanted Mary to assume some of those court functions for which his much-adored young wife was temperamentally unsuitable. When the crash came, and Henry became convinced of Catherine's infidelity in November 1541, she was arrested and her household dismissed. Mary was then conducted 'to My Lord Princes with a convenient number of the Queen's servants'.[13] There is no mention of her own servants, or of Elizabeth, which presumably means that the old joint household, while remaining in theory, had in fact reverted to serving Elizabeth only. Mary's chamber certainly remained in existence, and was presumably taken for granted in this relocation. Whether Mary did not wish to rejoin her sister, or was not allowed to do so, is not clear. Her situation over the next few months is uncertain, but presumably it became peripatetic again. In March 1542 she fell ill; not this time with her usual trouble, but with 'a strange fever'. Henry wrote, and sent his physicians, but she was not at court and he did not visit her. He was still very depressed following the revelations about Catherine Howard, and was always morbidly afraid of infection.[14] She was obviously not very far away, perhaps at Hunsdon or Richmond, but we cannot be sure.

It was not until the end of November that the king's spirits began to revive. This was probably because of the thrashing that his forces had given the Scots at the Battle of Solway Moss, but it may also have been partly inspired by the prospect of a new Imperial alliance. Eustace Chapuys was back in England, and his chatty despatches again become a prime source for illuminating events. On 17 December he reported that Mary and 'a great number of ladies' had been bidden to the court for Christmas. Henry had now been a widower for almost a year, and the prospect of a new 'petticoat presence' was clearly a cheering one. On the 21st Mary arrived, 'accompanied and met in triumphal manner'. She stayed for several months. This probably signalled the final break-up of the joint household with Elizabeth, because by the following summer the latter had been relocated to Edward's establishment, and with Mary normally resident at court there was no longer any reason to keep up two fully independent houses.[15]

In the spring of 1543 Mary was again close to her father, his black mood having finally departed. Chapuys was even at one point dependent upon her for information about the intentions of the French, and she was able to reassure him about the progress of negotiations with the Emperor. A treaty was signed on 11 February 1543, which committed Henry to a new war in France. It is unlikely that his daughter, now aged twenty-seven, had any influence on the negotiations, but the favour that he was now showing her was a useful sweetener from the Emperor's point of view, and the question of her status was not allowed to interfere. The king was, Chapuys reported, calling at her rooms in the court two or three time a day.

On 12 July 1543 the king married for the sixth and last time. Catherine Neville, Lady Latimer, had begun to interest him early in the year. Her husband was still alive at that point, but was known to be very ill, and he conveniently died in February. Catherine, better known by her maiden name of Catherine Parr, was thirty-one and had been twice married. As far as we can tell from her portraits she was no great beauty, and totally lacked the avid sexuality of her predecessor; rather she was a calm and dignified matron.[16] After Lord Latimer's death she was sought in marriage by Sir Thomas Seymour, the brother of the late Queen Jane, who may (or may not) have been in love with her, but who was certainly on the lookout for a rich widow. The king, of course, took precedence. He probably was not ideal for her, because she had already endured two almost sexless marriages, and Henry's fires were now spent, his once magnificent body an unwieldy hulk. She, however, was ideal for him. He no longer needed an energetic bedfellow, nor a sharp and idiosyncratic wit like that of Anne Boleyn. What he needed was a calm companion, who could become a nurse when the circumstances dictated. She had no great intellect and was certainly no scholar, but during Lord Latimer's last illness she had begun to learn Latin, probably to enable her to read devotional works in that language. She was already friendly with Mary through mutual acquaintances at court, and the princess helped her with her studies. Mary was no great intellect either, but she was an accomplished Latinist, and the two had become close even before the king decided to make Catherine his next bride. The fact that Mary was devoted to the mass and to the 'old ways' in the Church, while Catherine was sympathetic to the 'evangelical' movement (as the proto-Protestants have been termed), never seems to have come between them. In her later and fiercer mode, Mary would probably have regarded her stepmother as a heretic, but theology was not in question at this stage and at their level of discourse, and the mass was not yet an issue.[17]

Mary was therefore one of that very select band of those who attended the royal nuptials on 12 July. Shortly after, she moved back again into the 'Queen's side' of the court, and seems not to have left until after her father's death. As a scholar, Catherine developed all the zeal of a convert, and it was she who commissioned a new translation of Erasmus' *Paraphrases* into English. The humanist Latin was a bit beyond her, but Mary undertook one section. She did not complete it, allegedly because of ill health, but Nicholas Udall, the general editor, praised her efforts in his introduction:

A peerless flower of virginity doth now also confer unto [us] the inestimable benefit of furthering ... the more clear understanding of Christ's gospel ...[18]

Mary attracted similar eulogies from Henry Parker, Lord Morley, in works dedicated to her, but we have no first-hand evidence of her accomplishments. From Elizabeth we have a few translation pieces, and from Catherine herself the *Prayers and Meditations* (in English), but from Mary nothing. This was not because she lacked the time, so it must have been a question of inclination, and we do not know whether the eulogies were anything more than flattery. Her household accounts do not indicate any expenditure at all on books, or on the patronage of scholarship. They may be incomplete, but the signs do not suggest the normal apparatus of an enquiring mind.

What the accounts do show, however, are renewed health problems. Mary ran up considerable bills with her apothecary, and was often bled. In September 1543 she was reported to be 'very ill of a colic', and in June 1544 confided to a friend that she had 'byn nothing well' for several days. The nature of these ailments is much less clear than it had been in the days of her house arrest, and may have been mere hypochondria. What they were clearly not is stress related.

The court, though, was a fairly stressful place in the 1540s, as the conservatives and the 'evangelicals' squared up to each other, with the king apparently moving now one way, now another. The conservatives scored heavily in 1539 and 1540 with the Act of Six Articles (asserting several conservative doctrines, such as clerical celibacy), the fall of Cromwell and the Howard marriage; but thereafter the evangelicals struck back. This occurred first through the destruction of Catherine Howard, then through the marriage with Catherine Parr, and then in the frustration of attacks on Cranmer (the 'Prebendaries' plot') and – apparently – on the queen herself. This last (if it ever happened) may explain the king's increasing distaste for his conservative councillors in the last two years of his life, culminating in the fall of the Howards at the end of 1546.[19]

All this infighting, however, appears to have left Mary untouched. Even the story of the attack on Catherine, the substance of which was that some on the fringes of the court were burned as heretics, makes no mention of the princess.

At this stage of her life her piety was entirely conventional. Like many Christian humanists she approved of the English Bible, and of sermons, and had no particular affection for the shrines and pilgrimages that Henry had abolished. On the now-dissolved monasteries she was silent, and her enthusiasm for the mass was no greater than Henry's own, who was to ordain 30,000 'trentals' (each trental being a set of 30 requiem masses) for the repose of his soul. Her accounts show dozens of examples of almsgiving, but only a small proportion for the 'maintenance of God's service' and none at all for traditional local pieties. Having, apparently, come to terms with the royal supremacy, she had settled into an orthodoxy which, although conservative, was by no means militantly so – and she wisely steered clear of the partisan politics with which she was surrounded.

From 1543 to 1546 Henry was at war, and in 1544 he campaigned in person for the last time. The object of his intentions was Boulogne, and the campaign was eventually successful, but given the king's age and health it was a risky venture. Catherine was named as regent during his absence, and the Parliament that ended in March 1544 again took order for the succession. The Act of 1536, which was still in force, had bastardised both daughters, and settled the crown on any son who might be born to Queen Jane. Edward was therefore the undoubted heir, but what happened if he should die childless? To cope with such an eventuality, the new Act settled the succession first on Mary and the heirs of her body 'lawfully begotten', and then upon Elizabeth. In the remote contingency of all Henry's children dying without issue, the crown was to pass to the descendants of his younger sister, also named Mary, who had died in 1533.[20] This Mary had married, and had had children by Charles Brandon, Duke of Suffolk, the surviving one in 1544 being Frances Grey, the wife of Henry Grey, Marquis of Dorset. The children of Henry's older sister, Margaret, represented in 1544 by the infant Mary Stuart, Queen of Scots, were totally ignored. The Act also empowered Henry to alter this order, if he thought fit, by his last will and testament, but in spite of this, it was as complete a statement of 'constitutional' engineering as could well be imagined. It was determined neither by legitimacy, nor by hereditary right, but by the will of Parliament. Despite being named as heirs to the throne, neither Mary nor Elizabeth was legitimated, and Frances Grey was preferred to Mary Stuart. Chapuys did not

1. Mary from a group portrait of Henry VIII and his family, painted in about 1545. The female figure in the background is supposed to be her jester, Jane the Fool.

3. Princess Elizabeth at about the time of her father's death, aged twelve. By an unknown artist, in the Royal Collection.

2. Princess Elizabeth from the same family group, aged about ten. The figure in the background is supposed to be Henry's jester, Will Somers.

Above left: 4. Edward VI from the same family group as illustrations 1 and 2.

Above right: 5. Holbein's design for a jewelled pendant for Mary, probably executed during his first visit to England in 1527–8, when Mary was still the king's heir.

Left: 6. Margaret Tudor, Mary's aunt. She married James IV of Scotland, and after his death at Flodden in 1513, remarried Archibald, Earl of Angus. She was the grandmother of Mary, Queen of Scots. From a drawing by an unknown artist.

Opposite page top left: 7. Lady Jane Dudley (Grey). Put up by Edward as an alternative to Mary for the succession, she was defeated in July 1553, and executed after the Wyatt rising in February 1554, at the age of seventeen.

Right: 8. Edward's 'Device' for the succession, naming Jane Grey as his heir. The document is in the king's hand throughout, except for the amendments, which make all the difference to its meaning.

Below: 9. A page from Edward VI's journal, for 18 March 1551, in which he refers to Mary and his dispute with her over the mass.

10. A later pastiche of Henry VIII and Mary, based on portraits by Holbein and Hans Eworth. The figure in the background is again Will Somers.

12. Mary at the age of twenty-eight (in 1543), by the sergeant painter known as 'Master John'. In the National Portrait Gallery.

11. Thomas Cranmer, Archbishop of Canterbury, in 1546. A painting by Gerhard Flicke in the National Portrait Gallery.

Above left: 13. Thomas Wolsey, Cardinal Archbishop of York and Lord Chancellor. A drawing by Jacques le Boucq in the Bibilotheque d'Arras.

Above centre: 14. Stephen Gardiner, Bishop of Winchester and Mary's Lord Chancellor, by an unknown artist.

Above right: 15. John Fisher, Bishop of Rochester, by Hans Holbein. A fierce defender of Catherine's marriage and of Mary's legitimacy, he was executed by the king for treason in 1535.

16. A cartoon of Thomas More and his family, executed in 1527–8. A painting based on this cartoon was made by Rowland Lockey in 1593, and is now in the National Portrait Gallery.

Above: 17. An allegorical representation of the betrothal of Mary to the Duke of Orléans, the second son of Francis I of France, in 1527.

Left: 18. Third Succession Act (35 Henry VIII, *c.* 1), 1544. This was the act which designated Mary and Elizabeth to follow Edward if he should die without heirs, and broke new ground in that it authorised the succession of illegitimate children.

19. A nineteenth-century representation of Mary entering London on 3 August 1553, having successfully overcome the challenge of Jane Grey. The kneeling figures are Thomas Howard, Duke of Norfolk and Stephen Gardiner, Bishop of Winchester. The third figure, concealed by Norfolk, is Edward Courtenay, the son of the Marquis of Exeter, who was released on the same day.

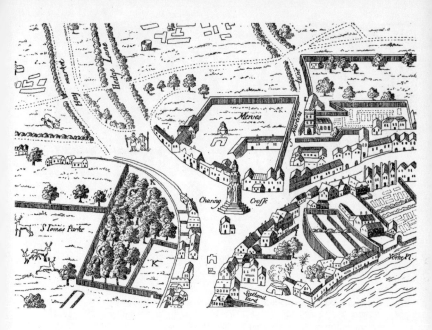

Above: 20. A plan of Charing Cross from the 'Ralph Agas' map. After a brief skirmish at the Cross on 7 February 1554, Wyatt led his force down the Strand and Fleet Street, only to find the gate of the City held against him.

Below: 21. Mary's instructions to John Russell, Earl of Bedford, sent to Spain in June 1555 to escort Prince Philip to England for his wedding. He is to brief Philip about the affairs of the kingdom.

Instructions for my Lorde previsel

furste to teli the kyng the whole state of this Realme,
wt all thynges appartayninnge to the same asrinche as ye
knowe to be trewe

seconde to obey hys comandment in all thynges

thyrdly in all thynges he shall aske vour advinse to declare
vour ovinion as becometh a faythfull conceyllour to do

Marye the quene

Above left: 22. Philip II as King of Spain, from a contemporary miniature.

Above right: 23. The reverse of the Great Seal of Philip and Mary, used for the authentication of important documents in both their names.

Below: 24. An equestrian portrait of Philip II.

25. Obverse side of the Great Seal.

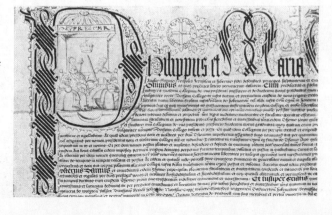

26. Passport for Richard Shelley to go into Spain, signed by both Philip and Mary. Shelley's mission was to have been to announce the safe arrival of Queen Mary's son, so the passport remained unused.

27. The charter of Philip and Mary confirming the foundation of Trinity College, Oxford, by Sir Thomas Pope, dated 28 March 1555. The ornate capital shows both sovereigns enthroned.

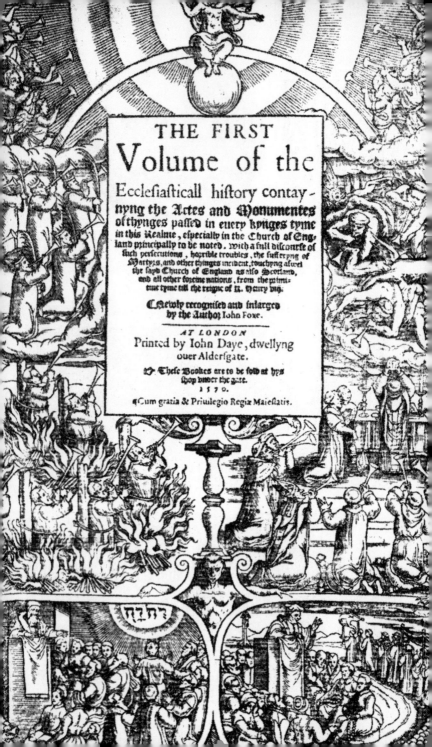

THE FIRST
Volume of the

Ecclesiasticall history contay-
nyng the Actes and Monumentes
of thynges passed in every kynges tyme
in this Realme, especially in the Church of England principally to be noted. with a full discourse of
such persecutions, horrible troubles, the sufferyng of
Martyrs, and other thynges incident, touching aswel
the sayd Church of England as also Scotland,
and all other forreine nations, from the primi-
tive tyme till the reigne of K. Henry viij.

¶ Newly recognised and inlarged
by the Author Iohn Foxe.

AT LONDON
Printed by Iohn Daye, dwellyng
over Aldersgate.

☞ These Bookes are to be sold at hys
shop under the gate.
1570.

¶ Cum gratia & Priuilegio Regiæ Maiestatis.

The burning of the bleſſed Martyr, Thomas Tomkyas.

¶ The cruell burning of George Marſh,Martyr.

Top left: 29. The burning of Thomas Tompkyns, from the 1570 edition of the *Acts and Monuments*. The same woodcut was used for a number of victims.

Top right: 30. The burning of John Hooper at Gloucester on 9 February 1555. Hooper, who was former Bishop of Gloucester, was burned on a slow fire. He was one of the first victims to suffer.

Above left: 31. 'The cruel burning of George Marsh'. Marsh was supposed to have been soaked in tar to make him burn more fiercely. From the 1570 *A & M*.

Above right: 32. The burning of Ridley and Latimer at Oxford on 16 October 1555. The sermon was preached by Richard Smith, who had been driven from his Regius Chair in Edward's time for his Catholic beliefs.

Opposite: 28. The title page of John Foxe's *Ecclesiastical History*, better known as the *Acts and Monuments of the English Martyrs*. This was a revised and expanded version of the work originally published by John Day in 1563.

The burning of M. Iohn Rogers, Vicar of S. Pulchers, and Reader of Paules in London.

The Martyrdome of Margery Polley.

The Martyrdome of Doctour Taylour, burned at Hadley for the testimony of the Gospell. February 9. Anno 1555.

The burning of Margaret Thurston, and Agnes Bongeor, at Colchester.

Top left: 33. The burning of John Rogers on 4 February 1555. Rogers was the first Protestant to be burned, and the example of his courage inspired many to follow him. From the 1570 edition of the *A & M*.

Top right: 34. The burning of Margery Polley. A number of Foxe's martyrs were women, and he emphasises how the Holy Spirit helped them to overcome their natural 'imbecility'.

Above left: 35. The burning of Rowland Taylor. Taylor was taken down to Hadley to suffer where he had ministered, with the intention of making an example of him. The evidence suggests that this did not work.

Above right: 36. The burning of Margaret Thurston and Agnes Bongeor at Colchester. Essex was a strong centre of Protestantism in Mary's reign, and a number of men and women deliberately provoked the authorities to act against them.

A true defcription of the racking and cruell handeling
of Cutbert Simfon in the Tower.

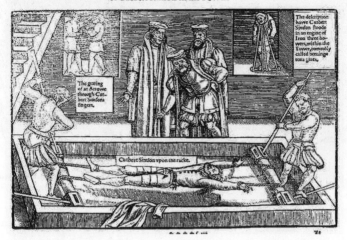

The picture defcribing the ftraight handling of the
cloafe prifonners in Lollardes Tower.

Top: 37. The racking of Cuthbert Simpson. The use of torture on the victims was unusual, but Simpson was the deacon of the London congregation, and he was racked (unsuccessfully) to make him reveal their names.

Above: 38. 'Strait handling' was more common, as this reconstruction of the ordeal of prisoners in the Lollards' Tower at Lambeth makes plain.

¶ The Martirdome of Thomas Haukes in Essex, at a Towne called Coxehall. Anno. 1555, Iune.10.

O Lord receoue my spirite.

Left: 39. An account of the disputation held at Oxford in April 1554. This extract is from the exchanges between Hugh Latimer and Richard Smith, with Dr Weston as Prolocutor. It was from this manuscript that Foxe printed his version.

Above: 40. A lively depiction of the burning of Thomas Haukes in June 1555. Haukes was one of the few gentlemen to suffer during the persecution. Most Protestants of that status fled abroad.

Below: 41. One of the most appalling atrocities of the persecution was the burning of a pregnant Margaret Cauches on Guernsey. The hapless woman gave birth in the flames, and her infant perished as well. An enquiry was launched under Elizabeth, from which most of our knowledge of the incident is derived.

A Lamentable Spectacle of three women, with a sely infant brasting out of the Mothers Wombe, being first taken out of the fire, and cast in agayne, and so all burned together in the Isle of Garnesey.
1556. July. 18.

The burning of Tho. Tomkins hand by B. Boner, who not long after burnt also his body.

42. The burning of Thomas Tompkyns' hand by Bishop Bonner. This example of Bonner's alleged cruelty was a part of Foxe's campaign against the bishop. Whether the incident actually occurred is uncertain.

43. Richmond Palace.

44. Calais and its harbour, from a sixteenth-century drawing. It was the loss of Rysbank (the tower in the middle of the picture) which sealed the fate of Calais during its capture by the French in January 1558.

45. Hampton Court, acquired by Henry in 1525, and subsequently much rebuilt. Edward VI was born there in September 1537.

know what to make of this. In a sense it gave the Emperor what he wanted – Mary was now in the order of succession – but it had been done in a fashion that he simply could not comprehend; and in any case a statute could always be repealed. Furthermore, Henry's preoccupation with Boulogne cost him the Emperor's good will, and almost as soon as the town was taken Charles made a separate peace with France at Crespy, leaving Henry to defend his conquest as best he could.[21] The war continued for another eighteen months – but that is not really part of this story.

HENRY REARRANGES THE SUCCESSION, 1544

His Majestie therefore thinketh convenient afore his departure beyond the seas that it be enacted by his Highness with the assent of the lords spiritual and temporal and the commons in this present parliament assembled and by authority of the same, and therefore be it enacted by the authority aforesaid that in case it shall happen that the King's Majesty and the said excellent Prince his yet only son Prince Edward and heir apparent to decease without heir or either of their bodies lawfully begotten (as God defend) so that there be no such heir male or female of any of their two bodies to have and inherit the said Imperial Crown and other his dominions according and in such manner and form as in the foresaid Act and now in this is declared. That then the said Imperial Crown and all other the premises shall be to the Lady Mary the King's Highness daughter and to the heirs of the said Lady Mary lawfully begotten, with such condition as by his Highness shall be limited by his Letters Patent under his Great Seal or by his Majesty's last will in writing signed with his gracious hand; and for default of such issue the said Crown Imperial and all other the premises shall be to the Lady Elizabeth the king's second daughter and to the heirs of the said Lady Elizabeth lawfully begotten, with such conditions as by his Highness shall be limited by his Letters Patent under his Great Seal or by his Majesty's last will in writing signed with his gracious hand. Anything in the said Act made in the said 28th year of our said Sovereign Lord to the contrary of this Act notwithstanding ...

[Statute 35 Henry VIII, cap. 1. *Statutes of the Realm*, iii, p. 955.]

Mary's role in all this was her marriage potential, and she was deployed as circumstances required, now to the Imperialists, now to the French; sometimes with her legitimacy negotiable, sometimes not.[22] The only one of these suitors whom she actually saw was Duke Philip of Bavaria, the son of the Elector Palatine. Philip was not an official candidate, and appears to have been acting on his own initiative. He arrived in England just before Christmas 1539, offering his military services to the King of England and asking for Mary's hand in marriage. Either charmed by his knight-errantry or dazzled by his effrontery, Henry allowed a negotiation to take place. As this was a private venture, Cromwell immediately sent a message to Mary to ascertain her feelings. Philip was a Lutheran, and her response was that she would 'prefer never to enter into that kind of religion'. Nevertheless, she would do as her father wished. On 26 December, while Mary was at court for Christmas, they met in the gardens of the Abbot of Westminster. The only account we have of their encounter comes from Marillac, the French ambassador, who must have got it from one of Mary's attendants. The duke had actually ventured to kiss her! This must mean marriage, Marillac concluded, because he was no kin, and no English nobleman would have dared so to presume.[23] They conversed partly in Latin and partly in German (the latter through an interpreter), and as they parted he swore that he would make her his wife. Mary responded prosaically that she would do as her father should determine. It must have been a chilly tryst and was not, on her part, very romantic; but it was the nearest thing to real courtship that she was ever to experience. Marillac expected a marriage within weeks, and indeed a treaty was drawn up, whereby Philip would have accepted her as incapable of succession, and with a modest dowry, but it was never implemented. Henry probably decided that he could not afford to lose so useful a diplomatic instrument so easily, and within a month Philip had departed, a disappointed man.

He did not give up easily though. In the spring of 1540 he wrote to renew his suit, but his letter went astray in the confusion that preceded Cromwell's fall, and he had to be satisfied with the Order of the Garter. He came to England again in May 1543, with the same military and matrimonial agenda, but he did not see Mary; he departed with a gift, but no other satisfaction. In March 1546 Philip did finally obtain a contract to supply 10,000 foot soldiers and 1,000 horsemen, and also another interview with Mary, although nothing is known about this encounter. Finally, in September of the same year he came in response to Henry's initiative, and the old speculation of a marriage was immediately renewed. However, this time he was an emissary for his father, and the negotiation came to nothing.

Whether Mary ever had any inclination to marry Philip, we do not know, but by 1546 she was thirty and her unmarried state was becoming something of an anomaly, even a scandal. In spite of what she had earlier said to Chapuys, there are signs that Mary herself was beginning to feel this. She is alleged to have said that as long as her father lived 'she would be only the Lady Mary, and the most unhappy Lady in Christendom'.[24] She seems to have been convinced that none of the numerous negotiations that had been entered into on her behalf was sincerely meant, and she may have been right. She had been brought up to regard her chastity as a very precious asset, and had been denied, or had denied herself, all the flirtations that normally accompany the process of growing up. In spite of all frustrations, however, she never showed any sign of wanting to withdraw from the world. Legitimate or not, royalty was her birthright, and that meant, at some stage, a royal marriage, so she had little option but to wait and hope.

At this stage of her life, Mary is something of an enigma. Her virtue and godliness were praised by conservatives and reformers alike, but in spite of her excellent education, and the extent to which improving works of piety and theology had been pressed upon her, we know very little about her theological opinions. In public she was the king's obedient daughter, but in private it seems likely that, while she was strictly Catholic on such theological matters as transubstantiation and justification, she sympathised with the reformers on their desire for vernacular scripture, and she regarded religious orders with indifference. Whether she had any intellectual, as opposed to emotional, convictions we do not know. If she had they were probably rather similar to those that her cousin Reginald Pole tried unsuccessfully to defend at the Council of Trent, which met for the first time in 1545.[25]

The more strictly puritanical on both sides of the religious divide regarded Mary with suspicion. She loved jewellery and fine clothes, tastes that her father was happy to indulge, but which argued frivolity in their eyes. She also gambled compulsively, usually for small stakes, and accumulated debts of hundreds of pounds, not because she was especially unlucky but simply because of the frequency with which she bet. The accounts do not record her winnings, so we do not know how successful she was. She continued to enjoy music, and added playing the lute to her earlier accomplishment on the virginals, employing Philip van Wilder to improve her technique. She danced with great enthusiasm, and that offended the reformers who regarded such activities (rather ironically in her case) as encouraging 'carnal lust'. In May 1546 one of Prince Edward's more austere tutors encouraged the eight-year-old boy to send an admonition (in Latin, of course) to Queen Catherine, asking her to beg his dear sister Mary 'to attend no longer to foreign dances and merriments, which do not become a most Christian Princess'.[26] It is to be hoped that the queen was in a position to ignore such an unsympathetic message. More appropriate in Prince Edward's eyes was no doubt her renewed taste for hunting, which caused Henry on one occasion to send her a present of arrows, and inspired her to walk several miles a day, which must have been beneficial both to her health and to her spirits.

As Henry's reign drew to an end, what we know of Mary's daily routine suggests peace and good order. She was normally resident at court, so visits are no longer recorded, but she was not at this stage regarded as a factional leader or identified with any particular cause. At the same time she had no independence, no estates to manage, no body of dependents who owed her allegiance. All her costs were paid by her father, and although her place in the succession was guaranteed by statute, nobody expected her ever to succeed. Although it was clear by 1545 at least that Henry would have no more sons, his son Edward was a flourishing, healthy youth. He had already been contracted once to marry the infant Queen of Scots, and although the Scottish Parliament had repudiated the Treaty of Greenwich that had brought this about, the Scottish marriage was still a live issue and high on the king's agenda. Although mortality was uncertain, nobody in 1547 expected Mary to be queen.

5

THE KING'S SISTER

Neither Catherine Parr nor Mary were with Henry when he died on 28 January 1547. Even Archbishop Cranmer only just arrived in time. Henry's death had been anticipated for several days, but his personality continued to dominate those about him until speech failed him altogether a few hours before the end. So it must have been by his own wish that neither his wife nor his daughter were present – a measure, perhaps, of his reluctance to face the true situation.[1] Both claimed to be very distressed when the news reached them, but they were bound to say that, and their real feelings are hard to discover. Each was freed from constraints that they were bound to have found irksome. Catherine, in spite of three virtually platonic marriages, was still young enough to bear children and was now free (after a decent interval) to marry again. Mary, whose marriage prospects were not as improved as she might have liked, was nevertheless by the terms of Henry's will put in possession of a patrimony worth nearly £4,000 a year. For the first time she was independent: free to manage her own estates, to hire and dismiss her own servants, and to build a body of political clients if she felt inclined to do so.[2] Her marriage was now controlled by her brother's council, but in other respects she was free to manage her own life in a way that she had never been able to do before, even during her years of favour. At the age of thirty-one this was an exhilarating – and possibly daunting – prospect.

The late king's obsequies were a long and dignified process. His body was laid out by his household servants, and lay in state in the chapel at Westminster, where he had died, until 14 February. On the 15th he was transported with great solemnity to Windsor, and there on the 16th he was laid to rest in the Garter Chapel with a magnificent requiem mass. The chief mourner, by custom, was not his heir (who was not present), but the next nearest thing to a male kinsman that Henry possessed, his nephew-in-law Henry Grey, Marquis of Dorset, the husband of his niece Frances (née Brandon). Catherine watched the interment and mass from an enclosed part of the chapel gallery, known as the Queen's Closet, but whether Mary was with her no one noticed or recorded. It is reasonable to suppose that she was not present. The whole elaborate ceremony was curiously detached from the hectic political activity that was going on at the same time. It was organised and, in a sense, presided over by William Paulet, Lord St John, in his capacity as lord great master of the household. Although St John was also lord president of the council, he seems to have used the organisation of Henry's funeral as a means of distancing himself from the power brokering that was going on there.

Henry's death had not been announced at once. It was only on 31 January that a formal proclamation was made, and Parliament dissolved.[3] This had enabled Edward Seymour, Earl of Hertford, the young king's maternal uncle, to secure his person. There was nothing particularly sinister about this, because it has to be remembered that, in the eyes of Catholic Europe Edward was illegitimate, and Mary was the true heir. Consequently it was important to frustrate any move that she might make – or, more likely, any move that might be made on her behalf. Both the Emperor and his sister, Mary of Hungary, withheld recognition from Edward until it was clear that the English had accepted him without dissent. In the event nothing happened. Neither Mary herself nor anyone else gave the slightest hint of challenging Edward's claim, which rested not only on statute, but also (as the statute had specified) upon the king's last will and testament.[4]

Although the authenticity of the will that Sir William Paget, the late king's principal secretary, read out on 2 February was challenged subsequently (and its authenticity is still a matter of debate) it was not disputed at the time.[5] Mary's only known reaction was to complain that Hertford had kept her waiting several days before informing her of her father's death, although she must have understood the reason for the delay. The council immediately set about converting Henry's rather vague, and almost certainly incomplete, arrangements for the minority government into a workable form. The king had named a body of executors and assistant executors, which corresponded roughly with his final council. These executors (but not the assistants) were then given the power to make whatever provision they thought fit for Edward's welfare and that of the realm. They decided that executive authority required the appointment of a single person as 'Lord Protector and Governor of the King's Person', and selected the Earl of Hertford. It was agreed that the lord protector would not act without the assent of his colleagues, and there was little dissent at this stage. The executors then kissed hands with the new king, and he formally assented to them converting themselves into his privy council.[6] This they were bound to do, as they needed the power to govern, and their legal status as executors of a dead king was inadequate. At the same time Paget, who had worked closely with Hertford and Lisle in the last months of Henry's life, came forward with what he claimed were the late king's intentions for new peerage creations – intentions that had been left unfulfilled by his death.

Paget, whose testimony was supported by Sir Anthony Denny and Sir William Herbert, both gentlemen of the privy chamber who had been close to Henry, declared that in early December the king had confided to him that 'the nobility of this realm was greatly decayed, some by attainders, some by their own misgovernance and riotous wasting, some by sickness and sundry other means'.[7] There had then followed a discussion of possible promotions, a few soundings had been taken, and estimates drawn up for the additional lands that would be necessary to support the new dignities. Henry had returned to the subject just a few days before his death, and urged Paget to see the plan implemented if he should not live to do so. Although it is natural to represent this as the new elite simply helping themselves, the old king had made no secret of his intentions, and other members of the privy chamber supported parts of Paget's statements, according to their knowledge. The upshot was that on 17 February, the day after Henry's interment, there was a flurry of new peerage creations. The Earl of Hertford, the protector, became Duke of Somerset; William Parr, Earl of Essex, became Marquis of Northampton; John Dudley,

Viscount Lisle, became Earl of Warwick; and Lord Thomas Wriothesley became Earl of Southampton. Four new barons were also created, including Sir Thomas Seymour, the protector's brother.[8] A few days later, on 20 February, Edward was solemnly crowned at Westminster, a ceremony attended by both his sisters and his stepmother. Within a few days of Henry's death, the bulk of the new king's princely household had been merged into the royal household proper, and Elizabeth (now thirteen) joined her sister in the entourage of Catherine Parr, the queen dowager.

This was never intended to be more than a temporary arrangement, because Elizabeth, like Mary, had been generously provided for in her father's will and, once the proper arrangements could be made, would have her own estates to manage. For the time being, Elizabeth seems to have been quite content to stay where she was, but by April Mary was pressing for her own share of the endowment to be put in place. The reason for this was not any change in her relationship with Catherine, but rather the reappearance of Thomas Seymour, now Lord Seymour of Sudeley, the queen dowager's old suitor and the new lord protector's brother. Although a privy councillor, and since 17 February lord admiral, Seymour was a faintly disreputable character. Whether he was really in love with Catherine, or merely fancied the idea of laying hands on her generous settlement, is not clear; however, she was in a vulnerable state of mind, and found his attentions irresistible. They were married secretly at some time during May.

When he found out, Protector Somerset was furious. Not only did he consider his brother to have acted with indecent haste, but he also suspected there was an intention to undermine his own position. A quarrel quickly developed when Somerset demanded the return of a quantity of jewellery that he claimed had been loaned to Catherine, but which she protested, with her husband's support, had been a gift.[9] There was little else that the lord protector could do. The marriage was a *fait accompli*, and as he was soon to discover to his chagrin, Thomas had managed to wheedle the boy king into supporting his move, unknown to the council, which Thomas knew would back his brother in opposing the match.

By the end of April, Mary's patrimony had been allocated. The formal grant was not made until 17 May 1548, but the first warrant for a payment to her from these lands is dated 12 April 1547. It looks very much as though an interim arrangement was quickly put in place to satisfy her desire to get away from Thomas Seymour, because some of the properties were not identified until June, and it was July before she took up residence in one of them.

Although he was disappointed by Mary's failure to challenge Edward's legitimacy, the Emperor clearly instructed his ambassador, Francois Van der Delft, to keep an eye on her, because Van der Delft was soon reporting in the same querulous tone as his predecessor about the dishonourable way in which she was being treated. She had, he reported, never been shown her father's will, and had no idea what marriage portion would be allocated to her. In fact it was £10,000, but in the circumstances the point was academic.[10] She was being kept, he declared mendaciously, in miserable poverty and no respect was being shown her.

In fact Mary's estate, when it was finally assembled, was valued at £3,819 a year, which made her the third or fourth-richest person in England. Most of it consisted of former Howard properties in Norfolk, Suffolk and Essex, including the great house at Kenninghall, which had come to the crown on the attainder of the 3rd Duke of Norfolk just weeks earlier. Whether or not Mary was consulted about this allocation in advance is not clear, but it also included some royal houses where she had lived in earlier days, notably Hunsdon (which was one of her favourites) and Newhall in Essex, upon which Henry had spent a great deal of money in the early part of his reign. It may have been for simplicity's sake that the council decided to give her an estate much of which already belonged together and cohered, but this also had the effect of transferring many of the leaderless (and conservative, pro-Catholic) Howard supporters in East Anglia to the princess. Not only did Mary acquire a patrimony in the summer of 1547, she also acquired a clientage.[11]

This was probably not intended, because although no issue had so far arisen, it must have been known to the council that Mary's religious views were likely to be hostile to the direction in which they were proposing to go. A small hint of this had been given when Archbishop Cranmer had arranged for all his bishops to have their appointments renewed on the death of the old king. Stephen Gardiner had at once protested that this was inappropriate because bishops were ordinaries – that is their authority derived from their consecration and not from their appointment. It was a technical point, but highly significant in view of what was to come. Mary said nothing, but her views were well enough known to her brother. When Thomas Seymour had been angling for Edward's support in his pursuit of the king's stepmother, which must have been within a few weeks of his accession, the boy had jokingly suggested that Seymour should try his sister Mary instead 'to turn her opinions'.[12]

What Edward knew was certainly known to his council, and yet they took the risk of establishing Mary in what could easily turn out to be a conservative power base very close to London and the Home Counties. Van der Delft might refer to Kenninghall as though it was in Northumberland, but in fact it was within easy reach of the court, appropriate to the honour of the holder, but also – of course – making it easier to keep an eye on her. Perhaps it was felt that if she was going to have it out with the government, it was better to have her where they could see her, and also in control of an 'affinity', a support group, whose potential was (more or less) known. Although in a sense Mary inherited a ready-made situation in East Anglia, she did not in fact create her new establishment overnight. She now needed a council, stewards, estate managers and receivers (money collectors) as well as the chamber servants and domestic staff with which she was already familiar. What she seems to have done was to build around her existing household, recruiting particularly from those East Anglian gentry families who were now her neighbours – Robert Rochester, Edward Waldegrave and Francis Jerningham being the most prominent. Special warrants authorised payments to her for these purposes from 12 April to 15 August 1547.[13] After that they cease, and it must be supposed that by then she was collecting the revenues from her own lands. Her new establishment seems to have been completed by mid-September.

In spite of what Van der Delft might claim, Mary's interests were in fact being well looked after at this time, but the politics of the minority government were moving in a direction that was bound eventually to lead to conflict. The Duke of Somerset was not satisfied with the terms of his protectorate. Particularly he wanted to be rid of the restrictive clause that required him always to act with the consent of the council, and at the same time to clarify the procedure by which new councillors were to be appointed. In March 1547 he obtained a new grant of his office by letters patent that addressed these issues.[14] He was now required merely to consult the council, and was given the initiative in matters of recruitment. These changes were strenuously resisted by the lord chancellor, the Earl of Southampton, so he had to be removed from office in order that the new patent could be sealed, i.e. authenticated. This was achieved by exploiting a foolish error that he made in delegating his work in chancery to civil lawyers by an unauthorised commission. He claimed that he had the right to act so *ex officio*, without authorisation, but the judgement was against him. He was deprived of his office, fined heavily and sentenced to imprisonment. Both the fine and the imprisonment were remitted, but he lost his office and his membership of the council.[15] He was a difficult and cross-grained colleague, but more to the point he was a well-known and tenacious religious conservative who would almost certainly have been a tough opponent of the programme of change that the lord protector now had in mind. Some conservatives remained on the council – Cuthbert Tunstall, Bishop of Durham, and Sir Anthony Browne, master of the horse – but they had at this stage neither the will nor the ability to be difficult.

By the summer of 1547 religious doctrine was becoming an issue in a way that it had not been while the old king was alive. Cranmer issued a set of homilies. Many of these were innocuous enough, and the archbishop did not write them all, but he did write the one on justification, which Stephen Gardiner, the conservative Bishop of Winchester, immediately pointed out was heretical. It taught justification by faith alone, a Protestant doctrine that had been outlawed by the Act of Six Articles of 1539. The protector was also allowing heretical works to be published in London, and the mass was coming under increasingly abusive attack.

At some point late in the summer or early in the autumn, Mary appears to have written formally to the protector to protest against this direction of events. The letter does not survive, but it can be reconstructed from Somerset's response.[16] Her father, she claimed, had left the realm in 'Godly order and Quietness', which the council was now disrupting with innovations. At best they were negligent, and at worst pernicious, allowing 'the more part of the realm through a naughty liberty and presumption ... [to be] brought into a division'. Henry, the protector replied, had not left a peaceful and stable situation, but a half-completed Reformation. The only way to safeguard his great achievement of the royal supremacy was to abolish 'popish doctrine' as well as papal authority:

> It may please your Grace to call to your remembrance, what great labours, travails and pains his grace had before he could reform some of those stiff necked Romanists or papists, yea, and did they not cause his subjects to rise and rebel against him?[17]

Mary, it appears, agreed with Stephen Gardiner, who had earlier written in a similar vein, pointing out that the changes that were now appearing were contrary to the Act of Six Articles, and moreover that the council had no right to make any changes whatsoever. Only the king himself could do that, when he reached his majority in 1555. This last point was undoubtedly consistent with Henry's own view of the supremacy, but it was a limitation that the council could in no way afford to admit. To put the ecclesiastical supremacy on hold until 1555 would not only have been impracticable, it would also have cast serious doubts on the remainder of the protector's authority.

So similar were Gardiner's and Mary's arguments that the council suspected collusion between them, but that is unlikely. In spite of the way in which Van der Delft chose to present the situation, neither of them was arguing for a Catholic Church, but rather for the sanctity of Henry's settlement regarding the status of the Church in England, which had always owed more to the king's personal idiosyncrasies than it had to logic, either theological or political. Somerset was undoubtedly right when he argued that the settlement which his government had inherited was unstable, although wrong to claim that the great majority of the people supported his changes.[18] Gardiner's position was undermined, both by his own admission that 'a king's authority never lacked, though he be in his cradle' and more specifically by the repeal of the Act of Six Articles in the first Parliament of the reign, late in 1547. Neither of these factors touched Mary. She never used the Act as an argument, but rather claimed (it would appear) that her father's position represented true religion, which no human authority had any right to touch. She later claimed that when he achieved his majority, Edward would find her 'his true subject in this as in all else', but since she consistently deceived herself about the reality of his position, and the circumstance never arose, too much weight should not be attached to that.

By the autumn of 1547 Mary was returning to the persecuted frame of mind that she had abandoned in 1536. At issue was the whole range of traditional rites and ceremonies that had been permitted by Henry but were repugnant to the Protestants who were now in power. Most specifically, the issue was the mass, and about that she would never retreat or compromise. As early as June 1547 Van der Delft reported that Mary was hearing as many as four masses a day.[19] He chose to represent this as a staunch defence of the old faith, but in truth it was a battle on a very narrow front. Four masses a day was excessive devotion, even by the most zealous standards, and suggests on the one hand that she did not have enough to occupy her time, and on the other that she was spoiling for a fight on her own chosen ground. There is no suggestion that her liturgical life was exceptionally rich in other ways, but it can be assumed that all the traditional rites were observed in her chapel, and that chapel was hospitably open to any who wished to participate.

Mary does not seem to have visited the court at all during 1548. Although her personal relations with Somerset remained amicable, she would no doubt have found the whole climate distasteful, and the council had many other things to think about. The English position in Scotland, apparently invincible after the victory at Pinkie in September 1547, was beginning to crumble as the garrisons that had been established in the wake of that victory were harassed and came under pressure. No progress had been made towards reinstating the Treaty of Greenwich.[20] After the death of Francis I in April 1547, the French started to make increasingly threatening noises about English-controlled Boulogne, and the Emperor was hostile and would not extend the existing defensive treaty to cover 'the new conquest'. Cranmer and Somerset were also pressing for the development of a vernacular liturgy, and an experimental English order of communion was authorised. Mary, of course, would have nothing to do with it, but it was as yet merely authorised, not mandatory.

During the summer of 1548 Elizabeth had left the Seymour household in disgrace, and taken refuge with Sir Anthony Denny. The fourteen-year-old princess had been found by Catherine in a compromising embrace with her husband. The main responsibility for this undoubtedly lay with Thomas, but it was convenient to blame Elizabeth – and she may not have been entirely innocent.[21] The Dennys provided only a temporary refuge, and the main immediate result was that the creation of Elizabeth's patrimony under the terms of her father's will was rapidly put in hand. Catherine had been pregnant at the time of this incident, and on 30 August was delivered of a healthy baby girl. Unhappily, like Jane Seymour eleven years earlier, she did not survive the experience, dying of puerperal fever on 7 September. Whether Mary attended her friend's obsequies or not we do not know; they had not met for about eighteen months. Nor do we know the princess's reaction to her sister's experience, except that she no doubt felt justified in having got out of Thomas' way as quickly as possible. The lord admiral himself may have been distressed by his wife's death, but if so his pain was of short duration. Within weeks he had renewed his pursuit of Elizabeth, this time speaking of marriage and the council woke up to the possibility of a serious challenge.[22]

Lord Thomas Seymour had been at odds with his brother since the beginning of the reign. He thought that the governorship of the king's person should have been his by right, since he was no less the king's uncle than the lord protector. He was not satisfied with a barony when his brother got a dukedom, and they had quarrelled bitterly over his marriage to Catherine. He had been spending his wife's money building a support base for himself, and appears to have been trying to create a party in the House of Lords to have the protector's patent annulled by statute. He had also been stalking Elizabeth. Just how substantial these ambitions were – and how treasonable – are still matters of dispute, but it would undoubtedly have been high treason to marry the princess without the council's consent. He was arrested, interrogated and his activities investigated in January 1549. He was attainted, and a few weeks later executed.[23] None of this touched Mary, unless she was concerned for her sister's reputation, which seems unlikely. In the early weeks of the reign, it transpired, Seymour had spoken of the possibility of marrying either princess, before he returned to Catherine, and it may well have been some suspicion of that which had caused her to decamp with such alacrity in April 1547.

Nevertheless 1549 was to be an eventful year in other respects. After considerable debate, and not a little posturing, in January the first Act of Uniformity was passed, the principal effect of which was to impose the English

Book of Common Prayer across the land from the forthcoming Whitsun. This book was not radically Protestant, but it was in English and did replace the mass with a communion of the people, which was quite enough to outrage Mary and Van der Delft, and to put the princess on her mettle. As we have seen, the council had been worried about Mary's intransigence since the summer of 1547, and by the end of 1548 was becoming highly irritated by the ostentatious nature of her traditional practices. Bishop Gardiner had been in and out of prison for his refusal to use the homilies, or to subscribe to the royal injunctions of 1547; at the beginning of 1549 he was in the Tower.[24]

Mary could not be dealt with in that way, and in any case had so far refused nothing, so the council waited, and hoped for the best. When Whitsunday arrived, she ordered mass to be celebrated with exceptional splendour in her chapel at Kenninghall, and she made sure that the whole countryside knew about it. On the same day at Ottery St Mary in Devon the congregation forced their curate (who seems to have had every intention of conforming to the law) to do the same, and within a few days the so-called 'Prayer Book Rebellion' had swept across the county. At first Mary's high-profile defiance was taken the more seriously. On 16 June the council wrote a restrained letter of admonition, 'giving her advice to be conformable and obedient to the observation of his Majesty's laws'. Mass was to cease forthwith and only the approved order of communion used.[25] This was a red rag to a bull, and on the 22nd Mary replied furiously, denouncing the so-called law under which they were claiming to act, 'a late law of your own making for the altering of matters of religion, which in my conscience is not worthy to have the name of law'. This was serious, because it meant that the princess was using the yardstick of her private conscience to decide which laws she would obey, and which not. This was as unacceptable a position to Edward's council in 1549 as it had been to Henry VIII sixteen years before – and as unacceptable as it would be to any modern government.[26] The council was alarmed, as well it might be, and summoned her principal chaplain, John Hopton, and two of her officers (Rochester and Englefield) in the hope of being able to pressurise her through them. On 27 June she wrote again, disingenuously accusing the council of being 'unfriendly', and of ignoring her superior status.

MARY'S LETTER TO PROTECTOR SOMERSET AND THE COUNCIL
27 June 1549

My Lorde, I perceive by letters directed from you and other of the kinges majesties Counsaile, to my Controller, my Chaplaine, and master Englefielde my servant, that ye will them uppon their alleagaunce to repaire immediately to you, wherin you give me evident cause to chaunge my accustomed opinion of you all, that is to say, to thinke you careful of my quietnesse and wel doinge, considering how earnestly I wryte to you for the stay of two of them, and that not without very just cause. And as for master Englefield, as soone as he could have prepared himselfe, having his horses so farre off, although yee had not sent at this present, would have perfourmed your request. But indeede I am much deceived. For I had supposed ye would have waited and take[n] my letters in better part, if yee have received them; if not, to have tarried mine answere and I not to have found so little friendship, nor to have bene used so ungently at your hands in sending for him upon whose travail doth rest the only charge of my whole house, as I wryt to you lately, whose absence therefore shall be to me & my saide house no little displeasure, especially being so farre off. And besides all this, I doe greatly marvaile to see your wrytinge for him, and the other two, with suche extreame wordes of pearill to ensue towardes them in case they did not come, and specially for my Controller, whose charge is so great, that he canne not sodainly be meete to take a journey, which woordes in mine opinion needed not (unlesse it were in some verye just and necessarye cause) to any of mine, who taketh myselfe subject to none of you all. not doubting but if the kings maiestie my brother were of sufficient years to perceive this matter, and knewe what lacke and incommoditie the absence of my said officer should be to my house, his grace would have bene so good Lorde to mee, as to have suffered him to remaine where his charge is. Notwithstanding I have willed him at this time to repaire to you, commaunding him to returne foorthwith for my very necessities sake, and I have geven the like leave to my poore sicke prieste also, whose life I think undoubtedly shall be putte in hasard by the wet and colde painefull travaile of this journey. But for my parte I assure you all, that since the king my father, your late maister and verye good Lorde died I never tooke you for other than my frende; but in this it appeareth co[n]trary. And sauving I thought verily that my former letters shoulde have discharged this matter, I woulde not have troubled myselfe with writing the same, not doubting but you doe consider that none of you all would have bene contented to have bene thus used at your inferiours handes, I meane to have hadde your officer, or any of your servaunts sent for by a force (as yee make it) knowing no just cause why. Wherefore I do not a little marvaile, that yee had not this remembraunce towards mee, who always hath willed and wished you as well to doe as myselfe, and both have and will pray for you all as heartily as for mine own soule to almightye God, whome I humblye beseeche to illumine you with his holy spirite, to whose mercy also I am at a full poynt to commit my selfe, what so ever shall become of my body. And thus with my commendations I bid you all fare well. From my house at Kenninghal, the 27 of June [1549]

Youre frende to my power though you geve me contrary cause, Mary.

[John Foxe, *Acts and Monuments* (1583), p. 1333.]

The protector did not respond with the harsh measures that the situation required. There were two reasons for this. In the first place the revolt in the south-west was apparently spreading out of control, while Somerset was still sending such troops as he had available to the north, hoping to redeem the situation in Scotland. Mary had no connection with the rising in Devon. A few of those who were in a sense her servants were involved, but it could conveniently be assumed that they had acted without her knowledge or consent. Difficult as she was being, there was no suggestion of physical resistance. Nevertheless, there was an urgent need for the protector to review his priorities.

The second reason was, of course, the Emperor. As soon as he heard of the passage of the Act of Uniformity he sent instructions to Van der Delft to tell the protector that he would not tolerate his cousin being forced to 'change her religion'. Even Henry had only belatedly and reluctantly told Charles to mind his own business, and the lord protector was in a much weaker position, especially in view of the threatening stance that was being adopted by Henry II of France. By March 1549 the ambassador was visiting Mary, as Chapuys had done, with messages of comfort and support from his master. On 10 May Charles instructed Van der Delft to demand written assurances from the English government that Mary might 'notwithstanding all new laws and ordinances made upon religion ... live in the observance of our ancient religion', and that neither king nor Parliament would molest her.[27] Charles may have hoped by this gratuitous bullying to have brought about the overthrow of a regime that he found obnoxious, and which he was assured was extremely unpopular.

However, no self-respecting government could afford to submit to such treatment, and Somerset replied pointing out that Mary's conformity was not, or not only, a question of her conscience, but also of the public order of the realm. A formal dispensation to ignore an Act of Parliament was therefore out of the question. He was, however, prepared to consider a compromise. In view of her status, and the tenderness of her conscience, he was prepared to allow her to retain mass privately, in her own chamber and in the presence only of her household servants, until the king came of age and took control of his sister's conformity.[28] The ambassador huffed and puffed, and made further threats, but Charles was no more willing in 1549 than he had been in 1533 to proceed to coercion, and there the matter rested for the time being.

When a new rebellion – Kett's peasant revolt – broke out in Mary's backyard in July 1549 the Prayer Book was not an issue, and the princess was not involved, or suspected of involvement – indeed some of her own property was destroyed. However, as the protector got into increasing difficulties during July and August, the prospect of 'regime change' began to be surreptitiously canvassed. The full story of this conspiracy does not concern us here, and will probably never be completely understood, but it is clear that by August 1549 several members of the council had had enough of Somerset's mixture of self-righteousness and ineptitude. That self-righteousness had made him autocratic and unwilling to listen to advice. He did not exceed the powers that his colleagues had given him in March 1547, but he did behave with a conspicuous lack of tact, and occasionally forgot that he was the lord protector, not the king.[29] His ineptitude sprang partly from the same root. So conscious was he of the royal responsibility to protect the poor that he regularly forgot that his own position depended upon the support and collaboration of those who were not poor – his colleagues and the gentry of the counties. He had probably given Scotland too high a priority. That had made him slow to respond to the risings of the summer, and when he was mired in rebellion, the French at last declared war.

There were also some who were out of sympathy with Somerset's religious policy, and inclined to agree with Mary and the imprisoned Stephen Gardiner.

This last group, which included the earls of Arundel and Southampton (restored to the council in December 1548), and possibly the lord president, has always loomed large because they featured in that way in the accounts of Van der Delft, which are some of the principal sources for the events of these days. The ambassador believed that the main objective of the conspirators was the restoration of 'true religion' – by which he meant the mass. In September he reported that Mary had been secretly approached to assume the regency when the protector should be overthrown. She had, he declared, declined to become involved.[30] Van der Delft believed that the ringleader was the Earl of Southampton, and he was disappointed by the princess's reaction; but it seems quite likely that she understood better than he did that Southampton was not the real leader, in spite of his grievance over losing the chancellorship, and that the main motive of the plotters was negative rather than positive. Their religious stance was still to be revealed.

After a confrontation in early October, which involved the protector whisking a frightened king away to the defences of Windsor Castle, Somerset resigned his office in the face of the almost unanimous demands of the council, and upon certain conditions of immunity.[31] The office of lord protector was abolished. Mary may, or may not, have been approached again. If she was she did not respond, and executive authority reverted to the collective entity of the council. Van der Delft waited expectantly for 'true religion' to be restored and the imprisoned bishops – Stephen Gardiner and Edmund Bonner of London – to be released. Nothing happened. In theory the new situation should have placed executive authority in the hands of the president of the council, but the president was Lord St John, a distinguished but extremely elderly and canny civil servant, who had no desire for such exposure.

The 'strong man' who did gradually emerge after the coup was not Southampton but John Dudley, Earl of Warwick. Warwick had probably been the key man throughout. He had retained near London the army with which he had suppressed the East Anglian uprising in August, and that force gave the council a critical edge in its dealings with the protector. He had also been thought of until the last minute as a close ally of Somerset, and his leadership of the 'London Lords', the council members except for a few associated with Somerset, gave them a strong psychological advantage. As October turned into November, and the main preoccupation of the council was the defence of Boulogne, a low-key stalemate developed over religious policy. However, Southampton retreated from the council owing to ill health in mid-October, and by early November it was clear that Warwick's supporters were in a majority.[32] Warwick supported continuing reform, and several new appointments were of like-minded men. Mary metaphorically shrugged her shoulders. She had never expected any improvement, she told Van der Delft, because 'the people were so infected' – an accurate conclusion upon a false premise. As worried Protestants plucked up courage again, Mary confided to the ambassador that she feared a fresh assault upon her own immunities, such as they were, and was beginning to think seriously of escape.

Just before Christmas there was a showdown between the two groups in the council. The ostensible issue was the treatment of the fallen protector. Should he be charged with misgovernment and punished, and, if so, how severely? However, it seems clear that the real conflict was over the leadership of the council. The ascendancy of Warwick was becoming increasingly obvious, and several of his colleagues, particularly Arundel and Southampton (who had returned from illness), were seeking to get rid of him. To call them religious conservatives, and to represent religion as the main issue, is to beg several questions, although if they had succeeded, the reforms of the previous year would probably have been abandoned. Their plan, apparently, was to proceed severely against Somerset, and by implicating Warwick in the charges against him (plausible enough in view of their association) to discredit him as a leader, and perhaps to imprison him as well.[33] Warwick was known to favour leniency towards Somerset – in other words honouring the conditions upon which he had resigned – and if skilfully managed Warwick's lenient attitude could be used against him. In view of the balance of power within the council, this plan could only have succeeded with careful handling and an element of surprise.

It got neither, because about the middle of December the Earl of Arundel approached Lord St John, thinking him to be a kindred spirit, and solicited his participation. To have secured the support of the president would have meant a distinct tactical advantage. However, the innocuous St John for once acted decisively, and immediately told Warwick what was afoot. This put the tactical advantage on the other foot, and just before Christmas Dudley was able to ambush the plotters in a full council meeting, declaring that whoever sought the protector's blood sought his also.[34] As a result the leading plotters were dismissed and placed under house arrest. Soon after, a settlement was agreed with the Duke of Somerset, and after a few months he returned to the council.

These developments were bad news for Mary. The new men whom Warwick began recruiting to the council in place of the disgraced plotters were all (more or less) Protestants. She declined an invitation to court for Christmas, lamenting to Van der Delft that the only reason for the summons had been to deprive her of the nativity mass: 'I would not find myself in such a place for anything in the world ...' Van der Delft began to drop pointed hints, as Chapuys had done, that the time had come for the Emperor to intervene, or at the very least to rescue the beleaguered woman from her predicament.[35] Charles was unimpressed. From his point of view Mary's value was as a pressure point, a means whereby he could apply leverage to the English government. He had neither the will nor the resources to invade England, rightly mistrusting his ambassador's assurances that 'all good men' desired it; and Mary in the Low Countries would be of no use to him at all. From his point of view she would be deserting her post.

A desultory negotiation for a Portuguese marriage went on through the spring of 1550. The princess would no doubt have been pleased and gratified – if anyone had asked her – but neither of the main parties was keen. The Emperor was not opposed, but would prefer her to remain in England, while Warwick wanted her where he could see her. Meanwhile the increasingly Protestant English council was becoming restive in the face of Charles' covert bullying, and Warwick decided upon a sharp reversal of policy. He had defended Boulogne more effectively than anyone had expected, but it was ludicrously expensive and he now needed to fend off the Emperor by bringing the war to an end. In March he sold Boulogne back to the French for 400,000 crowns (about £130,000), thus easing his financial problems and executing a political *volte-face* at the same time.[36]

Mary either did not read these warning signs, or she was busily reacquainting herself with a taste for martyrdom. The compromise agreement of the previous year had been for the princess to enjoy the mass within her household, but she had regularly been opening her house and chapel to anyone who cared to attend, apparently convinced that she had a sacred duty to provide for the spiritual needs of all and sundry. The council considered this to be an abuse of privilege and was by April proposing measures to put a stop to it. Both Mary and Van der Delft protested vigorously that the council was going back on the protector's given word.

At the end of April the ambassador visited her at her own request at one of her minor residences, Woodham Walter near Maldon in Essex. He found her in a state of agitation bordering on hysteria. The Marquis of Brandenburg was seeking her hand in marriage, and she had informed the council that she would not marry without the Emperor's consent. The marquis was a Lutheran – what else should she do? There was little that he could say, but while he was thinking how to say it, he had been treated to an inconsequential tirade against the iniquities of the English government. The council was determined to martyr her as her father had done: 'such persons fear no God and respect no persons, but follow their own fancy, and my cause is so righteous in God's sight, that if His Majesty favours me [he will not delay] until I am past all help'.[37] Van der Delft did his best to calm her down, but he was genuinely worried. He did not seriously fear that Mary would be martyred in any literal sense, but she was clearly cracking up under the strain.

Charles was sufficiently convinced by this to allow a plan of escape to be drawn up, although he left the details to his sister, Mary of Hungary. A window of opportunity was created by the fact that Van der Delft was about to be recalled on the (perfectly genuine) grounds of ill health. He could thus set up the whole plan before withdrawing and his successor, Jehan Scheyfve, would know nothing about it. Van der Delft withdrew in the middle of May, and the attempt was begun on 30 June.

The Imperial agent was Jehan Dubois, the embassy secretary, and the only evidence we have of what transpired comes from a detailed report that he made to Mary of Hungary in mid-July.[38] It is highly specific, and there is no reason to doubt its accuracy. The plan was for Mary to go to Woodham Walter, and for two Imperial ships to lie off the coast at Maldon on the pretext of looking for pirates. Dubois would then land in the guise of a corn merchant, display his wares in Maldon and make contact with the household at Woodham Walter. Under cover of darkness the princess would make her way down to the river, and be taken off in one of the ships' boats. The only difficulties appeared to be that the watches had been increased on the coast, and that the local population might not have been quite as sympathetic to the Imperial cause as the old ambassador had believed.

Dubois landed very early on the morning of Wednesday 2 July, and immediately sent a note to Robert Rochester, Mary's controller, at Woodham Walter. To his dismay, Rochester then turned up in Maldon and endeavoured to put him off the whole enterprise. Supposing, he argued, that the king should die while Mary was out of the country – what would then happen to the succession? He was unconvinced that his mistress was in any pressing danger. Dubois responded that all this ground had been covered between Mary and Van der Delft before the latter's departure, and that the princess had placed herself unreservedly in his hands, saying: 'I am like a little ignorant girl, and I care nothing for my goods or for the world, but only for God's service and my conscience.' All this Rochester knew perfectly well, because he had been present.[39] Apparently persuaded, Rochester then returned to Woodham Walter, agreeing to send for Dubois as soon as Mary was ready.

After a few nervous hours word was duly brought by a servant, and Dubois made his way inland. What he found was not a state of readiness, but chaos. The princess was busy packing all sorts of possessions into long hop sacks, and protesting that she could not be ready until Friday – two days away. Controlling his impatience as best he could, the secretary pointed out that she had no need of all these possessions, and that speed was of the essence. Word then arrived that the townsmen of Maldon were proposing to impound Dubois' boat, because they were suspicious of the ships lying off the port. Dubois argued that this merely increased the need for speed, but he was overruled, the controller declaring that the whole process was now too dangerous. Mary, whose decision this should have been, was simply standing among the chaos saying, 'What shall I do? What is to become of me?' while the men made up her mind for her. After some discussion it was agreed that Dubois would withdraw and try again in ten or twelve days when the alarms had died down. He managed to make his way safely back to his ship, but no further attempt was made. Rochester's servant never kept an agreed rendezvous in Antwerp, and it looks very much as though the controller had sabotaged the whole enterprise.[40] Dubois had no particular incentive to make Mary look like a dithering idiot, but that is what he did.

Although given to emotional outbursts, the princess was not normally indecisive, at least not to this extent. The explanation for her strange conduct on this occasion probably lies in two unrelated but acute dilemmas that confronted her. The first was a problem of conscience. By running away she would be relieving the pressure on herself at the cost of abandoning her people, most of whom would not be able to accompany her. The mass that they could enjoy under her protection would be denied them, and their salvation would be imperilled. Could she betray them in such a fashion? The second dilemma was more practical. Rochester knew perfectly well that there were council spies in the household. He did not know who they were, or how much they knew, but they were certainly there. He took the strengthening of the watches to be a sign that the council suspected what was afoot, and believed (with reason) that if an escape was frustrated, his mistress would find herself in a worse condition than before. Mary also liked and trusted her controller, who was conspicuously loyal to her. She could not simply ignore his advice, especially as she did not know Dubois at all well.

Rochester's fears were probably justified, because on 13 July – at just about the time when the second attempt was due – the council sent Sir John Gates into Essex with a troop of horse 'to stop the going away of the Lady Mary, because it was credibly informed that Scipperus should steal her away to Antwerp'. Cornille Scepperus was the captain who had commanded the Imperial ships.[41] It is quite likely that Rochester's caution had helped to prevent a major disaster, at the cost of making his mistress look a fool in the eyes of her Imperial protectors. He also knew what Van der Delft would not see, and Dubois would have had no chance to learn, that although Mary was popular in that part of Essex, there would have been no shortage of men prepared to frustrate her flight abroad.

MARY'S ATTEMPTED ESCAPE, mid-1550

Report of Jehan Duboys on the matter concerning the Lady Mary, drawn up in full and as nearly as possible in the actual words spoken.

The men-of-war arrived off Harwich after much bad weather on the evening of Monday, 30th June, and I, Jehan Duboys, left M. d'Eecke* the next morning, as the passage I took was not navigable during the night, to go to Maldon. M. d'Eecke was to follow the next day, and proceed to Stansgate† five miles from Maldon, with only one ship ... the said Henry, the lady Mary's servant and my brother [then] made their appearance. From them I learned that they had spoken with the Controller‡ late the evening before, and that he had raised several difficulties tending to delay us in taking our load on board. He told me that as soon as I came he would visit me and give me a fuller explanation ... We went to the house and the Controller and I walked up and down in the garden. The gist of his talk was that he saw no earthly possibility of bringing my Lady down to the water side without running grave risks, because of the watch that was posted every night at all the passages, the suspicions of certain of her household, which was not so free from enemies to her religion as she imagined, and the danger she would incur of being held back ... And since then, at the late ambassador's§ leave taking, while the risks and perils of staying or going were being discussed, I had heard her, in his presence, say these words:

'I am like a little ignorant girl, and I care neither for my goods nor for the world, but only for God's service and my conscience. I know not what to say; but if there is peril in going and peril in staying, I must choose the lesser of two evils. What gives me most pain is the thought of leaving my household, which, though small, is composed of good Christians, who may, in my absence, become lost sheep, and even follow these new opinions ...'

... Soon after six in the evening my brother returned with the aforesaid Henry, who brought me a horse to carry me to my Lady, saying that he would lead me by a secret way. This he did without anyone seeing me who could possibly recognise me. I was met by the Controller and had a long talk with him while my Lady made ready to receive me ... While we were talking we were summoned to my Lady's presence ... [I said] that I had written in bad Latin to her Controller. 'I have your letter here,' she said, and also the one you wrote before; but I am as yet ill prepared, and it seems that you wish it to be for to-night' I replied 'Any time your Majesty** pleases; but I have spoken and written to your controller the reasons for which prolonged delay appears to me dangerous'. She then mentioned the preparations she had made, packing up some of her property in great long hop-sacks, which would not look as if they contained anything heavy. I made so bold as to say that once she had crossed the water she should lack nothing, and that her effects did not matter so much, for the great thing was to conduct her person in safety, which was the point upon which she must now make up her mind ... She then spoke with her Controller and also called in her principal woman of the bed chamber, who was keeping the door. They all three then appeared to come to a decision, and my lady turned to me, saying that she would not be ready until the day after next, Friday; but that she could then leave her house at four in the morning ... While we were consulting as to how the affair might best be managed for Friday, and how we might let M. d'Eecke know so that he might retire for a day or two, there came a knock at the door ... [news had arrived] 'Some men from the village have been to see the ship, but were not allowed to go on board. Therefore they intend to send expressly on behalf of the village by the next tide to ask the ship its business, holding you and your men in the meantime to examine you here.' In fact [the Controller] represented the matter as so serious that we might expect to see the beacon fires, that are wont to be lit on the approach of enemies, blazing along the coast by the following evening. He added that he was thankful he had not stayed to dinner, for it would have proved the destruction of his friend Schurtz.[‡‡] We were greatly troubled by these tidings, and knew not what to do or say ... Meanwhile my Lady said 'What shall we do? What is to become of me?' ... So finally we decided, my lady still repeating 'but what is to become of me?' that within ten or twelve days the Controller should send me one of his servants, called Baker ... and would write the exact day when they could be ready to put the plan into execution ...

[Undated but mid-July 1550. *Calendar of State Papers, Spanish*, ix, pp. 124-35. Original (French) Brussels R. A. Prov. 13.]

* Cornille Scepperus, Sieur d'Eecke.

† Stansgate Abbey, six miles from Maldon by water, and twelve by road.

‡ Robert Rochester.

§ Francois Van der Delft.

** Imperial representatives carefully used this form of address, because in principle they recognised Mary as the ruler rather than Edward.

‡‡ Not identified. The Flemish form of an English name. Rochester had used him as an intermediary with Dubois.

The attitudes of Mary's supporters and opponents were not necessarily incompatible: even her supporters needed her in the country to ensure the succession. Within weeks the abortive flight was being discussed in diplomatic circles all over Western Europe. The French ambassador claimed to have learned from English sources that Charles' intention had been to have married Mary to his son Philip, the prince of Spain, and then to have pressed her claim to the English throne on the grounds of Edward's illegitimacy.[42] This was probably an accurate reading of the ambition of Mary of Hungary, but a long way from any feasible Imperial policy, even if the escape had succeeded. Towards the end of August Mary wrote to Scheyfve, the new Imperial ambassador, mendaciously denying the whole adventure, and claiming that the council was putting such reports about as a pretext for taking further action against her.

Such action as was taken was low key, and seems to have been intended mainly to demonstrate to anyone who was watching the extent of her dependence upon a foreign power. Two of her chaplains were indicted for saying mass, presumably outside of the house where she was resident. Mary at once complained to Scheyfve, and on 4 September Charles instructed his ambassador again to demand unconditional assurances – with menaces. In the circumstance this was little more than an empty gesture and, having achieved their objective, the council allowed the matter to drop.

A brief truce then ensued, which lasted until December. However, Mary was then confronted by a new phenomenon. The Duke of Somerset had dealt with her sympathetically if condescendingly, but the Earl of Warwick was prepared to be more ruthless, and this can be directly linked to the steady development of the king's own religious convictions. Edward was now thirteen, and full of adolescent assurance and self-confidence. He was beginning to find his sister's conscience as offensive as she was finding the actions of his ministers. On 1 December what could easily have been another routine skirmish developed over a further indictment of two of the princess's chaplains, whom she claimed were covered by her immunity. This took a different course from the earlier indictment, however, firstly because the council wrote on Christmas Day a long letter to Mary that was more than half Protestant sermon, but which also pointed out that her immunity was a private matter, covering only masses said within the household, and in her presence. The alleged offences had been committed outside the household, and when she was not there.[43] Secondly, the king intervened in person. On 24 January he wrote, upbraiding her for her errors:

> ... in our state it shall miscontent us to permit you, so great a subject, not to keep our laws. Your nearness to us in blood, your greatness in estate [and] the condition of this time, maketh your fault the greater.[44]

The threat was implied rather than explicit, but it landed a heavy punch. Mary's case had always rested upon the assertion that she was dealing with ministers, and that the king ('that tender lamb'), even if he knew what was being done in his name, was far too young to appreciate it. When he came to full years, he might command her, but not before. Now for the first time she was faced with unequivocal proof – the letter was written partly in his own hand – that she was likely to find the adult Edward as uncongenial as his minority council.

Mary was deeply distressed by this prospect, so much so that (according to her own account) she became too ill to write a full reply. The conflict that now developed was not about jurisdiction, or about the definition of the king's power, but about faith. To Mary the mass and its traditional accompaniments represented true religion, which no one had any right to alter. She had supported her father's supremacy, not because she believed that he was right, but because he had safeguarded these fundamentals. If Edward would do the same she would obey him, but if not, not. To Edward, on the other hand, the mass was blasphemous idolatry – an abuse of the word of God – and his father had been woefully misled. Between these two iron-shod positions of conscience no compromise was possible, and if Edward had lived to achieve his majority his sister might well have found herself in prison. Meanwhile, she ceased to profess her willingness to obey him when he came of age, but continued, as best she could, to take refuge behind the circumstances of his minority.

Meanwhile, the council continued to parade its routine arguments. Her immunity covered only herself and her chamber servants, not her household at large, and certainly not anyone else. In response she tried to take refuge in implying that the king's words were not really his own, and even that he had no authority at all. She was wisely warned off this line of argument by Scheyfve, who saw that it could be construed as treason, but it is a measure of her disturbed state of mind that she even contemplated it.[45] Inevitably, Scheyfve was soon as embroiled in this dispute as Van der Delft or Chapuys had been before. He helped her to write her letters (or thought that he did) and made endless and tedious protests to the council about the way in which she was being treated.

However, the situation was not entirely static. The Earl of Warwick now became prone to say that he and his colleagues were only doing the king's bidding, and he pointed out meaningfully that whereas the ambassador enjoyed a licence to have mass said in his residence in London, no similar indulgence was extended to Sir Thomas Chamberlain, the English ambassador, in Brussels. Indeed an application for such had been treated with insulting contempt. The atmosphere became decidedly tense, but neither side wanted to be responsible for breaking off relations, and so the standoff continued.

On 15 March 1551 Mary was summoned to see her brother, an order that she could not possibly ignore. She made a grand entry to London, her entourage displaying rosaries and other symbols of the old faith, and told the king flatly that her faith was not to be constrained. He replied with equal candour that he was not interested in her faith, but only in her behaviour, and that disobedience to his laws would not be tolerated.[46] One or two of her gentleman servants were imprisoned, and her officers were summoned before the council and ordered on their allegiance to secure her conformity. Even if they had been willing there was no way in which they could have achieved that – and in any case they were not willing.

There were rumours that conservative nobles were conspiring on Mary's behalf, and at the end of March a crisis seemed to be about to break. However, at the last moment both sides backed off. Cranmer and Nicholas Ridley, Bishop of London, advised the council that although to license sin was also sinful, 'to suffer and wink ... for a time might be borne'. At the same time the Emperor, casting an anxious eye over his deteriorating relations with France, decided that he would postpone making an enemy of the English, and instructed Scheyfve that he should advise the princess to be satisfied with her private licence, and not to press for public concessions.[47]

This damped down the fire for a few months, but at the beginning of August it sprang up brightly again – not this time through any action of Mary's, but because the Earl of Warwick had decided to grasp the nettle. At that point the Emperor was clearly hamstrung by the threat of renewed war with France, and Warwick (who had been lord president of the council since February 1550, but declined to take the title of protector) decided that the time had come to take issue with his conservative opponents.[48] The Duke of Somerset, unreconciled to his own marginalisation, had apparently been conspiring with them, and Mary's household was increasing in importance as a symbolic focus of resistance. Moreover the young king was becoming steadily more querulous about this blot on the godliness of his government. It was necessary to destroy such a centre of defiance, and on 9 August the council decided to withdraw the princess's mass licence altogether. At the same time they threatened Scheyfve with the termination of his own licence, because Chamberlain had again been refused a reciprocal arrangement in the Low Countries.

On 14 August Rochester, Englefield and Waldegrave were again summoned before the council and ordered to convey the unwelcome tidings to Mary. She refused to listen, and instead sent her officers back to London with a personal letter to the king. In addition to repeating a number of familiar arguments, this made it clear that she simply refused to acknowledge any issue of law or public authority in the dispute. It was a quarrel between her private conscience and the private consciences of the Earl of Warwick and his cronies. What was in her eyes a bad law was no law at all, and there was no duty to obey it.[49] When they refused to act as the council's messengers a second time, the officers were imprisoned for contempt. That was the easy bit. Policing Mary's household while leaving her at liberty was an altogether more challenging prospect, and since the council had no desire to provoke another conservative demonstration by summoning her to London, they sent a commission to visit her at Copthall.

This mission, which consisted of the lord chancellor, Lord Rich, Sir Anthony Wingfield and Sir William Petre, arrived on 29 August. The king's patience, they declared, was exhausted, and henceforth no service might be said in any of her houses other than that authorised by law. Mary, while making a great show of humility when presented with Edward's letters, treated his representatives with contempt. They had, she said, no valid authority for their actions, and most of them were simply her father's creatures.[50] In a sense that was true, but their authority was as great as that of any minority government could be

– and her assertion was both perilous and untrue. It had been foolish, she went on, to seek to control her through her officers, when those were of her own free choosing. Moreover, it was ridiculous to represent the king as being old enough to make decisions in matters of religion, while denying it in respect of the government in general.

So far the honours had been about even, but the princess then turned from reason to histrionics. She would report them to the Emperor's ambassador. 'I am sickly,' she went on, 'and yet will not die willingly … but if I chance to die I will protest openly that you of the council be the causes of my death …' They gave her fair words, but their deeds were unfriendly. She wanted her officers back, because she had never been brought up to count loaves, and so on. As they rode away, having accomplished nothing, she leaned out of her window and shouted after them, 'I pray God to send you to do well in your souls and bodies, for some of you have but weak bodies …' It had been a performance of great panache, but little dignity, and the councillors might well have wondered whether they were dealing with a madwoman.[51]

A VISIT FROM THE COUNCIL, 1551

A NOTE OF THE REPORTE OF THE MESSAGE DONE TO THE LADYE MARYES GRACE BY US, THE LORD RICHE LORD CHANCELLOR, SIR ANTHONY WINGFELD, KNIGHT [COMPTROLLER OF THE HOUSEHOLD] AND SIR WILLIAM PETER, KNIGHT [PRINCIPAL SECRETARY] AND OF HER GRACE's AUNSWERS TO THE SAME … THE XXIXTH OF AUGUST 1551.

First, having received commaundement and instruccions from the Kinges Majestie, we repaired to the sayd Lady Maryes howse at Copthall in Essex on Fryday laste, being the xxviiith of this instant, in the morning, where shortly after our cummyng, I the Lord Chaunncellor, delyvred his majesties lettres unto her, whiche she received upon her knees, saying for thonour of the Kinges Majesties hand wherewith the said lettres were signed she would kysse the lettre and not for the mattier conteyned in them, for the mattier (sayed she) I take to procede not from his Majestie but from you of the Counsell.

In the reading of the lettre, which she did rede secretely to her self, she sayd thies wordes in our hearing, Ah! Good master Cecyll tooke muche payne here.'

When she had red the lettres we began to open the mattier of our instruccions unto her, and as I, the Lorde Chaunncellor, began, she prayed me to be shorte, for (sayed she) I am not well at easse, and I will make you a short aunswer, notwithstanding that I have alredy declared and wrytten my mynde to his Majestie playnely with myn owne hande...

We tolde her further that the Kinges Majesties pleasure was we shuld also gyve strayte charge to her chaplains that none of them shuld presume to say any Masse or other Devyne Servyce then is sett forthe by the laves of the realme ... Hereunto her aunswer was this; first she protested that to the Kinges Majestie she was, ys and ever wolbe his Majesties moste humble and moste obedient subject and poore sister, and wold most willingly obey all his commaundementes in any thing (her conscyence saved); yea and would willingly and gladly suffer death to do his Majestie good, but rather than she will agre to use any other servyce than was used at the death of the late King her father, she would laye her hed on a block and suffer death; but (sayed she) I am unworthy to suffer death in so good a quarrel. When the Kinges Majestie (sayed she) shall come to such yeres that he may be able to judge thies thinges himself, hys Majestie shall fynde me redy to obey his orders in religion; but now in thies yeres, although he, good swete King, have more knowledge then any other of his yeres, yet it is not possible that he can be a judge in thies thinges... The payne of your lawes is but emprysonnment for a short tyme, and if they will refuse to saye Masse for feare of that emprisonnment, they may do therein as they will; but none of your nue Service (said she) shalbe used in my howse, and if any be sayd in it, I woll not tary in the howse ...

After this we opened the kinges majesties pleasure for oone to attende upon her grace for the supply of Rochester's place during his absence, & as in thinstruccions. To this her aunswer was that she would appointe her own officers, and that she had yeres suffcyent for that purpose; and if we lefte any suche man there she would go out of her gates, for they two would not dwell in one howse. And (quoth she) I am sickly, and yet I will not dye willingly, but will do the best I can to preserve my life; but if I shall chaunce to dye I will protest openly that you of the Councell be the causes of my death. You gyve me fayre wordes, but your dedes be always ill towards me ...

Fynally, when we had sayd and done as ys aforesaid and were goone out of the howse, tarrying there for one of her chaplaynes who was not with the rest when we gave the charge aforesaid unto them, the Ladye Maryes Grace sent to us to speake with her one worde at a wyndowe. When we were comme into the courte, notwithstanding that we offred to come upp to her chamber, she would nedes speake out of the wyndowe, and prayed us to speake to the Lordes of the Councell that her Comptroller might shortly returne; for, sayd she, sythens his departing I take thaccoumpte myself of my expenses and learne how many loves of brede be made of a bushel of whete, and ywys* my father and my mother never brought me up with baking and bruyng, and to be playne with you, I am wery with myne office ... And I pray God to send you to do well in your sowles and bodies to, for somme of you have but weake bodyes ...'

[*Acts of the Privy Council*, III, pp. 348-52. Original TNA PC2.]

* ywys = I think.

Mary's officers remained in prison until the spring of the following year, so presumably she learned to count loaves – and other things. But in a sense her performance achieved its objective. The ban on her household mass was never lifted – but neither was it enforced. Scheyfve made his ritual protest on 4 September and was told that the king insisted upon obedience, and would in no wise change his mind. However, having learned some discretion, in practice Mary went on having mass celebrated in her closet and in the presence of a few of her ladies, and this pragmatic stalemate lasted for the remainder of the reign – a matter of nearly two years.

By the autumn of 1551 the council had probably decided that, short of imprisoning her, there was nothing more that they could do about this obstinate woman, and that it was better to tolerate a low-profile nonconformity than to stir up further international trouble. However, by failing to enforce a full submission they had left her credibility intact, and paradoxically that spelt a new danger when Franco-Imperial hostilities were renewed in October. Charles had always been reluctant to go beyond words in using Mary against her brother's government, but the Emperor's health was now poor and control of policy was coming increasingly to rest with Mary of Hungary and with his chief minister, Antoine Perrenot, Bishop of Arras. Mary of Hungary took English support for France in the new conflict for granted, but was absolutely contemptuous of England's military capability, and planned to use her namesake as a means of taking England out altogether. There is no reason to suppose that the princess was in any way a party to these plans, and we have no means of knowing what her attitude might have been. Writing to the bishop on 5 October, Mary of Hungary pointed out what an immense advantage it would be to have one or more English harbours at their disposal, and went on:

> Many people are of the opinion that the kingdom of England would not be impossible to conquer, especially now that it is a prey to discord and poverty. It seems that there are three persons who might try their fortune, conquer the country and marry our cousin ...[52]

A pretext for intervention would be easy to find. 'Taking the king out of the hands of his pernicious governors ... [or] of avenging him, or some other excuse easily to be devised ...' The three gallants in question were the Archduke Ferdinand (Charles' nephew), Dom Luis of Portugal (brother of the king), and the Duke of Holstein (brother of the King of Denmark). Mary was both a bait and a pretext – in fact no more than a pawn. Mary of Hungary had no particular sympathy with her predicament. If she were finally deprived of her mass altogether 'she will be obliged to put up with it. She has no means to resist, and would be a victim of force, so that she would be blameless in God's sight ...'[53] Charles, although he had never done anything very tangible to help, had at least taken Mary's conscientious scruples seriously – as they deserved. This extremely cynical plan was never implemented, perhaps because England's capacity to resist was reappraised, or perhaps because the Emperor vetoed it. But it does serve to emphasise what a dangerous person Mary had become, in spite of the fact that she made no move to destabilise the government, nor offered any encouragement to those who did.

The Earl of Warwick had in any case no intention of supporting France in the new war. His policy was one of disengagement. He had given up the English position in Scotland, and surrendered Boulogne, specifically to be able to concentrate on the difficult tasks of domestic government and retrenchment. Apart from his dealings with Mary, he was reasonably successful. The crown's debts were reduced, and in spite of continuing tensions there were no repetitions of the rebellious outbreaks of 1549. At the end of October Mary was invited to court to meet Mary of Guise, the Queen Dowager of Scotland, who was returning overland from France. She declined, on the grounds of her 'constant ill health, which at present is worse than usual', but admitted privately that the real reason was that she would not be able to hear mass if she was at court. Interestingly, when he heard of this the Emperor admonished her that it would be better to attend when invited, and she replied that she would go after Christmas as usual, but would refrain from contaminating herself with the rites of the Chapel Royal.[54] Mary continued to allege that her chaplains were being harassed, and in January both she and Scheyfve made ritual protests, but the impression given is that of force of habit rather than of any new or specific grievance.

In November 1551 the Earl of Warwick had himself created Duke of Northumberland, and the timing of this may have been significant. Edward had turned fourteen on 12 October, and this represented in some contexts a coming of age.[55] The king would not achieve his actual majority until he was eighteen, but Warwick was anxious to bring him into the political process as soon and as fully as possible. Apart from anything else, Edward was being very carefully educated for his future responsibilities, and only he stood any chance of prevailing over his sister. Warwick was carefully preparing himself for the day when he would step aside as regent and become instead the trusted first minister of an adult king. The enhancement of rank has to be seen in that context.

At almost exactly the same time Northumberland destroyed the Duke of Somerset. The ex-protector was accused of all sorts of plottings and treasonable intentions, most of which were fictitious, as Northumberland later admitted.[56] He had, however, threatened to divide the council at a time when any lack of unity could have been disastrous. Plotting with Mary's supporters was probably just another fiction, but in any case he was not convicted of treason. He was convicted of felony for assembling an armed band at his house in contravention of statute law – and of that he was guilty as charged. It was of course a pretext, but he was the king's uncle and a man of great political experience. Edward might have turned to him rather than to Northumberland as he approached his majority – if Somerset had still been around. If Edward's reaction to his uncle's death is anything to go by (a succinct, emotionless note in his journal), it was probably a misplaced fear, and in any case the circumstances did not arise.

What Somerset's execution in January 1552 demonstrated to Mary was that she was dealing with a man who was capable of being completely ruthless, especially if he sensed that the king was alienated from his victim, even temporarily. Her officers returned to duty in mid-April 1552, and there seems to have been a noticeable relaxation of tension. Edward was genuinely fond of his sister, infuriating as he found her, and it was important to keep him in that frame of mind. Although nothing fundamentally changed, by the summer of 1552 Mary was refraining from provocative actions or abrasive words, and when she visited the court in June she was honourably received – and the subject of religion does not seem to have been mentioned.[57]

A new Act of Uniformity reached the statute book in April 1552, imposing a liturgy far more explicitly Protestant than that of 1549, but this made little difference as far as Mary was concerned. For those who had struggled to convince themselves (as Stephen Gardiner did for a while) that the first Prayer Book was capable of a Catholic interpretation, this was a blow; but Mary had never suffered from any such delusion.[58] The English Prayer Book was heretical in whatever guise it came; and cocooned in her closet with her sympathetic priests, she did not have to endure it. What the second Act of Uniformity did make abundantly clear, however, was that the royal supremacy as a bulwark of traditional belief was a dead concept. If the supremacy was to be accepted, then it must also be accepted that the king (and the king's government) had the right to impose beliefs and practices that were traditionally regarded as heretical. We have no specific evidence, but it may well have been at this point that Mary – like Gardiner – came to the conclusion that the defence of the Henrician settlement was a pointless strategy. Only the Universal Church could protect true doctrine from sacrilegious hands. What we know is that as late as August 1551 she was arguing that her father's Church had represented the true faith, while by August 1553 she was privately arguing for the restoration of the papal jurisdiction.

At what point Edward's health began to give grounds for serious anxiety we do not know. He had a bad cold at Christmas 1552, but he had thrown off such infections before without great difficulty. Contrary to what is sometimes said, he had never been a sickly child, and although he had shown no great aptitude for them, his enthusiasm for war games and other physical recreations was immense. At some time early in 1553 he drew up the document called his 'Device for the succession', but this was a school exercise, not an attempt to address a pressing issue. It did indeed envisage the possibility of his dying without heirs (that was its whole point), but it did so with a long and indefinite time span. For example, the 'heirs male' of his cousin Jane Grey were included, although Jane, who was sixteen, was as yet not married.[59] What is significant about it is that it ignored Henry's Act of Succession of 1544, which had laid down quite clearly that if Edward were to die without heirs, he should be succeeded by Mary. Now this may have been in response to a tutorial instruction – 'suppose that act had never been passed, what then?' In other words it was a hypothetical exercise. Or it may have been that there was already an understanding between the king and his tutors that the statute would be disregarded. We do not know. What is clear is that the matter was being thought about some time before there was any urgent need for an answer. Northumberland was certainly not spoiling for a fight, in fact he was going out of his way to make conciliatory gestures to Mary, although admittedly these related to payments of money and exchanges of lands, not religious matters.

In February Mary visited the court in some state, and if she made any provocative religious gestures no one commented upon them. Edward was sufficiently unwell by then to postpone seeing her for a few days, but if her visit demonstrates anything it is that most of the court still thought of her at that stage as the heir to the throne.[60] In March, according to Scheyfve, she asked him to press the Emperor to secure a relaxation of the tight restrictions upon her worship, but that was in the context of making sure that her lines of communication were still intact and (probably) that Charles was still sufficiently *compos mentis* to be appealed to if necessary.

Parliament met from 1 to 31 March, and the king was not well enough to perform the usual opening ceremony, but the succession was not discussed, and the 'Device' was never mentioned. It seems unlikely that anyone except the king, and possibly the Duke of Northumberland, knew of its existence. During March Edward's health improved. He closed Parliament in the usual way, and on 11 April was able to 'take the air'. At this stage only Scheyfve seems to have thought that his life was in any danger, and that may tell us more about the ambassador than it does about the king. His sources of information were good, but not special, let alone unique. More significantly, he coupled these pessimistic messages with the news that Northumberland was keeping Mary carefully informed of every change in the king's condition. He was poorly again at the end of April, but by the middle of May all the talk was of a complete recovery.[61]

On the list of that month a marriage took place that was to loom large in the conspiracy theories of the forthcoming crisis, but no one seems to have seen it in that light at the time. Guildford Dudley, Northumberland's fourth (and only unmarried) son wedded Jane, the eldest daughter of Henry Grey, Duke of Suffolk. This was later represented as a crafty plot to hijack the crown, but at the time even Scheyfve merely commented that Jane was 'the king's kinswoman'.[62] She was not even Northumberland's first choice for his son, but the Earl of Cumberland had rejected his approaches in respect of his daughter Margaret. At the same time Guildford's sister, Catherine, married Henry Hastings, heir to the Earl of Huntingdon, and Jane's sister (also Catherine) married Henry Herbert, heir to the Earl of Pembroke. In other words this was a routine dynastic 'wedding circus' of the kind that was common between aristocratic families, and had no significance beyond that. The king was not present, but gave his full approval to the ceremonies. Unfortunately, Jane had had no desire to marry Guildford, who was her inferior in both character and intellect, and this was not to be without its relevance in due course.

Meanwhile Scheyfve's gloomy view of the king's health had also led him to believe that Northumberland was plotting against Mary's right to the succession. He could adduce no firm evidence for this – it was what might now be called a 'gut reaction' – and he did not connect it with the marriages on 21 May, which suggests that he had no clear idea of what was intended. His views would have been just so much spilled ink if it had not been for the fact that in the first week of June Edward became dramatically worse. Pulmonary tuberculosis is one of those diseases that develops fitfully, with many remissions, and sixteenth-century diagnostics were extremely underdeveloped. Consequently no one had known what to expect. By 11 June a crisis had clearly developed, and Scheyfve's informant in the privy chamber was able to give him an account of the king's condition that left little to the imagination.[63] This was a deeply unpleasant shock, not only for the wretched boy himself but also for the Duke of Northumberland, all of whose elaborate preparations were now in jeopardy. It was not only possible but likely that the king would die within a matter of weeks, and a decision had to be made. Was Mary to succeed in accordance with statute law and her father's will – or not? And if not Mary – who?

It used to be believed that the Duke of Northumberland used his Svengali-like influence over the young king to persuade him to name his own daughter-in-law, Jane Grey, but the actual decision was almost certainly Edward's own. Not only was he deeply committed to the religious changes over which he had presided, he was also obsessed with the idea of male succession. In spite of the fact that he had no male kindred, his whole 'Device' had been designed for the heirs male of the various women by whom he was surrounded – starting with any son who might be born to Henry and Frances Grey. It was at this point that Edward produced his school exercise and instructed his law officers to draw up a will embodying its provisions. However, as it stood it was useless. Frances Grey was not pregnant, and had not conceived for several years. Jane was newly married, but her relations with her husband were so bad that there was no chance that she could be even in the very early stages of pregnancy. Something had to be done immediately, and the wording 'the heirs male of the Lady Jane' was altered to read 'the Lady Jane and her heirs male'.[64] This may well have been done by Northumberland, but with the king's full support and consent. It was the only solution if his Godly Reformation was not to come to an untimely end. Jane was a Protestant with excellent credentials, and Edward liked her. If he had to be succeeded by a woman, better her than any other. Elizabeth was, of course, excluded from any consideration. She was illegitimate, and if the 1544 Act was to be ignored, she had no claim.

And so the great conspiracy that Scheyfve had shadowed for weeks became a reality in the second half of June. Although secrecy was impossible as Edward struggled to give some constitutional force to what was in effect a decision *mere moto suo*, by his will alone, without the consent of Parliament, Mary did not immediately find out what was afoot. She realised by this time that Edward was really committed to his religious settlement, and was half expecting a conditional offer of the throne in return for preserving it. She asked Scheyfve what she should do in those circumstances, and the ambassador dutifully referred back to headquarters for instructions on 19 June. The Emperor's advice, which never reached Mary, was to accept such an offer if it was made, on the grounds that there were many ways to invalidate an ungodly oath.[65]

As the month of June drew to an end, both parties were in difficulties. Edward's condition was now desperate, but his law officers were being obstructive. Not only was parliamentary consent required for the change that he was proposing, but as a minor he was not even capable of making a valid will. As the days ticked by Northumberland became increasingly desperate, even threatening violence against the obstructors. Eventually it was agreed that the only way to proceed was by letters patent, which would have to be retrospectively confirmed. Such letters were drawn up, but they never passed the seals, and thus were never properly validated, and so remained technically invalid. Mary's problem was that she knew that a plan was in existence to deprive her of her right, but had no details, nor could she know how much force such a dispensation might have. The signals were mixed. Northumberland would back it to the hilt; and so (she supposed) would the Protestant bishops and other committed heretics like the Duke of Suffolk. On the other hand there was plenty of evidence of dissent. Could she do anything to turn that dissent into actual support for her cause?

Although Mary did not know it, she was on her own in this dilemma. On 23 June Charles sent a special mission, ostensibly to commiserate with Edward in his sickness, but really to watch events when he died. He probably did not intend to supersede Scheyfve, but that was the effect, and his instructions to his envoys are illuminating. They were not to intervene, even indirectly, on Mary's behalf, but were to monitor the situation closely. If Northumberland prevailed (as most observers expected) they were to do business with him. Only if Mary was clearly about to triumph should they declare the Emperor's support.[66] The princess might appeal to them, but they were not to respond unless or until that situation was reached. By 1 July rumours were already circulating that the king was dead. Mary was at Hunsdon, and rightly apprehensive that as soon as the breath was really out of Edward's body Northumberland would move rapidly to arrest her. She declined an invitation to come and visit her sick brother, and, warned that the end was now finally near, on 6 July moved rapidly from Hunsdon to Kenninghall in Norfolk – the heart of her estates and the stronghold of her body of support. The same day Edward died, but when Northumberland's men tried to intercept the princess at Sawston in Cambridgeshire, they were already too late.

6

MARY THE QUEEN

Edward died on 6 July 1553, and his death was concealed for two days in accordance with normal practice. The council now had to make a critical decision. The king's last wishes were well known, but he had not succeeded in giving them any legal force. Mary was still the heir by law, but Mary was unmarried, well known to be a creature of the Emperor, and belligerently conservative in her religious views. This last consideration did not make her unpopular – quite the reverse – but it did threaten the overthrow of the Church settlement to which Edward had been so thoroughly committed, and of which many of the council also approved. If it came to a showdown, most of those in the best position to know believed that Jane Grey would prevail. The Duke of Northumberland, easily the most powerful man in the realm, was completely committed to her cause – although whether out of self-interest or loyalty to his late master, nobody knew. Antoine de Noailles, the French ambassador, had spoken to the duke just a few days before Edward died, and been told 'that they had provided so well against the Lady Mary's ever attaining the succession, and that all the lords of the council were so well united, that there is no need for you, Sire, to enter into any doubt on this score'.[1] Simon Renard, the brains of the Imperial mission, had come to the same conclusion: 'The actual possession of power,' he wrote, 'is a matter of great importance especially among barbarians like the English.'[2] Northumberland, he believed, had that power. On 8 July the council proclaimed Jane queen in London, to a less than enthusiastic reception from the largely Protestant citizens. Even a sermon from their bishop pointing out the dangers of an unmarried queen with such strong foreign proclivities failed to stir them to any show of zeal for the married, and undoubtedly Protestant, Jane.

Meanwhile Mary was in Norfolk, on the way to Kenninghall. There at some point, probably on 7 July, 'she was told of the king's death by her goldsmith, a citizen of London newly returned from the City'. But Mary, we are told, did not believe the tidings, and would not allow the news to be spread abroad. She clearly did not trust the messenger, and her caution was wise, because if she had proclaimed herself while the breath was still in Edward's body that would have been high treason.[3] The following day, when she had reached her destination, the tidings were confirmed by one John Hughes, a physician. It seems unlikely that he could already have known of the proclamation in London, so she must have had some good reason to trust him better. That same night she consulted her council and household officers, and the next day, the 9th, declared the news to her assembled household, and proclaimed herself queen.

> Roused by their mistress's words, everyone, both the gently born and the humbler servants, cheered her to the rafters and hailed and proclaimed their dearest Princess Mary as Queen of England …[4]

That was, of course, the easy bit. The same day she wrote to the council in London, demanding their allegiance. The following day the council received her letter and responded, declaring their allegiance to Queen Jane and demanding her submission.

According to Robert Wingfield's highly partisan account, the country folk of Norfolk and Suffolk 'every day flocked to their rightful Queen, ready to lay out for her in this worthy cause their wealth, their effort and life itself'.[5] In fact what seems to have happened was that her East Anglian 'affinity' was extremely well prepared. Men like Sir Henry Bedingfield and Sir John Shelton did not command large followings, but when the call came their men were armed and ready to ride. Within a few days Mary had a force at her disposal, not large or led by experienced soldiers, but fully equipped and well supplied. At the same time proclamations were sent out far and wide, announcing her accession and demanding recognition. These documents could not have been prepared overnight; they had clearly been many days, or even weeks, in the penning. Wingfield's tale of spontaneous enthusiasm is persuasive but untrue. Mary had been planning for this eventuality for some time, probably since she had first learned of the plot against her, and her supporters had been preparing.

By contrast, in spite of his bold words to the French ambassador, Northumberland was markedly ill equipped. It seems that he seriously underestimated his opponent, because when it was first known that Mary had left Hunsdon and was heading east, he gave it out that she was in flight to the coast to do what she had sought to do before – take refuge with the Emperor.[6] Moreover, Northumberland was much less powerful than he appeared. His own men were comparatively few. The bulk of the forces over which he appeared to have command owed their primary allegiance either to the crown or to one or other of his colleagues of the privy council. In the circumstances the household troops were not to be relied upon, and the trustworthiness of most of the others depended upon the council remaining united.

The council's reaction at first conveyed no great sense of urgency. The lord mayor and the aldermen of London were sworn to Queen Jane, and letters were sent out to sheriffs and justices of the peace, announcing her accession and ordering them to suppress any 'stirs or disorders', very much the sort of letter that would have been sent out at the beginning of any new reign.[7] The first reaction of most local authorities, even within East Anglia, was to do as they were told, and several borough records have entries of Jane's accession, hastily erased a few days later. The council knew by the 10th that Mary was posing a challenge, but were inclined to dismiss it as insignificant. Lord Robert Dudley, Northumberland's son, was based in Norfolk and could, it was felt, contain the situation there. Meanwhile, on the same day, Jane was brought through London and installed in the royal apartments at the Tower. Her passage, like her proclamation two days earlier, was received with a mixture of indifference and hostile demonstrations.[8] In retrospect this looks ominous, but it need not have mattered. There was no resistance, and no powerful nobleman had as yet rejected her.

However, the council's complacency was misplaced. Henry Radcliffe, one of the sons of the Earl of Sussex, was persuaded (or forced) into Mary's camp, and his father was quickly making overtures in the same direction. 'Now that fortune was beginning to smile on sacred Mary's righteous undertaking', wrote Robert Wingfield, other gentlemen flocked to join her – John Huddleston, Sir Richard Southwell, Sir John Mordaunt, 'amply provided with money, provisions and armed men'.[9] Lord Robert Dudley was simply swept aside, even some of his own men declining to follow him. By 13 July it was clear that a military expedition of some power would be needed to deal with Mary's growing band – and the sooner the better, because as yet she had no captain of skill or experience to lead her forces if it should come to action, certainly no one who could match Northumberland as a soldier. Unfortunately the duke was now required in two places at once. He needed to remain in London to make sure that his colleagues stayed in line, and he needed to be in Norfolk to confront Mary. Having failed to persuade the Duke of Suffolk to undertake the East Anglian mission, he decided that there was no option but to go himself, and set off from London on 14 July with about 1,500 men and a small artillery train.

In normal circumstances a disciplined force of this size would have been sufficient – but the circumstances were not normal. By 15 July the Earl of Sussex, the Earl of Bath and Lord Thomas Wentworth had joined Mary's camp, and five royal warships that had been sent to the Essex coast to prevent any possible escape by the princess had defected to her cause. According to Wingfield one of Mary's agents had worked on the seamen and they had mutinied against their officers to bring this about.[10] It may have been otherwise, and the ships themselves were of no great significance, but their crews and guns were, and this may have been the turning point. At the same time, events in London were moving in the same direction. On 12 July Lord Cobham and Sir John Mason had waited upon the Imperial ambassadors to point out that their commission had expired. They clearly suspected Renard and his colleagues of being behind Mary's unexpected defiance. Renard was pained, pointing out (truthfully) that they had no such instructions. On the other hand (he said) he was able to demonstrate that French support for Jane was a sham; they wanted Mary excluded in order to make way for their own candidate – Mary Stuart. According to the ambassador the councillors were impressed. They withdrew their ultimatum and arranged for a further meeting with a larger group the following day.[11] Neither Cobham nor Mason was close to Northumberland, and the duke – who was still in London – was not informed. Even before he left the capital that unity upon which so much depended was beginning to crack.

Events moved fast. On the 14th, when Northumberland left London, it was believed that Lord Clinton and the Earl of Oxford would reinforce him as he moved north, but on the 15th Oxford joined Mary, and Clinton did not move. At this point Mary was still expecting to have to fight, and moved her headquarters from Kenninghall to Framlingham Castle, which was more defensible. There she was joined by more men of substance – Lord Windsor, Sir Edward Hastings, Sir John Williams – and convened her first council meeting.[12] As late as the 16th, after an inconclusive meeting with a number of councillors, Renard still believed that Jane would survive, and he consequently ignored an appeal from Mary for his assistance. In so doing he probably served her cause better than he knew, because the weak spot in the princess's position was her probable dependence upon foreigners, and if that could have been demonstrated at this critical stage it might have done her untold harm. However, nothing happened and the appeal remained unknown.

By the 18th Mary was reported to have 30,000 men behind her banner, and the confidence of the council in London disintegrated. The initiative was seized by Henry Fitzalan, Earl of Arundel, no friend to the Duke of Northumberland, who had readmitted him to the council only as a last-minute gamble.[13] Arundel had been thought to favour Mary, but had sworn to Jane with the rest. Now, on 18 July he convened a meeting of those councillors who were clearly wavering, including the Earl of Pembroke. Apparently he denounced Northumberland as a tyrant, and urged the recognition of Mary. Those present agreed with him, and the council divided at that point. The following day the majority group proclaimed Mary queen in London, amid scenes of overwhelming relief and joy.[14] Without Northumberland's resolute leadership, the remainder simply gave up, and the Duke of Suffolk himself informed his daughter that she was no longer queen. Then, with a fatalism that strikes the modern eye as extraordinary, they simply waited to see what would happen. The French ambassador, Noailles, wrote: 'I have witnessed the most sudden change believable in men, and I believe that God alone has worked it.'

A similar thought probably crossed Northumberland's mind when news reached him of what had happened in London. He was at Cambridge, and although he still had several hundred loyal men with him, many had deserted, and he now had no cause to fight for. He could have sought to escape, but there was nowhere to go, and defiance does not seem to have crossed his mind. He proclaimed Mary himself and, like his allies, simply waited. The new queen did not at first realise that her enemies had simply evaporated. The news was brought to her at Framlingham on the 21st by Lord Paget and the Earl of Arundel himself, bearing from their colleagues a letter of unparalleled obsequiousness:

> ... we your most humble, faithful and obedient subjects, having always (God we take to witness) remained your highness's true and humble subjects in our hearts ever since the death of our late sovereign lord and master your highness's brother, whose soul God pardon, and seeing hitherto no possibility to utter our determination therein ... have this day proclaimed in your City of London your Majesty to be our true natural sovereign liege lady and Queen ...[15]

The writers then went on to ask for pardon – what else could they have done? The resolute Protestants whom Northumberland (and Renard) had expected to rally to Jane had done no such thing. Even the duke's favourite bishop, John Hooper of Worcester and Gloucester, had immediately recognised Mary, and even sent a contingent of men to her support.

What might have happened if Mary had been opposed by a competent man with some sort of a claim instead of a hapless girl, or if the Duke of Northumberland had not been so universally unpopular, it is probably pointless to speculate. By 21 July the issue was decided. Mary was queen, and no blood had been shed. This has been described as 'the only successful rebellion against a Tudor government', but it succeeded precisely because it was not against a Tudor government; it was on behalf of a Tudor against a Grey/Dudley government. A few may have backed the princess out of personal loyalty, or because they recognised her as Henry's only legitimate child. Some probably looked to her to restore 'true religion', but the great majority supported her because she was the heir by what everyone acknowledged to be the law

– a statute.[16] Her success was momentous, not because it upheld inviolable hereditary succession, but because it represented the triumph of statute law over the undoubted wishes of an incumbent monarch. Had Northumberland succeeded, the whole authority of Parliament to resolve issues such as the succession would have been brought into doubt, and the legislative authority of that institution undermined. Of course if Edward had lived a little longer, and if Parliament had endorsed his 'Device', that issue would not have arisen, and Mary's success would have had a quite different significance. As it was she began her reign with a ringing endorsement of what would later be called a 'constitutional' succession, and that was to be very significant for the way in which she conducted her government.

Meanwhile, Mary was in the position of the leader of a hopeless opposition party who suddenly finds herself prime minister. Her council, the core of her government, presented the most urgent problem. Unlike a modern cabinet, it had no collective responsibility because all decisions of importance were made by the monarch personally, but its composition was nevertheless critical both to her image and to her capacity to govern. As soon as she had proclaimed herself queen, she needed a body that could be recognised as a privy council – and for that reason there came into being the so-called 'Framlingham council', which consisted of her existing household officers (such as Robert Rochester) and her very first adherents (Sir Henry Bedingfield and the Earl of Bath). This body was strong on loyalty, but woefully short of political experience.[17] Then the councillors in London submitted, and she had to decide what to do about them. They were all contaminated by association with the previous regime, but some more than others, and without their assistance the processes of government would have been virtually impossible. So over the next fortnight, while she moved from Framlingham to London, most of them were pardoned and reinstated. Paget and Arundel were the first, and they were followed by the earls of Pembroke, Sussex, Derby and Bedford, the Marquis of Winchester (lord treasurer), Lord Rich, Sir William Petre (principal secretary) and a number of others. When she reached London, there awaited her various 'prisoners of conscience' – the Duke of Norfolk, Edward Courtenay, and the ex-bishops of Durham, Winchester and London – all of whom she released 'with loving words'. Norfolk, Durham and Winchester were immediately sworn into the council, and Winchester was appointed lord chancellor.[18]

This gave her a council of over forty members, about 25 per cent larger than Edward's, and very variously made up. The members ranged in age from twenty-six to eighty and in experience from Rochester (nil) to Norfolk (vast and over more than forty years). There was no expectation that they would be unanimous about anything (saving their allegiance), but Mary, because of her own inexperience, wanted consensual advice – and this she hardly ever got. The first and most obvious division was between the 'Framlingham council' and the rest. The former regarded the latter as mere time servers, and quasi-heretics because they had accepted Edward's religious settlement. The latter regarded the former as mere bumpkins with no knowledge beyond household management.[19] Both groups, up to a point, were right, and their quarrels bedevilled the political functioning of the council throughout the reign.

The other immediate issue was what to do about those who had been caught in the open by the collapse of Jane's party. This included not only the Duke of Northumberland, his brother Andrew and all his five sons, but also the Marquis of Northampton, the Duke of Suffolk, the Earl of Huntingdon and about a dozen knights and senior ecclesiastics – as well, of course, as Jane herself. They were rounded up without resistance between 23 and 26 July, and interrogated by members of the new council, including some who had moved fast enough to avoid the drop. Mary seems to have decided very early that Northumberland was responsible for the whole plot. This explanation had the great advantage both of exonerating her brother and of focusing the blame on a man who was already unpopular. In spite of all the evidence to the contrary, the queen persisted in believing that Edward had simply been led astray by the duke and Archbishop Cranmer in respect of his religion, and by the duke alone in respect of the succession.[20] Although she allowed her brother to be interred with the rites that he had professed, she insisted, in spite of all advice, in celebrating a requiem mass for him in the privacy of the Chapel Royal.

About a dozen men and one woman (Jane) were tried for treason as a result of the succession dispute, but only three – Northumberland himself and two relatively minor adherents, Sir John Gates and Sir Thomas Palmer – were eventually executed on 22 August. Northampton and the Dudley sons were also convicted, but they were eventually pardoned. Jane's father, the Duke of Suffolk, very surprisingly, was pardoned without trial. Guildford and Jane were convicted and held in the Tower. They might also have been released in due course if it had not been for the events that would follow in January.[21] The Emperor's advice, conveyed to Mary by Renard early in August, was to strike hard at the ringleaders and to be lenient with the rank and file, but whether she was following his guidance, the advice of her council or her own instinct is not clear.

MARY ENTERS LONDON, 1553

Now indeed her retinue reached its greatest size. On her arrival the queen was received by all ranks of society, lords and commons alike, with remarkable honour and unutterable love. First, nothing was left or neglected which might possibly be contrived to decorate the gates, roads and all places on the queen's route to wish her joy for her victory. Every crowd met her accompanied by children, and caused celebrations everywhere, so that the joy of that most wished-for and happy triumphal procession might easily be observed, such were the magnificent preparations made by the wealthier sort and such was the anxiety among the ordinary folk to show their good will to their sovereign. Thus came the Queen, so welcome to everyone, with her sister Elizabeth, and with the leading men of the realm, the lord mayor and aldermen going before her, she was followed by her gentlewomen. On 10 August she arrived with magnificent pomp at the Tower of London, the strongest castle in the kingdom. The queen dismounted and was passing through into her private apartments when she came upon a number of prisoners strategically positioned to beg mercy from her; in her incomparable goodness she not only gave them liberty, but also restored their original honours and positions. This most appropriately prompts me to list their names.

Most important among them was Thomas Howard, duke of Norfolk, a scion of the renowned houses of Mowbray and Bigod, but an old man with one foot in the grave; the duchess of Somerset;[*] Edward Courtenay, the only son of the marquis of Exeter and grandson to one of the daughters and heirs of King Edward IV.[†] The deprived bishops were as follows: Cuthbert Tunstall, bishop of Durham, a man of illustrious origin and notable for his exceptional scholarship and purity of life; Stephen Gardiner, bishop of Winchester, a man of great intellect and astonishing learning, first imprisoned by Somerset and then deprived of his see and offices by Northumberland, but appointed Lord Chancellor by the queen because of his unusual wisdom; Bishop Day of Chichester, a retiring and highly learned man; Heath of Worcester, an unassuming man of great intellectual gifts; Bonner of London, skilled in civil and canon law.

This most notable example of mercy did much to win her subjects' affections ...
['The Vita Mariae Angliae Reginae of Robert Wingfield of Brantham', translated and edited by Diarmaid MacCulloch, *Camden Miscellany*, 28 (1984), pp. 271-2. Original Latin, pp. 222-3.]

* Anne Seymour, widow of Edward, Duke of Somerset, beheaded in 1552.

† Catherine, who had married Sir William Courtenay.

On 29 July, while Mary was still making her way slowly towards London, the Imperial ambassadors waited upon her, and Simon Renard was accorded a secret audience. Blandly ignoring the fact that they had offered her no support during the crisis itself, he set out to exploit a debt of gratitude that went back twenty years, and immediately began to advise her about all the issues that confronted her – Edward's funeral, what to do about the offenders, her coronation, religious policy and her marriage.[22] This was a portentous interview, because within a few weeks the ambassador had established himself in the role of confidential adviser, capitalising upon (and further exacerbating) her uneasy relations with her council.

At a very early stage, probably in the course of this initial audience, Mary expressed to Renard her intention to rectify the religious situation 'even to the Pope's authority'. Within a few days she had also confided in some, at least, of her council. This was not quite what they were expecting. Mary had not mentioned the pope or his jurisdiction in public for many years, and the issue with her brother's council had always been the defence of her father's religious settlement. Consequently, while everyone was expecting her to restore the mass and other traditional rites, they were not expecting her to revoke the royal supremacy over the Church. Her council appears to have taken the news stoically, some with joy, others, no doubt, with resignation; but Renard was disconcerted. He could not do anything but applaud such a pious intention, but he was worried. He believed the queen to be insecure, and her subjects deeply sunk in heresy, so that, if provoked, they would remove her as quickly as they had installed her.[23] He begged her to be careful, and conveyed his anxiety to his master. When Mary issued a proclamation on the subject on 18 August it was bland, promising no more than a settlement in due course, a settlement that would be consistent with her known wishes.[24]

Apart from religion and the punishment of Jane and her followers, there were two other issues of urgency: her coronation and her marriage. There was debate as to whether the former should precede a Parliament or not. The problem was that her legal title to the crown could be challenged, because although the Act of Succession of 1544 had been unequivocal, it had not repealed the earlier statutes declaring Mary to be a bastard, and it could therefore be argued that in theory the 1544 succession act had been invalid. In fact no one was arguing that way, but it remained a possibility. Consequently some cautious members of the council were suggesting that it would be tidier to have Catherine's marriage reinstated by Parliament before the queen was crowned. Such doubts were not allowed to prevail, and although Parliament was convened on 14 August, it did not meet until 5 October. Meanwhile, Mary had been crowned with great solemnity – and a traditional mass – on 1 October. It was an act of filial piety rather than a legal requirement when Parliament repealed the 1534 succession act, as one of its earliest priorities.[25]

Marriage was a different sort of issue altogether. For more than twenty years Mary had been kept in a state of enforced celibacy, first by her father and then by her brother's council. Now she was entirely free to marry whom she pleased – and as she was already thirty-seven there was no time to waste. Not surprisingly, this unprecedented situation daunted her. As a virgin of impeccable credentials, she did not want to appear too keen, and began to make deprecating noises. She did not really want to marry at all, but she realised that it was her duty in the interests of her realm – and more in the same vein. Only her cousin Reginald Pole, with a worldly wisdom that few have given him credit for, urged her to remain single and trust in God.[26] In this predicament, Mary remembered (and repeated) her old promise never to marry without the Emperor's consent, and asked Renard what she should do. Charles knew what he wanted, but did not know whether it would be possible. His only son, Philip, the Prince of

Spain, was a widower, deep in negotiations with the Portuguese for the hand of the infanta. He might no longer be available; moreover the Emperor was very aware of English xenophobia. Philip was notoriously hispanophile, and this had stirred up considerable trouble in the Low Countries not very long before. Briefly Charles toyed with the idea of entering the lists himself, believing that he might be acceptable to the fickle islanders, but he quickly decided that he was too old, and that his health was uncertain. His candidate would have to be Philip, but until the Portuguese negotiation could be put aside, he instructed Renard to hint at the desirability of a domestic marriage.[27]

This option was also the preference of a number of members of Mary's council, including her lord chancellor; they were keenly aware of the points that her opponents had scored in the summer by harping upon the danger of a foreign king. Unfortunately, the only available candidate was the feckless Edward Courtenay. Courtenay was the son of the Marquis of Exeter, who had been executed in 1538, and he had grown up from boyhood in the Tower of London. Aged twenty-seven in 1553, he was well educated, personable enough and reputed to be a Catholic; but he had no self-control, and not the faintest idea of how to behave in the world. Mary created him Earl of Devon on 3 September, but refused to show the slightest interest in marrying him.[28] As Charles succeeded in blocking off the only other plausible candidate – the perennial Dom Luis of Portugal – by October it was clearly a case of Philip or nobody. The prince had by this time declared his availability, and Renard was instructed to open a formal negotiation.

The ambassador feared a stiff battle with Courtenay's supporters, being particularly suspicious of the 'chatter' of the queen's ladies, but it turned out to be no contest. Renard presented a portrait of the prince, and, as he put it, caused the queen to fall 'half in love' with him. After years of repression, Mary was both excited and terrified at the prospect of having a man of her own. On 28 October she accepted the Emperor's proposal, saying that she trusted him with her life – and promptly burst into tears. The following day she swore on the sacrament that she would marry Philip.[29] Unfortunately this highly emotional commitment was entered into without consulting – or at first informing – her council. When they found out, they accepted her decision with a good grace, but it had not been a wise way to proceed.

There were good arguments in favour of the Prince of Spain. He was impeccably royal, and Catholic, and experienced in the ways of the world. Although only twenty-six, he was already a widower with one son, and he represented the traditional Habsburg alliance. However, there were also good arguments against, and these were given no countenance – by Mary at least. He was purely Spanish, had no knowledge of England or its customs, and spoke no word of the language. He was also his father's heir in respect of Spain and the Netherlands, which meant that he would shortly have enormous resources and (probably) no time to devote to England. There were also other considerations. While he liked the idea of being a king, he did not particularly fancy a spinster eleven years older than himself, whom he persistently described as his *muy cara y muy amanda tia* ('dear and beloved aunt'). He had also played no part in the negotiations, which had been conducted entirely by Charles, and (like Renard) regarded England as a country of barbarians and a land riddled with heresy.[30]

THE DRAFT ARTICLES OF MARRIAGE, 7 December 1553

As soon as may be a true marriage shall by words of the present tense be contracted and consummated between the prince and the queen in person in England. Prince Philip shall so long as the matrimony endures enjoy jointly with the queen her style and kingly name and shall aid her in her administration. The prince shall leave to the queen the disposition of all officers, lands and revenues of their dominions; they shall be disposed to those born there. All matters shall be treated in English. The queen shall be admitted to the society of the dominions the prince has or as during the matrimony may come to him. For her dowry, if she outlives the prince, she shall receive £60,000 at 40 Flemish groats the £ from the realms of the emperor, £40,000 from Spain, Castile and Aragon and their appurtenances – Brabant, Flanders, Hainault, Holland, as Margaret, widow of Charles, Duke of Burgundy, received – provided the lands are still in the prince's patrimony; otherwise adjoining lands of the same value to be substituted within three weeks.

Lest controversy for the succession arises, it is ordered: in England males and females of the marriage shall succeed according to law and custom. There shall be reserved to Don Carlos of Austria, Infante of Spain,* and his heirs general, all rights which belong or shall belong to the prince by the death of the queen his grandmother or Charles V in Spain, Two Sicilies, the Dukedom of Milan, and other dominions of Lombardy and Italy, with the burden of the said dowry. If Carlos dies and his issue fails, the eldest son of this marriage shall succeed there and in all the emperor's dominions in Burgundy and Lower Germany – the dukedoms of Brabant, Luxembourg, Gelderland, Zutphen, Burgundy, Friesland, the counties of Flanders, Artois, Holland, Zeeland, Namurs-Friesland – the land beyond the isles and all others. If Carlos or his heirs live and there is any male child by this marriage, Carlos and his descendants shall be excluded from the Lower Germanies and Burgundy, which shall descend to the eldest son of this marriage. Other children of the marriage shall he allotted portions in England and Lower Germany. No sons of the marriage shall pretend any rights in Spain or other dominions reserved to Carlos other than given by the father or grandfather. If only females are born of the marriage, the eldest shall succeed in Lower Germany. Should she marry outside England or Lower Germany, without Carlos's consent, the succession shall revert to him and his heirs general, but she and other daughters shall be endowed of lands in Spain and Lower Germany. If Carlos's issue fails, and women only remain by this marriage, the eldest daughter shall succeed in Spain, England and the rest. Whoever succeeds shall leave to every dominion their privileges and customs to be administered by their natives. The dominions of the emperor, the prince and his successors, and the queen shall aid one another according to the treaty at Westminster [February] 1543 and declared at Utrecht 26, January 1546.[†]

[Paraphrase. *Calendar of State Papers, Domestic Series*, Mary I, 1553–1558, edited by C. S. Knighton (1998), no. 24. Original MS TNA SP11/1, no. 20.]

[*] Philip's son by his first marriage.

[†] The treaty of alliance by which Henry had entered his last war with France.

Meanwhile, Parliament had (mostly) done what was expected of it. It had reinstated Catherine's marriage to Henry, thus removing the anomaly of having a sovereign lady who was technically illegitimate. It had also repealed both the first and second Acts of Uniformity, and the other statutes that had made up Edward's religious settlement. As from 20 December the Church of Henry VIII was resurrected. Parliament had not, however, touched the royal supremacy, and it had declined to reinstate the see of Durham, in spite of the fact that the queen had restored Cuthbert Tunstall as its bishop. It had also petitioned the queen to marry within the realm, having no means of knowing that she had already decided otherwise. Mary's reaction was an emotional tirade, telling them to mind their own business.[31] Technically, as her council realised, she was perfectly within her rights. Although a royal marriage was a matter of state, it was also intensely personal, and the decision was the monarch's own. Nevertheless she was not the only person to feel strongly about this issue. As Renard had realised from the beginning, one of the principal difficulties with the Spanish match would be to sell it to 'the people', by which he meant not the man and woman in the street, but the nobility and gentry without whose cooperation the country could soon become ungovernable. Mary had dealt with this problem by ignoring it, and it remained to be seen whether her gamble would pay off. Before the end of the parliamentary session, surreptitious meetings were being held in London, and a conspiracy was forming. Some of those involved were MPs, most had some association with one or other of the Edwardian governments, and all were resolute opponents of the Spanish marriage.[32]

Because of the sporadic way in which this conspiracy developed, there are a number of uncertainties about its precise aims. According to later testimony, one of the conspirators (William Thomas, a former clerk of the privy council) had spoken of assassinating the queen, but he was immediately ruled out of order. The government later claimed that it was a Protestant plot, intending to rescue and reinstate Jane Grey, but Jane was already a thoroughly discredited cause, and although some Protestants were undoubtedly involved, no one attempted to make an issue of religion at the time.[33] During the planning of the rebellion, and through the rebellion itself and the trials that followed its collapse, the protagonists claimed that their sole aim had been to force the queen to abandon her intended marriage by a display of political and military force. They may have been honest, but some of them at least must have known Mary's famous obstinacy and realised that it would be easier to break her than to make her bend. They were alleged to have been in touch with Elizabeth, and had certainly consulted the French ambassador.[34] Had the plot developed the momentum that its originators had hoped to find, it would probably have resulted in Mary's overthrow, with French support, and her replacement by her younger sister – in which case Mary might well have been 'sent to the Emperor' as she had once desired.

However, everything went wrong. One of the plotters – it is not known who – approached the Earl of Devon, who was deeply and rather publicly chagrined that the queen was showing no interest in him. He expressed sympathy, and apparently offered support. How much Courtenay knew is unclear, but he knew that dissent was stirring and that rebellion was intended. Both the lord chancellor and Simon Renard had their ears to the ground, and picked up tremors. Knowing his man, Gardiner sent for Courtenay and extracted from that weak and foolish young man whatever it was that he knew. At the same time Renard, overreacting as usual to rumours of French machinations, advised the queen to take urgent steps to protect herself against a mixture of invasion and insurrection.[35] In so doing he wrong-footed the lord chancellor, who was by no means convinced that the situation was either desperate or urgent, and who was trying to protect Edward Courtenay from himself. On 12 January 1554, when the council first began to exhibit signs of anxiety about rumours emerging from Devon, he tried to calm things down, and as a result was later accused (by Renard) of having been in league with the conspirators.

The rebels' plan, which was still embryonic at this stage, was for a threefold demonstration of force, to be raised in Leicestershire, Devon and Kent, and converging on London. This was not supposed to happen until Easter, by which time it was hoped that French backing would also be in place. However, as Noailles reported on 12 January, 'the Queen and the Lords of her Council are working to break up the plot ... and thus those who are in [it] will have to take up arms sooner than they think'.[36] One of the plotters, Sir Peter Carew, had been testing the water in the south-west by circulating alarming rumours about what the soldiers accompanying a Spanish prince would get up to on their arrival. He created some panic, but no will to resist. However, when he was summoned to the council to explain himself, his fellows naturally assumed that all was about to be revealed. Attempts were therefore made to create premature explosions in both Leicestershire and Kent, where mines had supposedly been laid. The protagonists in Leicestershire were the Duke of Suffolk and his two brothers, Thomas and John Grey. The duke's involvement was an act of both folly and ingratitude, and was to prove fatal to himself, his daughter and his son-in-law, but it accomplished precisely nothing. No one responded to their trumpets, and within days all of them were lodged in the Tower.

Only in Kent did the cry 'no foreign king' awaken an actual physical response. The plotter in this instance was Sir Thomas Wyatt, and he had a network of friends and considerable influence in the county.[37] On 19 January a group of disaffected gentlemen met at Wyatt's home – Allington Castle – and the following day mobilisation began. By the 22nd the council had been alerted. 'We do understand that they pretend to be ... our loyal subjects and that they have assembled our people only for the impeachment of the marriage ...' Influenced by Gardiner, negotiation was offered, but that was the last thing Wyatt wanted. He was trying to raise a power, and sweet reasonableness did not suit him at all. He rejected the overture, and by the 28th had about 3,000 men under arms. On the same day that venerable warrior, the Duke of Norfolk, set out from London with a hastily assembled force to confront what was now clearly a rebellion. Unfortunately most of his troops consisted of the London militia, the so-called trained bands, who were strongly sympathetic to Wyatt. On the 29th at Rochester Bridge they deserted *en masse* to the rebels, leaving the duke and a handful of the royal guard to extricate themselves as best they could.[38] This was not only a major setback in itself, it also cast considerable doubt upon the loyalty of the capital, and the loss of London would have been a major disaster. Loyal retinues had been summoned, but hardly any had yet arrived, and if Wyatt had followed Norfolk's defeat with an immediate advance upon London, he might have won. However, he delayed for three days and in that time his opportunity (if it ever existed) disappeared.

After the desertion of the Londoners, Mary was bombarded with conflicting advice. Most of her council appear to have thought that she should abandon the city and retreat to a place of greater safety. Renard thought otherwise, and in this case he was right. Mary was never short of courage when her mind was made up, and on 1 February she went to the Guildhall and made a rousing speech, calling upon the citizens' loyalty. Much of what she said was disingenuous, if not dishonest, but it did not matter.[39] The Tudor magic worked, and when Wyatt reached Southwark on 3 February, he found London Bridge closed against him. For three days he hesitated, trying to make contact with his friends in the city, and then on the 6th he marched up river to Kingston Bridge in order to approach London directly from the west. By this time the retinues of such loyal peers as the Earl of Pembroke and the Marquis of Winchester were in place, and when Wyatt reached Temple Bar he found a sizeable force arrayed against him. The court was at St James', and there was a brief panic, but almost no fighting.[40] When it became clear that all the city gates were securely held, and there was not going to be a sympathetic rising in London, Sir Thomas and his colleagues surrendered, and as many of his men as could do so simply faded away, leaving about 500 in government hands. In spite of this anticlimax, the danger had been acute for a few days, and it remained to be seen what lessons the queen would draw.

MARY'S GUILDHALL SPEECH, 31 January 1554

But her Highness doubting that London, being her Chamber and a city holden of dear price in her princely heart, might, by WYAT and such ruffens as were with him, be in danger of spoil, to the utter ruin of the same: her Highness therefore, as a most tender and loving Governess, went the same day in her royal person to the Guild Hall to foresee those perils.

Where, among other matters proceeding from her incomparable wisdom, her Grace declared how she had sent that day two of her Privy Council to the traitor WYAT: desirous rather to quiet their tumult by mercy than by the justice of the sword to vanquish: whose most Godly heart fraight[ed] with all mercy and clemency. Abhorred from all effusion of blood, Her Highness also there showed the insolent and proud answer returned from WYAT: whereat the faithful citizens were much offended; and in plain terms defied him as a most rank traitor, with all his conjurates.

And touching the marriage, her Highness affirmed that nothing was done herein by herself alone, but with consent and advisement of the whole Council, upon deliberate consultation, that this conjunction and Second Marriage should greatly advance this realm (whereunto she was first married), to much honour, quiet and gain.

'For,' quod her Grace, 'I am already married to this Common Weal and the faithful members of the same, the spousal ring where of I have on my finger: which never hitherto was, nor hereafter shall be, left off. Protesting unto you nothing to be more acceptable to my heart, nor more answerable to my will, than your advancement in wealth and welfare, with the furtherance of GOD'S glory.' And to declare her tender and princely heart towards them she promised constantly not to depart from them, although by her Council she had been much moved to the contrary: but would remain near and prest to adventure the spense* of her royal blood in defence of them.

[John Proctor,[†] *The History of Wyat's Rebellion: With the Order and Manner of Resisting the Same* (London, 1554). Reprinted in A. F Pollard, *Tudor Tracts* (1903), pp. 239-40.]

* Shedding.

[†] The schoolmaster of Tonbridge School.

In spite of its ephemeral nature and limited impact, the Wyatt rebellion had some lasting effects. The Spanish marriage remained unpopular, even though the actual terms of the treaty in which the agreement was embodied were generous. Philip was to enjoy no authority in England apart from the queen, was not to employ his own servants in government, and was not to embroil England in his current war with France. In fact it seems clear that Charles was seeking a short-term advantage, to secure his son's position in the Netherlands, rather than any long-term aim to obtain Habsburg control over England.[41] Although the envoys who came to sign this treaty were pelted with snowballs by the London schoolboys, and beat a hasty retreat when the rebels threatened the city, knowledge of this treaty certainly took some of the edge off the indignation that news of the intended match had caused, and deflated the rebels' pretensions. It was proclaimed in London on 16 January. Philip was told merely that there had been a little local difficulty over religion, and Mary herself was understandably reluctant to believe that her subjects could feel so badly about her choice of partner. Religion was a convenient pretext. It expressed the queen's own conviction, and relieved the lord chancellor of any suspicion of complicity. Gardiner, as Bishop of Winchester, seized the opportunity, and preached fiercely against the 'rotten and hurtful members of the commonwealth', meaning the Protestants.[42] In the long term, this backfired. Most of those who disliked the marriage were not Protestants or fellow travellers, but supporters of 'the Queen's proceedings'. They did not regard Wyatt and his fellows as heretics, but as patriots, and the government's attitude presented the Protestants with xenophobic credentials that they did not really deserve.

The rebellion also left a fog of suspicion behind it. Courtenay's complicity was more or less proved, but it had not extended far, and hard evidence was elusive. Elizabeth was equally suspected. Arrested some time about 18 February, she was interrogated and intimidated, but the princess would admit nothing, and all that could be proved was that the conspirators had written to her.[43] Mary heartily disliked her sister, had bullied her into a show of conformity in attending mass, and had made it clear that she did not wish her to be included in any plans for the succession. On the other hand Mary's sense of justice would not allow her to dispose of this troublesome sibling without incontrovertible evidence – and of that there was none. After several very frightening weeks for her, Elizabeth was released into house arrest at Woodstock. Renard suspected everybody, and became deeply frustrated as both Elizabeth and Courtenay escaped. He even threatened to advise a delay of the wedding if security were not improved.

Nevertheless, in relation to the scale of the rising, the toll of executions was heavy. About 150 died, out of some 3,000 who had been at one time or another under arms – a far higher percentage than had suffered for the Pilgrimage of Grace under Mary's father.[44] Among those who lost their heads were Wyatt himself, the Duke of Suffolk, and the unfortunate seventeen-year-old Jane (Grey) and Guildford Dudley. About a hundred Londoners were hanged, and a smaller number at various places in Kent. For a time Mary and her council had been seriously alarmed, and 'inclined to severe justice', but the mood passed and turned instead into a longer-term resolution to exterminate heresy – of which more anon.

7

MARRIAGE

Philip and Mary were formally espoused by proxy on 6 March 1554. But when he had learned the terms that his father had negotiated for him, the prince had been horrified and nearly called the whole thing off. This was not his idea of what being a king meant, and the reservation about war with France was inexplicable. Why else marry the Queen of England, if not to belabour the French? However, he had great respect for his father's judgement, and on calmer reflection could see that it was one thing to sign a treaty, and quite another to abide by its terms. He satisfied himself with a secret disclaimer, declaring that he had no intention of being bound by the terms that he had just signed up to.[1] This was exactly what his opponents in England had suspected he would do – but fortunately they never found out. By the end of March Mary was impatient for his arrival, but he was now rather less than ardent. As late as 16 February he was writing as though he intended to come quickly with just a small entourage, and to use the English household that he knew would be prepared for him. However, over the following month he changed his mind. He may have got wind of the fact that Mary had no plans to present him with any English estates, but more likely his political priorities changed under pressure from his servants and from the development of the war. Charles now wanted him to bring money and reinforcements from Spain, and both required time to assemble. There was also the need to make arrangements for the government of Spain in his absence. He was his father's regent there, and there was considerable uncertainty as to who should be installed in his place, given the fact that his absence was going to be of indefinite duration. Eventually his sister Juana was agreed upon, but all this took more time and it was high summer before he was ready to move north.[2]

Philip was not the only party to be uneasy about the marriage treaty. The terms were explicit enough. If Mary died first, and there were no children, Philip's interest in the kingdom came to an end, and it passed by English law to the next heir. But what was English law in this respect? The law regarding real estate was that when an heiress married, her property passed to her husband in full ownership, for the span of his life – not hers. In other words, the wife's estate only passed to her own heirs once her husband was dead. England had never had a ruling queen before (Matilda had only been *de facto* queen for a short period in 1141), and no one knew certainly whether the 'woman's estate' applied to the realm, as it would have done to a private lordship. Renard reported early in 1554 that English lawyers were muttering unhappily about this, and believed that their doubts had helped to fuel the rebellion.[3] There is no evidence of that, but the doubts were real enough. It was all very well to welcome Mary as their 'Sovereign Lady', but there was a sense in which this was a contradiction in terms, and that needed to be resolved.

Consequently, when Parliament met on 2 April, this was one of the matters on the agenda. It was dealt with simply enough by a bill that declared that the queen's authority was identical with that of her predecessors, the 'Kings of this realm' – in other words, that the gender of the monarch was irrelevant to the powers of the office, or the processes of its transmission. A 'woman's estate' did not apply to the realm. This was a decision of the utmost importance, both for Mary's relatively short lifetime, and even more for the much longer and higher profile reign of her sister that followed.[4] At the same time, the marriage treaty was ratified by converting it into a statute. This was unprecedented, and was a reflection partly of the unprecedented situation of having a ruling queen, and partly of suspicions that Philip would do exactly what he had (secretly) done in refusing to be bound by its limitations. As king he would have to respect the laws of the land – and his marriage treaty was now enshrined among the laws of England. By the time that Parliament was dissolved on 5 May, everything possible had been done to protect England from the long-dreaded advent of a foreign king.

Mary must have been aware of this legislation in more than a formal sense. Bills were not always drafted in full council, but nothing reached the floor of either House without having been discussed with the monarch. We do not know what her input into these discussions may have been, but from her later actions it seems clear that her concern to protect the interests of her kingdom from the fragility of her own condition was real enough. Some members appear to have thought that the bill about gender equality was designed to prevent her from using her sex as an excuse to escape the limitations imposed on earlier rulers – such as Magna Carta – but that was never part of the intention.[5] The purpose of both this bill and the treaty ratification was entirely positive, and Mary certainly saw them in that light. Keenly aware of her own lack of political experience, she was only too pleased to have such issues resolved.

In one respect, however, Mary's zeal betrayed her. The Church, from her point of view, was in an unsatisfactory limbo. She had told both Henry Penning (Cardinal Pole's envoy) and Gianfrancesco Commendone months before that she considered herself to be the pope's obedient daughter; but in April 1554 she was still legally the supreme head of the Church in England.[6] She had stopped using the title, but continued to exercise the power, and in March 1554 a royal visitation had been conducted to weed out the remaining Protestant bishops and clergy. Stephen Gardiner, the Bishop of Winchester as well as lord chancellor, was the top-ranking bishop since both Canterbury and York were vacant, the former by the attainder of Thomas Cranmer, and the latter by the deprivation of Robert Holgate following the visitation. Gardiner was anxious to resolve the jurisdictional issue as quickly as possible – a view with which the queen entirely concurred. Unfortunately, there were other aspects to this problem. In the first place large amounts of monastic and chantry land had now passed into secular hands – usually by purchase – and the return of the papacy would inevitably invalidate the statutes by which that land had been acquired. Secondly, the Emperor (partly persuaded by Renard) not only knew this but believed that 'the heretics' were politically powerful. He was anxious (as he saw it) to protect the queen from rushing into a restoration of monastic lands that would stir up major political problems. He was also keenly aware that it would be an enormous coup for his son to negotiate the Catholic reconciliation after he was married to the queen.

Charles was therefore preventing Reginald Pole, who was named by the pope as his cardinal legate to the kingdom, from proceeding to England and thus forcing the issue. In his view the marriage must come first, followed by an agreement with the pope, before Pole could be called upon to discharge his mission.[7] Gardiner understood both aspects of Imperial policy, and was extremely anxious to forestall it, because he was keenly aware that the pope was widely regarded in England (and not just by Protestants) as an interfering foreigner. To have the pope brought back on the coat-tails of a foreign king would do the Church considerable damage. It would be much better to resolve the religious issue (with or without Pole) before Philip set foot in England. After all, Philip would not want to come to a schismatical throne – would he?

Gardiner therefore set out in this second Parliament of the reign to resolve the issue of the royal supremacy. His bill does not survive, so we can only reconstruct its contents from second-hand accounts. One of its aims was apparently to revive the heresy laws, dating back to the early fifteenth century, which had been repealed under Edward VI. Another was 'setting up again the power of the bishops, and dealing with the Pope's authority'.[8] As Gardiner had no authority to negotiate on the part of the papacy, this could only have meant a unilateral submission. Such a move would no doubt have suited Mary very well, but it would have left unresolved the whole issue of the Church lands. The bill was debated in council, where there were strong differences of opinion, but Gardiner must have prevailed in order to get the bill before Parliament at all, where it was read in the Commons for the first time on 9 April. The queen had, of course, been consulted, but what some of her advisers do not seem to have realised was the strength of her commitment to the measure. The bill, probably in an amended form, passed the Commons on 25 April.

For some reason that is not entirely clear, Lord Paget and several noblemen, including some other councillors, were seriously alarmed by this development. Paget, who was close to the Imperial ambassador, was probably aware that such an act, if it were to pass, would largely derail the Emperor's agenda. Other nobles seem to have been mainly concerned at the prospect of a challenge to their property rights, and possibly by a major revival of episcopal authority.

Paget was also deeply suspicious of the lord chancellor's intentions for other reasons. He suspected him of a scheme to smuggle through a measure that would have had the effect of disinheriting Elizabeth, since Gardiner had failed to deal with her by the more drastic means of execution following the Wyatt rebellion.[9] Paget even appealed at one point to Renard to persuade the queen to dissolve Parliament, apparently in order to avoid a confrontation.

Parliament was being difficult, but no more difficult than usual. It ratified the marriage treaty, and tidied up the anomalous position of the Durham diocese, which its predecessor had refused to do. On the other hand, it reduced the protection offered to Philip by the treason laws to an absolute minimum, and the Lords wanted nothing to do with Gardiner's bill on ecclesiastical authority. Noailles had predicted as early as 23 April that what he revealingly described as the queen's plan for restoring the Roman obedience would founder in the House of Lords and so it proved. The bill was rejected on the third reading on 1 May, and the Parliament was dissolved four days later.[10]

Paget had undoubtedly led and orchestrated the opposition to this measure, and Mary was furious. Whether he had deliberately taken an enormous risk, or genuinely did not know the extent of the queen's involvement, we do not know, but he found himself seriously out of favour. He was not dismissed from the council, but was forced to retire to his estates for several weeks. Rather surprisingly, he also fell out with Renard. The two had worked together since August 1553, when Paget had been the first English councillor to embrace the idea of a Spanish marriage, and the ambassador had been deeply suspicious of Stephen Gardiner. Now that situation had changed. This was partly because of the fact that Renard and Gardiner were agreed about the need to get Elizabeth out of the way, if not by execution then certainly by exclusion, while Paget was protective of the princess. But it was also partly due to Paget's actions in this Parliament.[11] In spite of the fact that what Paget had done was clearly in the Imperial interest, Renard appears to have suspected that he was in league with 'the heretics', and that his loyalty to the queen was consequently questionable. On 13 May he wrote that 'the Queen is being urged to imprison Paget', along with the earls of Arundel and Pembroke. There was (and is) no evidence to support such suspicions, but the ambassador actually persuaded Mary to allow Imperial agents to open the correspondence of Sir John Mason, her ambassador in Brussels, on the grounds that he was intriguing with Paget. That she should have agreed to such a proposal says a great deal about Renard's influence during the first year of her reign, and helps to explain why some of Mary's own council should have voiced the opinion that this was an unprecedented and undesirable situation. As the time for Philip's arrival began to approach, therefore, Gardiner's star was in the ascendant, while Paget's was definitely in eclipse.

Meanwhile the Church remained legally in schism. In fact Pole had been exercising his function as the pope's representative, the cardinal legate, since about March (quite unlawfully). Thus he was secretly confirming the episcopal appointments which Mary made after the visitation of that month and issuing dispensations to anxious laymen to commit such sins as eating meat in Lent.[12] Nevertheless, and in spite of the queen's best efforts, the issue of the relationship between the English Church and the Holy See remained unresolved.

Philip was being infuriatingly uncommunicative. His proxy at the betrothal ceremony in March had been his father's servant, the Count of Egmont, and Philip himself had sent neither word nor token. Charles became anxious, and sent a private letter to the Duke of Alba, whom he knew was to accompany his son to England, in an attempt to ensure that Philip behaved 'in the right way'. The difficulties in which Philip was enmeshed were real enough, but he was making not the slightest effort to appear the ardent bridegroom. April passed into May, and still no word came from Valladolid. Below the surface, tension was beginning to increase again, and early in April a commission was put in place to resolve disputes between Philip's Spanish courtiers and the English among whom they would be settled, bearing in mind that they would be accustomed to different legal systems.[13] Early in May royal ships were sent out to scour the Western Approaches for any sign of his coming, and there must have been unexpressed doubts as to whether he would ever come at all. The French had made vague threats of intercepting him en route, and there were still mutterings about his arrival being greeted with armed insurrection. Renard, understandably, became increasingly neurotic, and worked out his unease on Paget and his friends. By the end of May an English household had been nominated for the king, numbering about 350 men headed by the Earl of Arundel as lord steward. Arundel was also steward of the queen's house, so there was clearly an attempt to ensure unity of control, but otherwise the two establishments were distinct.[14] Early in June word was finally received, although not from Philip himself, that he had actually set out from Valladolid on his way to the coast, and the Earl of Bedford was despatched as a special envoy to escort him on his voyage. On 11 June Philip's harbinger, the Marquis of Las Navas, reached Southampton, and there were no doubt sighs of relief all round. Mary met Las Navas at Guildford on the 16th, and received from him the magnificent jewel that the Prince had now (at last) sent as a token of his affection. At the same time his English household was mobilised and despatched to the south coast to await his coming.[15]

The speed of that coming was, however, another matter. June had become July before he reached La Coruña and made contact with the Earl of Bedford. The main reason for this snail-like progress was the laborious effort that was needed to assemble a fleet of sufficient size to transport not only Philip and a retinue of several hundred but also the thousands of troops destined for the fighting front in the Low Countries. At the same time the whole operation was thrown into doubt by an urgent message that Charles sent to his son on 29 June. Marienbourg had fallen to the French, and the prince was therefore instructed to spend only a few days with his bride before proceeding to the Netherlands to shore up his father's position. It was only when he was on the seas, and almost within sight of his destination, that these orders were rescinded. The French had retreated and Philip could therefore enjoy his nuptials in peace. One of the advantages of the poor communications was that none of this was known in England.

July dragged on, and everyone's patience was wearing thin. The awaiting fleet was short of victuals and afflicted by squabbles between its English and Flemish components. Some of Philip's household simply upped sticks and went away, complaining that they could not afford to hang about at their own expense.[16] Renard had run out of excuses, and was thoroughly miserable. Finally, on 20 July in pouring rain the prince's ship dropped anchor off Portsmouth, and a slightly seasick Philip landed at Southampton. Mary had been at Bishop's Waltham, near Fareham, for nearly a month, but she had allowed herself no expression of impatience. Instead she had spent some of the time overseeing the goldsmith who was creating the magnificent Garter insignia 'worth 7 or

8,000 crowns' (£2,500) that she intended to bestow upon her royal husband, and with which the Earl of Arundel girded him on board his own ship, even before his landing.

It was almost exactly a year since Mary had been proclaimed queen in London, and as she stood on the threshold of the second most momentous development of her life, Mary might well have reflected that God had (at last) been good to her. Against all the apparent odds, she had secured her throne and successfully defended it against heretics and rebels. The French had threatened war if she married a Habsburg, but she had outfaced them. The mass, and all the traditional rites that she had fought so hard to defend, were now received again throughout the realm – and Philip had come, to share her life and burdens, and hopefully to beget an heir. There was much still to do. The tangled problem of ecclesiastical jurisdiction had yet to be resolved. Heresy was defeated, but not eliminated; the enigmatic Elizabeth still posed a threat; and her children were still to be begotten. Only she knew what an exciting and alarming prospect that presented.

Apart from the weather, Philip could hardly complain about his reception. Several councillors, including the earls of Arundel, Derby, Shrewsbury and Pembroke, had gone out in a richly gilded barge to bring him ashore, and a distinguished retinue of courtiers awaited his arrival. The 'vii score ships' that had accompanied him from Spain proceeded straight to the Netherlands. Contrary to what many had feared and anticipated, no Spanish troops landed in England. Among those awaiting Philip's landing was a messenger from his father, bearing a patent conferring upon him the kingdoms of Naples, Sicily and Jerusalem, 'whereat the English lords were greatly pleased'.[17] Philip was soon complaining that the actual powers of government did not appear to have followed the grant, but at the time everyone was gratified by the gesture, because it meant that the marriage that was about to take place would now be between technical equals.

Having received the homage of his English officers through the agency of Sir Anthony Browne, master of the horse, the new king went straight to the Church of the Holy Rood in Southampton to give thanks for his safe arrival. The same evening he treated the council to what is described as 'a long discourse of the occasion of his coming into this kingdom', no doubt intended to reassure them of the honourable nature of his intentions. Presumably he spoke in Latin, since he had no English and the councillors (with one or two exceptions) no Spanish.[18] Philip, 'with such noblemen as had accompanied him', remained in Southampton that night, and the Saturday and Sunday following, to recover from their journey. On Monday 23 July he proceeded to Winchester, where he was lodged in the deanery. Mary, meanwhile, had come down from Bishops Waltham to Winchester on the Saturday, and was lodged at the bishop's palace.

It was on Tuesday the 24th – the day before their wedding – that the royal couple first met each other. At about three o'clock in the afternoon, accompanied at a discreet distance by numerous lords both English and Spanish, 'he went to the queen from the Dean's house afoot ... in a cloak of black cloth embroidered with silver, and a pair of white hose', and, according to one source, wearing his Garter.

> After that he had entered the court, where all kinds of instruments played very melodiously, and come within the hall where the Queen's Majesty was standing on a scaffold, her highness descended, and amiably receiving him, did kiss him in presence of all the people. And then taking him by the right hand, they went together in[to] the Chamber of Presence, where after they had, in sight of all the Lords and Ladies, a quarter of an hour pleasantly talked and communed together under the cloth of estate, and each of them merrily smiling on [the] other, to the great comfort and rejoicing of the beholders, he took his leave of her grace ...[19]

What either of them really thought or felt at this time, we do not know, but the public display of affection was a vast relief to the spectators – as it was intended to be – and conducted in accordance with the strictest protocol. Philip, indeed, behaved admirably throughout what must have been a rather trying experience. He was not accustomed to making himself agreeable for the benefit of people whom he neither knew nor liked, but during these days he made an excellent impression, not only on the courtiers (who were disposed to be impressed) but also on the crowds that hung around the fringes of these events, catching sight of him as they could. Although he was quite small and slightly built, they seem to have found him 'manly', and very splendidly turned out. He was courteous, very correct, particularly in his religious observances, and his display of affection for Mary, although brief, was very well received.

What Philip thought of Mary he seems not to have confided, even to his closest servants, which probably tells its own story. His servants were frankly unimpressed, and their letters home present an unflattering picture of a dowdy spinster, 'not as young as we had been led to suppose', who loved flashy clothes and jewellery, but who had no taste or dress sense.[20] They were even more unflattering about the queen's ladies, who they generally describe as plain and elderly, although there is some evidence to suggest that that was distinctly unfair. In fact a number of Philip's courtiers had had their arms twisted to come on this trip at all, and were disposed to be querulous and critical of everything that they found. 'We do not want to go courting in England,' one of their laments ran, 'there are far prettier girls at home'.[21]

The wedding duly took place in Winchester Cathedral on Wednesday 25 July. The date – St James' Day – seems to have been chosen as a compliment to the Spanish visitors, as Santa Iago (de Compostella) was the patron saint of Castile. The ceremony was lavish, and replete with symbolism. The king arrived first, accompanied by a large retinue of Spanish lords, 'the like of which has not been seen', but (as the commentator carefully notes) no sword borne before him (because he was not yet king), and took his place on the dais.[22] Half an hour later the queen arrived, accompanied by numerous lords, ladies and gentlewomen, and with a sword borne before her by the Earl of Derby. While the heralds and kings of arms took up their positions, she proceeded to the other side of the dais. Once they were in position, the Count of Feria stepped forward and formally confirmed the Emperor's grant of the crown of Naples to his son, presenting the patent. The lord chamberlain, Sir John Gage, then made 'a goodly oration to the people', full of flattering references both to Philip and his father, but also drawing careful attention to the terms of the marriage treaty, 'the articles whereof are not unknown to the whole realm'. If Philip felt any discomfort at this recitation of the limits imposed upon him, he gave no sign of it. The actual marriage was conducted by the Bishop of Winchester, assisted by his brethren of London, Durham, Chichester, Lincoln and Ely. The bans were called both in English and Latin, and Mary was given away in the name of the realm by the Marquis of Winchester and the earls of Derby, Bedford and Pembroke. There then followed a solemn high mass, but neither of the principals appear to have communicated, receiving instead 'hallowed wine and sops'.

Mary was married with a plain gold ring 'because so were maids wont to be married in old time', as she is supposed to have said, and when the ring was blessed Philip put three handfuls of fine gold 'upon the said book', which Margaret Clifford, performing the function of what would now be known as bridesmaid, carefully stowed in the queen's purse. And when they had enclosed their hands [that is, the marriage was complete] immediately the sword was advanced before the king by the Earl of Pembroke ...' Throughout the proceedings, we are told, the queen kept to the right hand, and the king to the left – a reversal of the normal positions – in case Philip should be left in any doubt that his status in England was primarily that of the queen's husband.[23] This was a role that, later, George of Denmark, Victoria's Prince Albert and the present Duke of Edinburgh would all have recognised, but it was without precedent in the mid-sixteenth century. What the king himself thought we do not know, but several of his councillors were outraged by the implied slight upon his honour. In spite of the euphoria with which (we are assured) the ceremony was greeted by the English, of all classes, the political symbolism of the marriage was not altogether encouraging.

THE QUEEN'S WEDDING, 25 July 1554

Then Wednesday, being Saint James's day, the xxvth of July, his Highness (at x of the clock) and his nobles before him, went to the cathedral church, and remained there (the doors being very straightly kept) until the Queen's Highness came: whose Majesty, with all her council and nobility before her, came thither at half hour to eleven. And entering at the West door of the said cathedral church (where her Grace was received the Saturday before, in like manner as his Highness was the Monday following), her Majesty ascended the foresaid steps, and came towards the choir door, where a little without the same door was made a round mount of boards, ascending also five steps above the scaffold. On which mount, immediately after her Majesty and the king were shriven, they were married by my lord the Bishop of Winchester, Lord Chancellor of England, her Majesty standing on the right side of the said mount, and the king on the left side. And this marriage

159

being ended and solemnised, which with the biddings and the bans thereof was declared and done by the said Lord Chancellor, both in Latin and English, his Lordship declared also there: How that the Emperor's Majesty resigned, under his Imperial seal, the kingdoms of Naples and Jerusalem to his son Philip Prince of Spain, whereby it might well appear to all men that the Queen's Highness was then married, not only to a Prince, but also unto a King. The Queen's marriage ring was a plain hoop of gold without any stone in it: because that was as it is said her pleasure because maidens were so married in old times. This (as I have said) being ended and done, the Earl of Derby before the Queen's Majesty, and the Earl of Pembroke before the King's Highness, did bear each of them a sword of honour. And so both their Majesties entered the choir hand in hand under a canopy borne by iiii knights towards the high altar, where after they had kneeled awhile with each of them a taper, they arose, and [the] Queen went to a seat or traverse of the right hand of the altar, and the King to another seat of the left hand, where they continued thus several in their meditations and prayers until the gospel was said, and then they came out, and kneeled all the high mass time openly before the high altar, the care cloth being holden as the manner is.* Where during the mass time the Queen's chapel matched with the choir and the organs, used such sweet proportion of music and harmony as the like (I suppose) was never before invented or heard. The high mass being done, which was celebrated and said by my lord the Bishop of Winchester, having to his co-adjutors the five bishops aforesaid, that is to say the Bishops of Durham, Ely, London, Lincoln and Chichester, (wherein both the princes offering rich jewels, and delivering their tapers, yea and the King's Highness at the Agnus Dei kissing the celebrator, according to the ceremonies of marriages used in the holy catholic churches), the King of Heralds openly, in presence of both their Majesties and the whole audience, solemnly proclaimed this their new style and title in Latin, French and English.

[John Elder, *The copie of a letter sent into Scotlande, of the arrivall and landynge, and most noble marryage of the moste illustre prynce, Philippe, prynce of Spaine...* (London, 1554). Printed by J. G. Nichols in *The Chronicle of Queen Jane* (Camden Society, 1850), Appendix x.]

* A canopy held over their heads.

46. Henry VII, Mary's grandfather, from the cartoon by Holbein in the National Portrait Gallery.

Next page spread, left: 47. Henry VIII. A statue in the great gate at Trinity College, Cambridge (a royal foundation), showing a mature Henry. About 1541.

Next page spread, right: 48. Catherine of Aragon, Mary's mother, showing her as a mature woman, about 1520. By an unknown artist.

KATHERINA VXOR HENRICI . . VI

Above left: 49. Anne Boleyn, Henry's second wife and Mary's *bête noire*. She was reckoned to be 'no great beauty'. By an unknown artist.

Above right: 50. Jane Seymour, Henry's third wife and the mother of his son, Edward. Painted in 1537 by an unknown artist.

Left: 51. Funeral effigy of Elizabeth Blount, Lady Tailboys, Henry's mistress and the mother of his son Henry Fitzroy.

52. A lady, supposed to be Mary at the age of about seventeen. By Hans Holbein, in the Royal Collection.

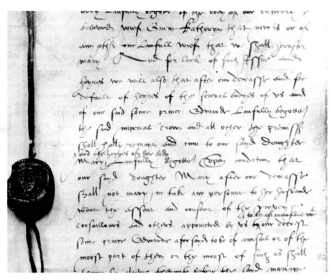

53. Henry VIII's will, dated 30 December 1546. It was signed with stamp rather than the sign manual, which was to cause problems in the future.

Above left: 54. Lady Anne Shelton, Anne Boleyn's aunt, and the governess of the household for the two princesses in 1533–4. From a stained glass window in Shelton church.

Above right: 55. Mary Stuart, Queen of Scots. Mary came to the throne of Scotland at just over a week old, in December 1542. Her claim to the English succession was ignored in Henry VIII's final Succession Act of 1544.

Left: 56. Edward VI as a child, playing with a pet monkey. A painting by Holbein in the Kunstmuseum at Basle.

57. Wolsey dismissed by Henry VIII. An imaginative Victorian reconstruction.

58. A view of Greenwich Palace, from a drawing by Anthony van Wyngaerde (*c*.1550), in the Ashmolean Museum at Oxford.

Posui ori meo custodiam: cum consisteret peccator adversum me. Obmutui et humiliatus sum. et silui a bonis: et dolor meus renovatus est.

59. A page from a book of hours (prayer book) once owned by Mary.

The spirit of Anglo-Spanish rivalry, foreshadowed in these ceremonies, seems to have surfaced as early as the banquet that followed the marriage. Edward Underhill, one of the gentleman servants who waited at that banquet, wrote afterwards:

> I will not take upon me to write of the manner of the marriage, of the feast, nor of the dancing of the Spaniards that day, who were greatly out of countenance, especially King Philip dancing, when they did see my Lord Bray, Mr Carew and others so far exceed them; but will leave it unto the learned ...[24]

We have only his word for it, but competition certainly seems to have been in the air. This was doubly unfortunate, because the two nations really did not like, or understand, each other at all. The Spaniards had a reputation throughout their dependent dominions for being arrogant and intolerant, while in their eyes the English were still (except the queen) the barbarous heretics who had rejected that good daughter of Spain, Catherine of Aragon. As far as we know none of Philip's retinue spoke a word of English, and there were only a handful of Spanish speakers in the English court. Except at the very highest level, where Latin provided a common medium, mutual incomprehension was absolute. Even at the wedding banquet this situation was exacerbated by the fact that Philip had two households – one Spanish, the other English – and two sets of officers. How this had arisen is a mystery, because it had always been clear that the king would have an English establishment – for which he would pay. Perhaps his Spanish servants had made it apparent that they would feel insulted if they were not allowed to accompany him, and he took the line of least resistance. However, the tensions were immediate and unavoidable.

Philip adopted a pragmatic attitude. Out of the public eye, he did not mind much who did his cooking and cleaning, so most of the 'below-stairs' Spanish servants were sent home. In the public eye, however, it was important to be correct, and he instructed that his public service should be performed by his English officers, and his private service by their Spanish equivalents. This sensible compromise offended everyone. The English complained that they had no access to the privy apartments, and the Spanish that they were made to appear redundant.[25] After a few weeks the issue simmered down, but it never entirely disappeared while Philip was in England. There were other problems. It was understood that the king would bring his own chapel staff, so none was provided, but it was not understood that he would bring his own stable establishment. Sir Anthony Browne lasted only a matter of days as his master of the horse. The chapel was not contentious because it was accepted that he preferred clergy who were familiar with his tastes and needs, but the real reason was that he regarded all English clergy as schismatics, and although he was prepared to grit his teeth and get through the marriage service, he would not willingly employ them if he did not have to.

About thirty Imperial noblemen attended the wedding. They were not all Spaniards; a few were Flemings or Italians, but they all found themselves at a loose end after the ceremony.[26] There were also a considerable number of *hidalgos*, Spanish gentlemen, and others, mostly dependents of one or other of the grandees, and equally at a loss. The obvious solution was to send them to join the Imperial army in the Low Countries, but Philip hesitated. Perhaps he felt that his honour required an attendance of his own countrymen. Meanwhile they became increasingly restive, complaining about the thieving ways of the English, and the general climate of hostility. 'We are all longing to be off,' one wrote, adding that in comparison 'Flanders looks like a paradise'.[27] After a few weeks, Philip yielded to their importunity, and they departed, greatly easing the tensions around the court.

Charles had warned his son against allowing his courtiers to bring their wives with them, observing that even soldiers would get on better with the islanders than these proud Iberian dames. The Duke of Alba ignored the warning, and the result demonstrated its wisdom. His duchess arrived unbidden, and complained bitterly that no suitable accommodation had been reserved for her. So grand a lady could hardly be refused an audience with the queen, but when they met, so sensitive (or competitive) was their sense of protocol that both ended up sitting on the floor, since neither was prepared to take a chair first!

The other main problem was at what might be termed the 'bottom end'. A considerable number of small traders, jobbers and hucksters of all kinds followed the prince from Spain and other parts of his dominions, hoping to make a quick profit from his visit to England. He had no responsibility for this, but once they had arrived, many of them endeavoured to set up stalls and booths around London and near to the court. This was directly contrary to the trading privileges of the City, whose officers wasted no time in pointing this out. Philip duly expelled them, but not before there had been several violent clashes, and a few deaths for which the English were not always to blame.

With marriage came, for Mary, another novel experience. If the queen was daunted by her first sexual encounter, she was too self-disciplined to show it. On the first night of her married life, the bride bed was duly (and publicly) blessed, but then the intrusive crowds retired, and even the most intimate servants were excluded. 'What happened thereafter,' one observer wrote, 'is known only to themselves,' but he added: 'God grant that they give us a son.'[28] According to custom, and perhaps need, Mary remained invisible for the next two or three days, while Philip did a little sightseeing around Winchester. What in a normal marriage would have been the honeymoon period was by no means relaxing for him, as the problems of his household and entourage began to appear. But Mary, according to contemporary accounts, was blooming. What must have been potentially a very difficult relationship for Philip with a totally inexperienced woman eleven years his senior appears to have started well. Shortly afterwards he seems to have confided to one of his servants that the queen was not very good *para la sensualidad de la carne* (that is, sexually), but if he felt dissatisfied he clearly never allowed his wife to see it. She was predisposed to find him pleasing, and it was on that basis that he developed the personal ascendancy that he clearly enjoyed over her during the remainder of his time in England.

Meanwhile, they were a long way from London, and everyone understood that Philip's reception there would be the first test of his kingship. On 31 July they set out from Winchester on a leisurely journey towards the capital, spending two nights at the Marquis of Winchester's seat at Basing, and one at Reading, before reaching Windsor on 3 August. Mary discharged a certain amount of regular business during the journey, because most of her council had been present at the wedding and were accompanying her on the journey. Philip met daily with his Spanish and other Imperial councillors, not about English business but about the war and other aspects of his far-flung Continental interests. Most pressing was planning the takeover of his inheritance from his father, who was now in visibly declining health and beginning to talk of abdication.

London was not yet ready for the royal couple. This was partly because the planned entry was very elaborate and expensive, and partly because the scaffolds bearing the victims who had suffered after the Wyatt rising had only recently been taken down. The more time that could be taken to erase that unpleasant memory, the better. At Windsor an extraordinary chapter of the Order of the Garter was held, and the king was duly installed. On 11 August the royal couple moved on to Richmond, and it was while they were there that the news arrived that the French were besieging Renty. This gave Philip the pretext to get rid of most of his disgruntled followers, and it was at this point that over eighty of them departed.[29] Then, London having declared itself prepared, on the 17th the royal couple moved to Suffolk Place in Southwark, ready to make a ceremonial entry on the following day.

8

A WOMAN'S PROBLEMS

Warmly as they had welcomed her, the English were not acclimatised to the notion of a woman on the throne. As Judith Richards pointed out a few years ago, their imagination did not extend much beyond virgins and amazons.[1] As long as Mary was unmarried, they could in a sense 'identify' her, because virginity conferred power as well as legal status. However, once she was wedded and bedded all that changed. This had nothing to do with the law, constitutional or otherwise, but was a question of image or perception. On the one hand, there was a feeling that England was now in a sense subject to Spain, and that was deeply unpopular. But on the other hand, their beloved queen had now found a mate who would please her and give her children (the true destiny of all women). Philip was well received by the crowds who lined the roads outside Winchester Cathedral for precisely that reason.[2] At the same time there was a feeling, particularly among the aristocracy, that government was man's work, and some were prepared to welcome Philip for no other reason than that he was male and would restore a semblance of the divine order. Many nobles still saw their service to the crown principally in military terms, and were much happier with a monarch who could lead them into battle – to say nothing of providing gainful employment in his international armies. There were therefore from the start those who were temperamentally disposed to be 'the king's men', both within the council and among the aristocracy at large.[3] It remained to be seen what Philip would do about this.

At first, in spite of the problems over his household and the recalcitrant mutterings of some of his followers, the public image was positive. On 18 August 1554, at two o'clock in the afternoon, the royal couple crossed London Bridge and processed through the City to Whitehall. Official London did its best to erase the memory of Wyatt with six or seven splendid set-piece pageants, starting with the figures of Corineus Brittanus and Gogmagog Albionus on the bridge itself. These pageants had been long in preparation (hence the delay) and must have been vastly expensive, but unlike those that had greeted the last Spanish royal visitor, Catherine of Aragon, in 1501, they were not particularly original or imaginative.[4] They were aimed rather obviously at the king: one of them concerned his descent from John of Gaunt, while others depicted the virtues of various historical and mythological Philips. Their captions were displayed only in Latin, which was probably a sensible compromise, but raises the suspicion that the City fathers did not want ordinary people to understand the extent of their flattery:

> Unica Caesareae stirpis spes inclite princeps
> Cui Deus imperium totius destinat orbis
> Gratus et optatus nostras accedes ad oras ...
> Te tamen in primis urbs Londoniensis honorat,
> Incolumenque suum gaudet venisse Pbilippum ...
> [O noble Prince, sole hope of Caesar's side,
> By God appointed all the world to guide,
> Most heartily welcome art thou to our land ...
> But chiefly London doth her love vouchsafe,
> Rejoicing that her Philip is come safe ...][5]

Philip later declared that he had been received with universal joy, which would no doubt have been a great relief to the aldermen, but in fact within two days of the entry the pageants were being vandalised and had to be taken down.

Hostility and mutual suspicion between the two nations were endemic, and neither was solely responsible. Even poor Simon Renard, the Imperial ambassador, was blamed by Ruy Gomez for the confusion over the households, for no better reason (apparently) than that he was not a Spaniard.[6] The real responsibility probably lay with Gomez himself. Just before the court entered London, it was reported that two noble Spanish ladies had not been received by the queen, 'and are not going to see her, for they have not joined the court because they would have no one to talk to, as the English ladies are of evil conversation'. Nor, of course, did they speak Spanish.[7] If the court was a simmering cauldron of hatred, controlled with difficulty by the joint commission, its environs were much worse. Innkeepers refused to accommodate Spaniards, or hurled abuse at them. Clergy, and especially the friars, were felt to be particularly vulnerable to anti-Spanish sentiment, 'for the English are so bad, and fear God so little, that they handle the friars shamefully, and the poor men do not dare to leave their quarters'. Most of the evidence for this animosity comes from the Spanish side, and may have been partly a nervous overreaction to the boisterousness and curiosity of a people whose tongue they did not understand. Some Englishmen were punished for robbery, assault and murder committed upon the visitors, but equally some Spaniards were punished for similar crimes against their hosts.[8] What seems clear is that the two nations were predisposed to fear and dislike each other before they ever came together, and that actual contact only made the situation worse.

Mary was said to be particularly distressed by this situation, and Philip was clearly irritated by it, but of any more specific reaction there is no sign. The fact that Simon Renard is one of the prime sources for these stories of hatred should make us cautious about taking them all at face value. Philip neither liked nor trusted him, and his confidential relationship with Mary had come to an abrupt end. He was soon complaining bitterly of his lot, and begging for recall, so his view of the political situation in September 1554 is nothing if not jaundiced:

> They loudly proclaim that they are going to be enslaved, for the Queen is a Spanish woman at heart, and thinks nothing of Englishmen, but only of Spaniards and bishops.

No doubt such words were being spoken on the streets, but they were not necessarily of much significance. Philip was unfazed by the hostile clamour – if he ever heard it – and got on with the business of building himself a position in England. On 23 August he issued patents conferring pensions upon twenty-one noblemen and councillors. These were drawn on his own revenues, and varied in amount from £75 a year to £500. Paget received £375, one of the highest awards, and the lord chancellor nothing – in marked contrast with their relative positions in the queen's favour at that point.[9]

Philip's personal relations with his wife appear to have been excellent, and it was not long before she was speaking rather coyly about being pregnant, but whether he could exploit that relationship so that he would acquire real political authority remained to be seen. Although the situation in the Netherlands had improved from the Spanish point of view, and there was no prospect of Philip being peremptorily summoned to join his father, he continued to be deeply interested in Imperial business, and daily concerned with it. For this purpose he had his own councillors, who were entirely distinct from the English council. He met regularly with the latter (or with some members of it), conferring in Latin, but since it was not the custom in England for the monarch to attend normal council meetings, it is unlikely that he attempted to do so. His 'Spanish council' was quite different, because he always attended and the business was conducted in that language. It must have been these meetings to which the Duke of Alba was referring when he declared that 'all public business is transacted in Castilian'. Alba's report makes it appear that he was referring to the privy council proper, but that would have been impossible since no English councillor spoke much Spanish.[10]

Philip's councillors and remaining courtiers were distressed by this situation, and by the king's general detachment from English affairs. He had not even been crowned, and the terms of the marriage treaty prevented him from conferring English offices upon any of them. Some of them were even trying to persuade him to withdraw until he could either force or persuade the English to show him more respect. What galled them most was the fact that he had been given no English resources, and this remains something of a puzzle. The consort of a king would have received a substantial estate – equivalent at least to that of a major peer – and all Henry's queens had been so endowed. But Philip received nothing. Perhaps Mary was persuaded to withhold this favour on the grounds that Philip had plenty of resources already, but the suspicion must remain that it was done deliberately to make sure that he had no independent English patronage. If the king himself felt slighted by this omission, he gave no sign of it. What bothered him, it later transpired, was the absence of an English coronation.

Meanwhile, Philip had two main preoccupations in his new kingdom – to keep Mary happy and to put the Church to rights. At this stage the former appeared to be the more straightforward: for the first, and probably the only, time in her life, during these months Mary was at peace with the world. 'The king and queen's majesties be in health and merry' ran a report from the court on 12 October, 'they danced together on Sunday night at the court. There was a brave maskery ...' The revels office had been stirred out of the torpor induced by Mary's indifference by Philip's arrival.[11] Philip knew that a brave show was required, and this is an early example of his impact. The queen was full of gratitude, both to her husband and to his father. 'This marriage and alliance,' she wrote to the latter, 'renders me happier than I can say, as I daily discover in the king my husband and your son, so many virtues and perfections that I constantly pray God to give me grace to please him.'[12]

Some of this happiness even rubbed off on the queen's subjects, jaundiced as they were by the sight of Spaniards on the streets of London, with their strange garb and incomprehensible speech. The rumours of Mary's pregnancy, which were widespread by November, awakened a warm response in many – somewhat paradoxically, as any child born to them would be three-quarters Spanish by blood. Whether this reaction was motivated by human empathy or the prospect of a secure succession, we do not know, but the observant Ruy Gomez noticed it, and took it for a good sign: 'If it is true,' he wrote, 'everything will calm down.' The loyal ballad mongers were also busy:

> Now sing, now spring, our care is exiled,
> Our gracious Queen is quickened with child ...[13]

It was a time of hope for everyone, except the beleaguered Protestants, who, with their services outlawed and most of their leaders in prison, now seemed to be deprived of the prospect of any long-term future.

That had, of course, been Mary's intention from the beginning, but it was only with Philip's arrival that the Emperor's opposition was withdrawn and the process of ecclesiastical restoration could begin in earnest. Discussions held during August and September had convinced Philip that it would be a mistake to allow Reginald Pole into the country with the brief that he then possessed. The king knew enough about Cardinal Pole's view of the English situation to realise that unless he were specifically instructed to do so, he would not make the concessions necessary to satisfy those whom he significantly termed 'the possessioners' (i.e. those now in possession of former monastic land). In Pole's opinion, such people were simply occupying stolen property, to the peril of their immortal souls.[14] Philip, however, appreciated that they had paid a fair market price for land to which they believed the king had a perfectly good title. He had himself some experience of extracting land from a reluctant Church, and also wanted the political support of the English aristocracy – so the last thing he needed was Pole's conscientious inflexibility. If the cardinal was given any discretion in the matter he would not negotiate, and as Philip suspected (with good cause) that Mary was of the same mind, he decided to take the matter in hand himself. He was in an excellent position to do so, because Charles was now willing to allow him to deploy the full weight of Habsburg influence in the curia. On 12 October he wrote to Francisco Eraso, the Emperor's secretary, saying that he had decided to make direct representations to the pope, and at the same time he sent Simon Renard to the Low Countries to exercise his persuasive skills upon the cardinal.[15] This had the double advantage of giving Renard a task well suited to his aptitudes, and getting him out from under the king's feet. For some time the ambassador's querulous flow was stemmed while he addressed himself to his new task.

By the end of October Renard had so far succeeded that Pole had agreed to surrender into the king's hands the discretion allowed him in his existing brief – provided that the pope agreed. Philip was confident enough of his own influence in Rome to accept this as sufficient for the time being. A Parliament had been called for 12 November, and could not be put off without great inconvenience. In this Parliament the issue of ecclesiastical jurisdiction would have to be addressed. Early in November word was received from Rome that a new and more specific brief would be issued to Pole, but there was no chance of it arriving before the Parliament opened. So Philip had to proceed on the basis of what he had already achieved, 'feeling sure that the Holy Father would ratify and approve my course, and indeed be very glad that I had adopted it'.[16] For the first (and only) time Philip accompanied Mary to the state opening, and a prayer for the pope was inserted among the religious formalities.

The cardinal's presence was now required, but there remained the small matter of an outstanding attainder for high treason against him. Philip, having consulted his advisers and theologians, decided to gamble. On 3 November the privy council invited Pole to return to England, in his formal capacity as papal legate, and as he made his way home with studied and ceremonial deliberation, the repeal of his attainder was rushed through all its stages. The process was completed by 22 November, when the king and queen took the most unusual step of going to the Parliament in person and in mid-session to give the royal assent.[17] Two days later the cardinal arrived by river at Westminster (thus ducking the issue of passing through London) and greeted the queen with the words of the 'Hail Mary'. It was an emotional moment, and she claimed, quite mistakenly, that the child in her womb had quickened in response. Pole took up residence at Lambeth Palace, untenanted since the imprisonment of Cranmer over a year before, and prepared to address himself to the arduous task of reconciliation. On the 28th he addressed both Houses of Parliament, his eloquence giving no hint of the reservations that he must have felt: 'My commission,' he declared, 'is not of prejudice to any person. I come not to destroy but to build. I come to reconcile, not to condemn. I come not to compel but to call again.'[18] The past, he went on, would be 'cast into the sea of forgetfulness'. He praised Mary, Philip and the Emperor in fulsome terms, likening the latter to David, who had been unable to build the Temple at Jerusalem but had been constrained to leave the task to his son Solomon. Two days later, on 30 November, Parliament presented a petition, in the name of both Houses, to the king and queen 'as persons unspotted by heresy or schism' to intercede with the papal legate for absolution and reconciliation. Pole pronounced his blessing, and the assembled company 'cried with one voice, Amen'.[19]

Tears of joy, we are told, flowed copiously. But of course in legal terms the process had only just begun, and on 4 December a committee was established to draft a bill that would have the effect of repealing all those acts by which the royal supremacy had been established. The committee was also briefed to safeguard the rights of the property holders. All this had been very much Philip's doing. Apart from taking her place in all the proper formalities, Mary hardly appears in these negotiations at all, and when she wrote to the Emperor on 7 December, informing him of the joy and enthusiasm with which her subjects had embraced the True Church, she rightly attributed this success 'largely ... to the wise guidance of my said Lord'.[20]

Philip soon became aware, however, that he could not yet sit back and enjoy his triumph. Hard questions remained to be answered. It was all very well to talk about 'seas of forgetfulness', but if the acts dissolving the small monasteries and conferring the property of surrendered large houses upon the crown were repealed with the rest, wherein did the property holders' title lie? A papal dispensation was fine up to a point, but the pope (like Parliament) was a sovereign legislator and could not bind his successors. If the next pope changed his mind and withdrew the dispensation, then the immunity of the new property owners from prosecution disappeared. Even the present dispensation was open to interpretation. It did away with earthly penalties, but suppose Pole claimed (as he probably would) that the actual sin of unlawful possession remained? A sermon by John Feckenham, the Dean of St Paul's, who was known to be close to Pole, on 25 November had promised no less.[21] This prospect of spiritual blackmail was both uncomfortable and unwelcome. What the Parliament needed was a new basis for title. Neither Mary nor Pole would see this – but Philip could, and did.

Philip therefore supported a plan, devised by anonymous lawyers, to include the full text of the dispensation in the statute of repeal. By so doing, it would become enshrined in English law, irrespective of future papal policy, unless or until the statute was itself repealed. This was hardly a perfect solution, but it met the immediate requirement. Pole was utterly opposed to the idea. In the first place he refused to acknowledge that any valid title to the property in question could be created by any positive law, and secondly it was contrary to the papal prerogative to attempt to constrain the freedom of future popes in this way. He had only reluctantly conceded the need for any statute of repeal, and to attempt to use it in this way was quite unacceptable. Mary, we are told, supported him, and between them they could have sabotaged the whole bargain. Detailed discussions took place, recorded (somewhat imprecisely) by Ludovico Priuli, Pole's secretary.[22] Both Pole and Gardiner lectured the lay nobility on the sinfulness of their ways, and called on classical antiquity to counteract modern precedent.

However, at some point between 22 and 27 December, Philip talked his wife round. He must have had magical powers of persuasion, because the issue touched her conscience, but she probably realised that it was a logical extension of the idea of a parliamentary settlement, which she had accepted as early as the previous August. The lawyers made some concessions, but without Mary's support the clerical position became increasingly untenable. The revised bill, having passed the Lords, was read in the Commons on 27 December and finally passed on 3 January 1555.[23] As Gardiner observed (not without a hint of irony), 'mercy and truth are met together; righteousness and peace have kissed each other'. To make the point more firmly, the fifteenth-century heresy laws, abandoned by Edward VI, were re-enacted. It became again a capital offence to deny any aspect of Catholic orthodoxy, and Mary and Pole, now armed with the latter's authority as papal legate, could begin the congenial task of exterminating Protestants.

THE RECONCILIATION WITH ROME, 21 December 1554

Sire. As I have heard that the King has sent to your Majesty the Act passed by the parliament of England on obedience to the Pope and the Apostolic See,* I have taken no steps to obtain and send a copy. Since that event, on the Sunday following, the King attended mass at St Paul's, in presence of Cardinal Pole. After mass the Chancellor preached in the pulpit outside the church and was listened to by a multitude of people that overflowed both the church and churchyard, as well as by the King and Cardinal. He explained to the people what parliament had done, and publicly confessed the error into which fear of the late King Henry had led him when he went to Rome and gave his consent to the rejection of the Papal authority, as he set forth in his book on true obedience.† No overt sign of displeasure was observed on his listeners' faces, but rather joy and satisfaction at seeing the King and the Cardinal, and hearing about the reconciliation. When the sermon was over the King and Cardinal returned to Westminster, accompanied by the English nobility and the king's guard, a fine sight to see. Since then parliament has been discussing several bills, among them one confirming the titles of holders of church property, which the English lawyers asserted to be unnecessary because since the earliest times the kings of England have held absolute and immediate jurisdiction over church lands. The holders, however, desired to be reassured, which caused a difficulty in that parliament wished the dispensation to be included in the statute on obedience to the Pope, and the Cardinal would not have this, lest it should seem that the realm's obedience had been bought, though he was willing to agree that the dispensation should be included in two other acts or statutes. This difficulty proved so serious that the Cardinal declared that he would go back to Rome without having accomplished that for which he came rather than make a concession so prejudicial to the rights of the holy see. Whereupon the King approached the Privy Council and certain private individuals with a view to persuading them to accept the concession of two statutes on some other controversial point. No decision has yet been reached, but it is hoped that parliament will arrange matters. Moreover several members of the Lower House who possess no church property, influenced by envy of the holders, political passion or conscientious scruples, have moved that no dispensation be granted, the question thus being left to the holders' consciences. But they will not prevail, because of the promise which the King and Queen have given to obtain the dispensation.

[Simon Renard] London, 21st December.

[*Calendar of State Papers, Spanish*, xiii, no. 131. The original manuscript, in French, is at Besancon]

* If the date on this letter is accurate this must refer to the bill rather than the Act, because the latter was not completed until it received the royal assent on 16 January. In the light of what he says later about controversy, it was presumably a draft.

† De vera obedientia. This high profile performance escaped Henry Machyn's notice altogether.

It must now have appeared to Philip that he had accomplished two, and those the most important, of his tasks in England. He had begotten an heir, and he had reconciled the Church. The opportunity for a propaganda coup was not to be missed, and in December and January a spate of pamphlets appeared celebrating his triumph. In English there was John Elder's *Letter into Scotland*, in Italian *I successi d'Ingbilterra dopo la morte di Eduardo Sesto* [The Successes of England since the death of Edward VI], by Giulio Rossi (printed in Ferrara), and five tracts under the general heading *La partita del serenissimo Principe* [The Challenge of the Most Serene Prince] (printed in Rome). Similar but briefer accounts appeared in Spanish, Dutch and German.[24] There was also an Italian account of the reconciliation alone, entitled *Il felicissimo ritorno* ... [The Most Fortunate Return ...]. The Spaniards, both in England and at home, temporarily forgot their complaints, and congratulated each other on *la bien aventurada*, which now seemed to be turning out so well. There is no doubt that the return of England to the Catholic fold was seen as a major achievement, and as the Emperor had hoped, his son got all the credit. *Te Deums* were sung, not only in Rome but throughout the Habsburg dominions. The sheep that was lost had been found.

However, in the midst of all this euphoria, Philip was uneasily aware that he was making uncertain progress in building up a party among the English aristocracy, and none at all in gaining more political power. The revels office put on a reasonably good show over Christmas, with one or two expensive masques and plays, the latter provided mainly by the gentlemen and choristers of the Chapel Royal. Mary danced and smiled and looked happy. On the other hand, an attempt to put on a display of a purely Spanish game, *juego da canas* ('cane play'), fell flat on its face. The spectators, who liked meatier stuff, mocked the players for 'hurling rods at one another'.[25] The king himself, although slightly built and no jouster, was a reasonably adroit swordsman, and took part in more than one passage of arms between January and March of 1555. There were also several Anglo-Spanish 'challenges', which involved conventional tilts, and these on the whole were well received, both by the participants and the onlookers. 'A great running at the tilt', recorded the London chronicler Henry Machyn under the date 'xxiiii Januarii'.[26]

Equally important was the religious pageantry, and that had the additional advantage that the queen took part as well. Mary never showed the slightest interest in her husband's war games, and the thought that she might have presided as the 'Queen of Faerie' never seems to have crossed her literal and sober mind. Solemn festivals of the Church were much more to her taste, and then she did usually appear, although the processions that marked St Paul's Day on 25 January seem to have been attended only by the king and the cardinal. It may have been the colour and glitter of these occasions that attracted the spectators rather than the significance of what was being celebrated: 'all the crafts in their best liveries' and 'copes very rich with tissue and cloth of gold' are examples of what contemporary observers noted. In addition to the dubious pleasure of seeing someone get hurt, the jousts attracted similar observations: 'goodly jerkins of blue velvet and hose embroidered with silver' were on display in the 'great triumph at the court gate' on 18 December.[27] The king was gracious in a rather distant way, generous with his money, and willing to pander (up to a point) to the uncultivated tastes of his English subjects. However, whether all this added up to very much in terms of his political agenda is another matter.

Ruy Gomez, who seems to have had a streak of cheerful common sense in his make-up, believed that he was making progress. The council, as he had frequently observed, was divided, but now the division appeared to be between Mary's men and Philip's men. On the one side stood the lord chancellor, Gardiner and the 'Framlingham councillors', Mary's old and trusted servants; and on the other Paget and the more military-minded peers, such as the Earl of Pembroke. The indications are that Philip involved himself actively but discreetly in English affairs, consulting with those members of the privy council in whom he had confidence. His name was conscientiously included in all commissions, and one or two from which it had been omitted were recalled and reissued.

However, in terms of what his Spanish courtiers had seen as sovereignty, all this did not add up to much, and it seems that the main source of Philip's input into English government continued to come through his personal ascendancy over Mary. The queen's apparent pregnancy was becoming more and more obvious, as was to be expected, and her active role proportionately less. Philip, however, did not push himself forward, and those who bore the face of the government in public were principally the officers of state. The Earl of Bedford, lord privy seal, died on 14 March, and was not immediately replaced. For the time being the functions of the office were discharged by Sir Robert Rochester, but he was not appointed to the post, and that may have been significant because his abilities were not much regarded by the king. In fact, by April Philip was becoming increasingly restless. He was consulting daily with his Spanish council, and the frustrations of his position in England were making him ever more anxious to leave. However, Mary's health was giving cause for concern as early as January, and Renard, exploiting his position as the Emperor's representative, read the king an unsolicited lecture upon his duty to stay in England until the queen was safely delivered.[28] If she bore a healthy son – or even daughter – his position would be transformed. If she died in the attempt, he would have interests to protect. He stayed.

On 20 April Mary withdrew into the customary female seclusion, but still Philip's role did not noticeably increase. An air of anticipation settled upon the court. At that point the birth was expected to take place about 9 May, and Renard was concerned that some statement should be made about the succession. Little as he liked the idea, he believed that Elizabeth should be recognised.[29] Nobody was much influenced by the once-powerful ambassador's opinion, but the princess was transferred from Woodstock to Hampton Court – more to keep her under close surveillance than for any more positive reason. Gardiner was still anxious to have her lawfully excluded, but his proposals made no progress either. On 22 May Ruy Gomez confided to Eraso that he could see no sign of an imminent birth, and anticipation began to turn to unease.[30]

Philip, meanwhile, was becoming worried about an entirely different development. Gardiner and Pole began to move against the Protestants as soon as Parliament was dissolved on 16 January. On the 22nd the lord chancellor had summoned the preachers who had been imprisoned to his house at St Mary Overy, and given them an ultimatum. Submit and receive the queen's mercy, or be proceeded against by the newly restored laws and jurisdiction. They all refused, and on the 28th Gardiner and several other bishops sat judicially in the Church of St Mary Overy by virtue of Pole's legatine commission. John Hooper, John Rogers and John Cardmaker were arraigned for heresy. The following day Cardmaker submitted, but the others refused and were condemned.[31] On the 30th Rowland Taylor, Lawrence Saunders and John Bradford were similarly condemned, and on 4 February John Rogers was burned at Smithfield. He publicly refused the queen's pardon, and died with great courage.[32] On 9 February John Hooper was burned at Gloucester, and Rowland Taylor at Hadley in Suffolk.

This was totally unexpected, at least by the government. Gardiner had firmly believed that the threat of fire would send all these rats scurrying for cover, and when his bluff was called, he was taken aback. For the time being, however, he had no option but to press on with the trials, and to hope that something would give. Up to a point he was justified, because although John Foxe, the Protestant historian/martyrologist, is cagey on the subject, Cardmaker was not the only one to recant. Hooper died, and John Ponet fled into exile, but several of Edward's bishops submitted, and even retained their sees, as Thomas Thirlby did.[33] Others, like Robert Holgate of York, were deprived of their bishoprics, but later sought reconciliation. Nevertheless, the number remaining defiant was far larger than anyone in authority had expected. Gardiner had gone for the leadership – not Cranmer, whose position was complicated by his canonical status, but leading preachers and other respected figures, on the assumption that their surrender would dishearten the rank and file so that the problem would disappear. In some places, like Norwich, that is actually what happened,[34] but at the national level and in London such expectations were disappointed. Within a few months, in Foxe's words, 'seeing that cruelty in this case would not serve', the lord chancellor 'gave over as utterly discouraged'. He ceased to sit in judgement, and vainly tried to persuade Mary to adopt a less spectacular form of coercion. Every burning was a defeat, and although the crowds were not necessarily as sympathetic to the victims as Foxe later made them appear, there is plenty of evidence that the burnings were unpopular. The Venetian ambassador, Giovanni Michieli, also reported hostile demonstrations, and Renard observed a worrying tendency for these crowds to blame Philip for what was happening. The loyal pamphleteer Miles Huggarde observed the same phenomenon. Religion, he declared, was simply being used as a pretext for the seditious undermining of authority:

> Cursed speakers also in using their tongues after a most vile sort, not only against the church, the spouse of Christ, but also against our princes ... And how abominab[ly] they have from time to time ill said of the king's majesty, reverence and shame constraineth silence ...[35]

Philip was not squeamish about burning heretics, but for him, as for Gardiner, it was a policy intended to suppress dissent – not encourage it. As early as 10 February (the day after Hooper and Taylor had suffered) Philip's confessor, Alonso a Castro, preached at the court advocating a different course of action. Castro had no personal aversion to persecution (he had written a book on the subject), and he was clearly expressing Philip's reservations.

No one seems to have been listening. Gardiner came round to Philip's point of view some months later, but neither Pole nor Mary were moved. Opinion among the king's Spanish advisers seems to have been divided. What Castro really thought we do not know, but Bartolome Carranza, who was close to Pole, was on the whole supportive of the action that was being taken.[36] As anxiety over Mary's condition began to mount in June 1555, the persecution began to spread, and to move away from the leaders to the rank and file. It was uneven in its incidence, being concentrated heavily in Essex, Kent and London. Reading between the lines of Foxe's hagiographical narratives, we can see personal scores being settled, harassed clergy getting revenge on prickly parishioners, and some highly provocative displays of defiance. Not all the victims were orthodox Protestants – they held all sorts of eccentric views – and some were clearly on bad terms with their neighbours.[37] However, many were responding in their own way to the kind of call that was to be issued in print by John Ponet in the following year:

> … to refuse to do that is evil for justice sake, to be slaughtered, spoken evil of, whipped, scourged, spoiled of their goods, killed of the worldly princes and tyrants, rather than they would disobey God and forsake Christ; this can neither papists nor Turks, Jews nor gentiles, nor none other do, but only the Elect of God …[38]

There was immense comfort to be gained from the conviction that you were among the elect of God, no matter what the price. In time, Pole came to see the force of this emotion, although he never accepted it. While remaining implacable against those whom he thought had 'deceived the simple' with bogus promises of salvation, he began to show some sympathy with those who had been deceived, and advised patience in dealing with them, even reprieving one or two from the stake without the kind of explicit submission that was normally required.[39]

None of this need have mattered in the long term, but thanks to the events that took place between May and July 1555, the regime suddenly lost momentum. On 30 April there was a false alarm, when:

> ... tidings came to London that the Queen's Grace was delivered of a prince, so there was great ringing [of bells] through London and divers places. Te Deum laudamus sung, but the morrow it was turned otherwise, to the pleasure of God ...[40]

The royal physicians were all at sea, obstetrics at that time being largely a matter of guesswork and experience. By mid-May they were saying that it could be any day, but Mary herself did not expect to give birth until early June. The uncertainty had a paralysing effect upon the Franco-Imperial peace negotiations that were going on at La Marque. The birth of an heir to the English throne would have given the Emperor an immense advantage, while if the queen and her child both died, the advantage would be to the French. On 30 May a number of blank letters were prepared, announcing the queen's safe delivery, and the following day signs of impending labour were reported. The physicians adroitly shifted their predicted birth date to 6 June. The day came – and went. In the bed chamber a cradle stood ready, 'very sumptuously and gorgeously trimmed', and a team of rockers, nurses and other domestic servants were prepared to do their offices. Still nothing happened, and scandalous rumours began to multiply. The queen was not really pregnant at all, but seriously ill – some said dead. The whole seclusion was a charade, a Spanish plot to pass off another infant as the queen's. On 11 June, we are told, a certain Isobel Malt was secretly approached by Lord North to surrender her newborn son – on generous terms. The lady apparently refused.[41]

The stakes were high. Michieli believed that if a prince were born, Philip's whole relationship with Mary and with the English council would be transformed, and he would no longer be 'like an alien' in the realm. Some apprehensive Englishmen thought the same: 'his father will bring into this realm his own nation, and put out the English nation'. In other words the marriage treaty would count for nothing. What Philip thought about all this fuss, and its immense implications for him, we do not know. He remained at Hampton Court, but whether he spent any time in his wife's company is not recorded – probably not, given the strictness of the taboos on male intruders.

Mary herself remained obstinately hopeful, and wrote to her ambassador in Brussels, Sir John Mason, as late as the middle of July instructing him to deny rumours that her pregnancy was false.[42] However, not even Mary could hope indefinitely. Even before she wrote to Mason, some of her council had given up, while as late as the 25th her women were still expectant. By the end of the month, the whole pathetic farce had collapsed, leaving Mary exhausted and distraught. Her first reaction on finally becoming convinced of her delusion was to blame the 'lies and flattery' with which she had been surrounded, but in fact it had been her own will that had driven the pretence on and made it virtually treasonable to share the doubts of French agents and heretics. No official pronouncement was made, but on 4 August the court moved to Oatlands, and the rockers and other nursery staff were dismissed.

Those who liked Mary – and they were numerous at all social levels – were deeply saddened. Protestants proclaimed a divine judgement on their persecutor, and politicians had to take stock of a new situation. No one knew (or knows now) whether this convincing phantom pregnancy had been the result of her own intense desires, or was a symptom of some serious illness.[43] Although no physician could then have named it, it looks suspiciously like the onset of the cancer of the womb that was to kill her three years later. Mary recovered her health slowly, and refused to give up the hope of offspring in the future, but Philip and most of her council began to face the probability that she would never have a child. The immediate beneficiary of this was Elizabeth, who was released when the court moved to Oatlands, and she returned to her own establishment at Ashridge. Nothing had been said about the succession, but then it hardly needed to be.

MARY'S 'PREGNANCY'
CONCERNING THE CHILDBED OF QUEEN MARY, AS IT WAS RUMOURED AMONG THE PEOPLE.
Long persuasion had been in England, with great expectation, for the space of

half a year or more, that the Queen was conceived with child. This report was made by the Queen's physicians, & other nigh about the court; so that divers were punished for saying the contrary. And commandment was given that in all churches supplication and prayers should be made for the Queen's good delivery; the certificate whereof you may read before in the letter of the council sent to Bonner, p. 1405. And also the same moreover may appear by provision made before in the act of Parliament made for the child, p. 1410.

And now for somuch as in the beginning of this month of June about Whitsuntide, the time was thought to be nigh, that this young Master should come into the world, and that midwives, rockers, nurses, with a cradle & all, were prepared and in a readiness, suddenly upon what cause or occasion it is uncertain, a certain vain rumour was blown in London of the prosperous deliverance of the Queen and of the birth of the child. In so much that the bells were rung, bonfires and processions made, not only in the City of London, and in most other parts of the realm, but also in the town of Antwerp, guns were shot off upon the river by the English ships, and the mariners thereof rewarded with an hundred pistolettes or Italian crowns by the Lady Regent, who was the Queen of Hungary. Such great rejoicing and triumph was for the Queen's delivery, & that there was a prince born. Yea, divers preachers, namely one, the parson of St. Anne within Aldersgate, after procession and Te Deum sung, took upon him to describe the proportion of the child, how fair, how beautiful, and great a prince it was, as the like had not been seen.

In the midst of this great ado there was a simple man (this I speake but upon information) dwelling within four miles of Berwick, that never had been before half way to London, which said concerning the bonfires made for Queen Mary's child. Here is a joyful triumph, but at length it will not prove worth a mess of pottage, as indeed it came to pass. For in the end all proved clean contrary, and the joy and expectations of men were much deceived, for the people were certified that the Queen neither was as then delivered, nor after was in hope to have any child. At this time many talked diversely. Some said that this rumour of the Queen's conception was spread for a policy; some other affirmed that she was deceived by a Tympanie* or some other like disease, to think herself with child, and was not. Some thought that she was with child, and that it did by some chance miscarry, or else that she was bewitched. But what was the truth thereof

182

the Lord knoweth, to whom nothing is secret. One thing of mine own hearing and seeing I can not pass over unwitnessed.

There came to me, whom I did both hear and see, one Isobel Malt, a woman dwelling in Aldersgate Street, in Home Alley, not far from the house where this present book was printed, who before witness made this declaration unto us, that she being delivered of a manchild upon Whitsunday in the morning, which was the 11th day of June an.1555, there came to her the Lord North and another Lord to her unknown, dwelling then about Old Fish Street, demanding of her if she would part with her child, and would swear that she never knew nor had no such child. Which if she would, her son (they said) should be well provided for, she should take no care for it, with many other fair offers if she would part with the child ...

[John Foxe, *Acts and Monuments* (1583), pp. 1596-7.]

* A tumour.

Philip faced the most serious dilemma because now, at the age of twenty-eight, it looked as though he was locked into a sterile marriage of indefinite duration. Mary was thirty-nine, and might well live for another twenty or thirty years. He had one son, who was not particularly robust, and apparently no prospect of redrawing the dynastic map of northern Europe. For the time being such sobering thoughts were set aside. Once the queen was back on her feet, he had to respond to the urgent situation that had been brewing up in the Low Countries. His father's health was deteriorating steadily, and Charles was less and less able to attend to business.[44] The time had come for Charles to begin handing over his responsibilities to Philip – but for that purpose Philip needed to be physically present. Everyone had agreed that as long as there was a prospect of an heir in England, Philip's place was in proximity to his wife. Now that had changed, and for a variety of reasons he was anxious to be off. On 26 August the royal couple 'came riding from Westminster through London unto Tower Wharf'. They only went as far as Greenwich, and the object was clearly to demonstrate that Mary was not only alive, but fit to discharge business. Three days later Philip set off for Dover 'with a great company', which included a number of his English gentlemen, and Mary went to Greenwich again to see him off.[45] There is no record of their parting, but it is reasonable to suppose that their emotions were very different.

9

MARY ALONE

Before he went, Philip had made arrangements to be kept in touch with English affairs by setting up a select council or council of state to act as a link between himself and the privy council.[1] This was unprecedented in England, but familiar in Spain and other dominions accustomed to being ruled from a distance. The idea was that the select council would extract from the privy council whatever business they judged to be of interest to the king, and minute it to him in Latin. They would also discuss and correspond with him about issues of policy that he wished to keep confidential. The oddity of this arrangement, and the reason why it did not work as intended, was that it took no account of Mary. Greatly as she respected and admired her husband, Mary had no intention of allowing herself to be bypassed in this way, nor would her own advisers have tolerated it. It may be that she also discussed matters of state with the select council rather than the privy council, but there is no direct evidence of that.[2] Consequently, although the select council worked effectively as a channel of communication, it had only the status of an informal advisory group in the government of England. If Philip had thought to increase his role in English government by manipulating it from a distance, then he miscalculated.

More successful was the surrogacy that Philip left to Reginald Pole. After several months of working with the cardinal, Philip's opinion of him had improved, and he came to appreciate the relationship that Pole had established with Mary. Philip was well aware that his wife was in a fragile condition, both mentally and physically, after her ordeal during the summer, and he privately instructed Pole to care for her wellbeing, as far as he could. Her occasional emotional storms needed to be calmed; she needed to be discouraged from overworking; and above all she needed the support and consolation of his unwavering Catholic faith. When Philip left, it was with soothing reassurances of a speedy return, and he left a large part of his normal household in England. Whether he ever seriously intended to come back quickly may be doubted. When Parliament was summoned on 3 September, it was expected that he would be present at the opening, but well before it actually assembled on 21 October he had sent his apologies. On 25 October, in an emotional and tearful ceremony in Brussels, Mary of Hungary stood down as regent of the Low Countries, and Charles handed over the sovereignty of the seventeen provinces to his son.[3] This can hardly have come as a surprise to Philip, and the elaborate preparations almost certainly went back before his actual arrival at the beginning of September. In other words, the king had known perfectly well that he was unlikely to be back in the foreseeable future, but did not wish to add to Mary's distress by being frank about it. In December the remainder of his household was quietly withdrawn, and Mary, we are told, was very upset. Not only did Philip have no intention of returning in the immediate future, but he had lied to her.

England was a depressing place in the autumn of 1555. The queen was in low spirits, both as a result of the failure of her pregnancy and because of her husband's absence. The late summer weather was appalling and the harvest failed. The Parliament had been called to grant a subsidy, and soon revealed itself to be in a difficult mood.[4] The religious persecution ground relentlessly on. Nicholas Ridley and Hugh Latimer, burned at Oxford in October, were only the most prominent of the many victims. And on 14 November Stephen Gardiner, lord chancellor and Bishop of Winchester, died after a short illness.

THE BURNING OF RIDLEY AND LATIMER

THE BEHAVIOUR OF D. RIDLEY AND M. LATIMER AT THE TIME OF THEIR DEATH, WHICH WAS 16 OF OCTOBER AN.1555.

Upon the northside of the town, in the ditch over against Bailly College,* the place of execution was appointed; and for fear of any tumult that might arise to let the burning of them, the L. Williams[†] was commanded by the Queen's letters, and the householders of the City, to be there assistant, sufficiently appointed, & when everything was in a readiness, the prisoners were brought forth by the Mayor and Bailiffs ...

M. Doctor Ridley as he passed towards Bocardo, looking up where M. Cranmer did lie, hoping belike to have seen him at the glass window, and to have spoken with him. But then M. Cranmer was busy with Friar Soto & his fellows disputing together,[‡] so that he could not see him through that occasion. Then M. Ridley looking back, espied M. Latimer coming after. Unto whom he said: O be ye there. Yea said M. Latimer, have after as fast as I can follow. So he following a pretty way off, at length they came both to the stake, one after the other, where first D. Ridley entering the place, marvellous earnestly holding up both his hands, looked towards heaven. Then shortly after espying M. Latimer, with a wonderous cheerful look, came to him, embraced and kissed him, and as they that stood near reported, comforted him saying; be of good heart brother, for GOD will either assuage the fury of the flames, or else strengthen us to abide it ...

Then Doctor Smith,[§] of whose recantation in K. Edward's time ye heard before, began his sermon to them on this text of St Paul, in the xiii chapter of the first Epistle to the Corinthians, *Si corpus meum tradam igni, charitatem autem non habeo, nihil inde utilitatis capio*. That is, if I yield my body to the fire to be burned, and have not charity, I shall gain nothing thereby. Wherein he alleged that the goodness of the cause and not the order of death, maketh the holiness of the person ...

Master Ridley took his gown and his tippet, and gave it to his brother-in-law M. Shipside, who all his time of imprisonment, although he might not be suffered to come to him, lay there at his own charges to provide him necessaries, which from time to time he sent him by the Sergeant who kept him. Some other of his apparel that was little worth he gave away. Other the Bailiffs took ...

M. Latimer gave nothing, but very quietly suffered his keeper to pull off his hose, and his other array, which to look unto was very simple; and being stripped into his shroud, he seemed as comely a person to them that were there present, as one should lightly see. And whereas in his clothes he appeared a withered and crooked little old man, he now stood bolt upright, as comely a father as one might lightly behold ...

Then the smith took a chain of iron and brought the same about both D. Ridleys and M. Latimers middles, and as he was knocking in a staple, D. Ridley took the chain in his hand and shaked the same, for it did gird in his belly, and looking aside to the smith said Good fellow, knock it in hard, for the flesh will have his course. Then his brother did bring him gunpowder in a bag, and would have tied the same about his neck. M. Ridley asked what it was. His brother said gunpowder. Then said he, I take it to be sent of God, therefore I will receive it as sent of him. And have you any, said he, for my brother, meaning M. Latimer? Yea sir, that I have (quoth his brother). Then give it unto him, said he betime, lest ye come too late. So his brother went, and carried of the same gunpowder to M. Latimer ...

Then brought they a faggot kindled with fire, and laid the same down at D. Ridleys feet, to whom Master Latimer spoke in this manner; Be of good comfort Master Ridley, and play the man; we shall this day light such a candle by Gods grace in England, as (I trust) shall never be put out.

And so the fire being given unto them, when D. Ridley saw the fire flaming towards him, he cried with a wonderfully loud voice: *In manus tuas Domine, commendo spiritum meum. Domine recipe spiritum meum*, and after repeated this latter part often in English: Lord, Lord, receive my spirit. M. Latimer crying as vehemently on the other side: O Father of Heaven, receive my soul, who received the flame as it were embracing of it. After, as he had stroked his face with his hands, and (as it were) bathed them a little in the fire, he soon died (as it appeared) with very little pain or none ...

But M. Ridley, by reason of the evil making of the fire unto him ... burned clean all his nether parts before it touched the upper ... Yet in all this torment he forgot not to call upon God still, having in his mouth Lord have mercy upon me, intermendling this cry, Let the fire come to me, I cannot burn. In which pains he laboured, till one of the standers by with his bill, pulled the faggots above, and when he saw the fire flame up, he wrested himself into that side. And when the flame touched the gunpowder, he was seen to stir no more ...

[John Foxe, *Acts and Monuments* (1583), pp. 1769-70]

* Balliol College.

† Sir John Williams, Lord Williams of Thame.

‡ Pedro de Soto, a Dominican at this time holding a chair of theology in Oxford, who was trying to persuade Cranmer to recant.

⁵ Richard Smith, who had been restored to the Regius Chair of Theology by Mary. He had been deprived of his see and had fled abroad for resisting the Protestant changes under Edward VI.

Irascible and difficult as he had sometimes been, Gardiner was a great loss to Mary, because he was a statesman of outstanding ability and long experience. He may, or may not, have been the author of a treatise on the coming of the Romans and Normans to England, which was a thinly disguised piece of advice to the king on how to secure his authority in England. This had been presented while Philip was still in England, and the only surviving copy is in Italian, so there is much doubt over its authorship, but it does appear to represent the position that Gardiner had reached after nearly two years of working with Mary.[5] We do not know whether Philip ever read the treatise, but he had developed a healthy respect for the chancellor's abilities. He was not going to be easy to replace, and since no appointment had been made to the office of lord privy seal (vacant since March), there were now two places to be filled. No other offices of similar importance had been filled since Philip became king, so a significant issue arose over how this was to be done. The Duke of Alba advised Philip that he must take control of both, adding: 'be careful whom you install, that they are not the Queen's men'. This confrontational view of the joint monarchy may have been peculiar to Alba, but was probably not,[6] and may help to explain why Mary, strong as her emotional attachment to her husband may have been, was determined not to be steamrollered. Eventually a compromise was negotiated, although we do not know exactly how. Paget was proposed for the chancellorship, but was opposed by many of those close to Philip, notably Carranza, who suspected his commitment to the faith. Eventually he was made lord privy seal, while the chancellor's position went to Nicholas Heath, the Archbishop of York. Heath may have been a 'queen's man', but Philip's servants gave him the credit for both promotions: 'The King's Majesty hath appointed ...'

With Philip still pressing surreptitiously for a more effective role in England, it is not surprising that the issue of his coronation became increasingly controversial. As long as there was a prospect of an heir, it was more a matter of honour than substance, but when that prospect disappeared the king's advisers began to look more seriously at a crowning. In November 1555 he is alleged to have written to Mary saying that he could not possibly return to England on the former terms, and suggesting a coronation as a way of giving him more equality.[7] Opinions varied as to what the significance of such a gesture would be. Renard had long ago written that the crowning was taken very seriously in England – more so than in any other realm – but legally it seems that it would have made no difference. Philip already had the name and style of a king, and the protection of the treason laws, so all that would be added was the oath that he would be required to swear to uphold the laws of England, which of course included the limitations imposed by his marriage treaty. Nevertheless, Philip seems to have set his heart on a coronation, and even wrote to Mary saying that he could not see his way to returning without it, thus causing her further distress. She was perfectly well aware that in some quarters it was being said that one of the main reasons for calling the Parliament was to arrange the king's coronation 'by force or fraud'. The issue had become symbolic on both sides. When Mary responded to his demand by pointing out that there was no way in which Parliament would approve such a move, he replied that it was none of Parliament's business, but rather a matter of prerogative. Technically he was correct, but Mary's sense of the mood in London and Westminster was also correct, and after the beginning of 1556 the matter was allowed to drop in official exchanges. Philip did not return, but 'the giving away of the crown' continued to be prominent in public discourse.[8]

PHILIP'S CORONATION, 1556

Is it not to be lamented that our Englishmen, for fear of change of religion, which cometh by God's ordinance, shall seek to plant such a nation in our country, as do seek the utter destruction of the same? But this is most detestable and abominable that so noble and provident governors as your lordships, should either for fair words, fair bribes, or any kind of covetousness, seek the subversion of our country, the ruin of our realm, the utter decay of our commonwealth, and the destruction of our own blood for ever. For if there might be any of the noble blood remain alive and bear rule, we should have some hope of restoring the realm and weal public. But if they deliver the Crown over out of your hands (I do not mean the

Crown of gold only but also the power that goeth with it) ye shall in short time have such a fall as there shall not be left one of your lineage living, that shall be able to defend his [own] or bear rule as his predecessors have done. For this you must needs grant, that it is necessary for the King to work the surest way for his own profit and preservation that can be devised by his own council. And then I am sure there is none of you, I think, that can bear rule in the commonwealth or near the King's Majesty. For the world speaketh against the detestable treason of our nobility, and therefore the Spaniards might be counted men of small wisdoms if they could not foresee such dangers. But they have provided for that well enough.

I would to God that your lordships knew as much as I have heard with mine own ears and seen with mine own eyes, or else would credit my words. For then your most prescient wisdoms could provide to withstand their pretensed treasons ...

Ye say the Queen hath power in her hands, we must obey her. That is true in all such laws as be already made and passed by parliament. But whether ye may lawfully consent [contrary] to the discretion of the whole realm and nation of Englishmen [to the giving away] of the Crown, and disannul the authority that was given by parliament, I leave it to your consciences. If the Crown were the Queen's, in such sort that she might do with it what she would, both now and after her death, there might appear some rightful pretence in giving it over to a Stranger Prince. But seeing it belongeth to the heirs of England after her death, ye commit deadly sin and damnation in unjustly giving and taking away the right of others. Remember what a miserable estate and end Achab had for unjustly desiring Naboth's vineyard. I think that you can never forget the unjust enterprise of the Duke of Northumberland and what miserable success it had. Be ye therefore wise and beware by other men's harms, for ye may perceive evidently that God will take vengeance upon wrongful doers. Otherwise the Queen's Majesty that now is had not been Queen of England at this present.

But peradventure her grace thinketh that the King will keep her more company, and love her the better if she give him the Crown. Ye will crown him to make him live chaste, contrary to his nature. For peradventure after he were crowned, he would be content with one woman, but in the mean space he must have three or four in one night to prove which of them he liketh best; not of ladies and gentlewomen, but of baker's daughters and such poor whores. Whereupon they have a certain saying The baker's daughter is better in her gown than Queen Mary without the Crown' ...

[John Bradford, *The copy of a letter ... sent to the Earls of Arundel, Derby, Shrewsbury and Pembroke* (1556). Taken from John Strype, *Ecclesiastical Memorials* (1822 edition), iii, p. 129.]

The Emperor was not pleased by this evidence of estrangement between Philip and his wife. Mary wrote to him, pleading for his good offices in bringing about her husband's return, and Charles wrote to Philip, urging him to go. There would be, Charles pointed out, no prospect of redeeming the failure of the summer, if Philip did not sleep with his wife. However, Charles had very little leverage, and Philip was not short of other women if he felt that way inclined. That he sometimes did feel so is reflected in the discreet comments made in diplomatic correspondence, usually with the warning that these things should be kept from his wife, 'who is easily distressed' (which would have been an understatement of the case should she have found out).

On 1 January 1556 Philip also took over from his father responsibility for the crowns (Aragon and Castile) of Spain, which added massively to his workload, and helps to explain the minimal attention that he seems to have paid to England over the succeeding months. Charles remained in theory Holy Roman Emperor, but in practice he had already handed over most of the responsibilities of that office to his brother Ferdinand. He did not finally retire to Spain until September, and continued to write letters of advice to his son and others, but there is little evidence that anyone was paying attention to them.

One of the first consequences of the handover in Spain was the Truce of Vaucelles with France, signed in February. The war had been going badly for the Emperor, and why Henry II of France was prepared to call a halt at this point is unclear. But when Philip sacrificed his honour by making the first move, Henry responded.[9] In so doing he left the pope temporarily frustrated. Julius III, the architect of the English reconciliation, had died in March 1555, and his successor (after the three-week pontificate of Marcellus II) was Paul IV. As Gian Pietro Carafa he had led the hard-line reformers in the 1540s, and as a Neapolitan he was bitterly anti-Habsburg. Charles and Philip had bungled the conclave that had elected him, and his incumbency spelled trouble. He was preparing to enter the war on the French side when the Truce of Vaucelles supervened. From an English point of view the truce was important, partly because it suspended Henry's desire to destabilise Mary's pro-Imperial government, and partly because it later provided a pretext to involve England in the war, when it was renewed (and from which England should have been excluded by the terms of the marriage treaty).

However, the most immediate consequence for Mary of the suspension of hostilities was that it took the wind out of the sails of what might have been a dangerous conspiracy. This is usually known by the name of Henry Dudley, a soldier and political adventurer who was one of the leaders.[10] The idea was for the English exiles in France, of whom there were between two and three hundred, mostly disaffected gentlemen, to launch an invasion of the south of England with French military and financial backing. A sympathetic rebellion would be raised at the same time to link up with the invaders, using the unpopularity of the Spanish connection – and particularly the threat of Philip's coronation – as an incentive. The objective, which was thinly disguised behind the xenophobic rhetoric, was to replace Mary with Elizabeth, and send the former to her husband, wherever he might be. It sounds wild and implausible, and so eventually it was, but in spite of strenuous efforts the English end of the conspiracy was never fully unravelled.

About Christmas Henry Dudley had been warmly received at the French court and promised generous (but apparently unspecified) aid. When he went back in February he got short shrift. Dudley, however, was not deterred by this rebuff. If he could find the money elsewhere he could still raise a mercenary force for a short campaign. Henry had not refused to allow him to recruit, he had merely refused to pay. In the hands of Nicholas Brigham, teller of the exchequer, there was some £50,000 worth of Spanish silver bullion, and that would do nicely if the plotters could lay hands on it. Astonishingly, they came within a whisker of success. Brigham himself was a man of unimpeachable integrity, but his wife was corruptible and they got an impression of his keys.[11] A small ship, a 'crayer', was hired to take the plunder to France where an illegal mint waited to turn it into coin. The thieves even got into the vault, only to find that the chests were too heavy to be moved, and they lacked the tools to break them open. Before they could try again the plot was detected, and on 18 March about twenty of the conspirators were rounded up and sent to the Tower. Henry Dudley and many of the other leaders were in France, but without money they were helpless, and the plot collapsed. Christopher Ashton and several of the other gentlemen turned their attentions to piracy instead, and made a considerable nuisance of themselves until they were caught by the queen's ships in July.[12]

Most of those whose complicity in the plot was proven were minor figures, but they did include Sir Anthony Kingston and Richard Uvedale, the captain of the Isle of Wight. There was dark talk of major noblemen, even councillors, being implicated, but nothing was ever proved.[13] The opportunity was taken to remove one or two of Elizabeth's servants from their posts, but the princess herself was merely informed that her name had been taken in vain. The plot collapsed principally because, after the signing of his truce with the Emperor, the French king was no longer interested in so provocative an action.

A CLIMATE OF FEAR AND SUSPICION
GIOVANNI MICHIELI, VENETIAN AMBASSADOR IN ENGLAND, TO THE
DOGE AND SENATE, 14 APRIL 1556.

The suspicion induced apparently by the conspirators on the Isle of Wight* has caused the government ... to send thither the Marquis of Winchester, the Lord Treasurer, and Lord Howard of Effingham, Lord High Admiral. The latter ... has had a large amount of guns and ammunition conveyed thither ... while the Marquis of Winchester, being a personage of great esteem and authority ... will consequently be better able than anyone to ascertain whether clandestine designs in favour of the conspirators were on foot there ...

Besides the precautions taken in the Isle of Wight ... it is told me that all the nobility and gentry of the country have been desired to keep on the watch, and ready to present themselves on the first summons; many persons adding that an order has been issued for the recall of all English absentees, both those who have permission to reside abroad and those who have not, without any exception, and that the proclamation will soon be printed.[†] And a certain rumour purporting that the conspirators had a special understanding with the King of France has been more rife than usual ... [because he fears] that the Emperor and the King his son will by force endeavour not only to render themselves stronger and more secure than they are at present, but to make themselves absolute masters of this kingdom ... a friend of mine ... having lately seen a letter from M. de James [sic], French resident in Luxembourg addressed to the French ambassador here, telling him that in that neighbourhood ... ten companies of infantry have lately been raised ... all which are to serve in England, the King intending to bring them with him, having to return hither. For the guard and security of his person, and he gives a preference to German and Flemish troops, because they are less hateful to the English than the Spaniards, or any other nation ... If, as premised by me, the advices be true, there would be cause for anxiety in every respect.

In the meanwhile here, not only does there not seem to be any expectation of the arrival of King Philip with these fresh troops, but on the other hand an irritation and anger is manifested against the Most Christian King ...‡ [because] of the harbour which it is understood he gives to English rebels, contrary to the agreements and express treaty between the two countries.

I am told that the Lord Paget will settle the mode to be observed in the heading of Patents and Public Acts, which all commence with 'Philip and Mary', enumerating first of all, the titles of their realms according to their order, it not seeming by any means proper to the English ministry that amongst these titles the Kingdom of Spain should take precedence of those of England and France.

[*Calendar of State Papers, Venetian*, vi, pp. 411-12. The original ms, in Italian and partly in cipher, is in the Vienna Staatsarchiv]

* The Dudley conspiracy. The Captain of the Isle of Wight, Richard Uvedale, was involved.

† No such proclamation survives, or appears to have been issued.

‡ Henry II.

For a while the council was seriously alarmed by the Dudley conspiracy. The regime had lost credibility since the previous summer, the succession was uncertain, and anti-Spanish sentiment was a force of unknown potential. Castro, Philip's confessor, who had left England in December, had later painted an alarming picture of 'foul language uttered by the English, indicating their ill will towards his majesty and the Spanish nation'.[14] There was, he observed, the greatest possible contrast between Mary's longing for her husband, and her subjects' rejoicing at his absence. Was Castro seeing spooks? And if not, what would it take to turn such ill will into action?

Renard had finally left England in the previous September, and he had not been replaced.[15] Without his self-interested but indefatigable reports, our picture of English politics during 1556 is relatively sketchy. In March, while the investigations into the Dudley plot were proceeding with feverish intensity, Thomas Cranmer, the highest-profile victim of Mary's mission against heresy, was burned in Oxford and Reginald Pole succeeded him as Archbishop of Canterbury. Cranmer's death, though, was another setback for the crown – and a completely unnecessary one. After his trial and conviction for heresy he had recanted, reluctantly but fully, and could well have been consigned to oblivion as a failed prophet. The damage that that might have done to his cause is incalculable. Instead, Mary was determined to have him dead, partly because she regarded his sins as unforgivable and partly out of personal revenge. His recantation was disregarded, and his execution duly proceeded. Having nothing to lose, he publicly and spectacularly renounced his surrender and reaffirmed his Protestant convictions – thus dying as an unlikely but extremely memorable martyr.[16] He was not the only person to die in that cause during these months, but he was by far the most conspicuous. Eight or nine gentlemen also died for their part in the Dudley plot, as the alarm gradually subsided and the hunt was called off.

In the midst of these depressing events, Mary made another attempt to persuade Philip to return. Sir John Mason was instructed to enquire pointedly whether the ships that were on standby to escort him should be stood down. In a direct message she pleaded that she needed him, and that he should not despair of getting an heir – although she was not getting any younger. He responded with excuses, and bland professions of affection. He certainly had enough to occupy him in Europe, but that was not really the point. In spite of all his efforts, and notwithstanding Mary's hints to the contrary, the government of England was managing perfectly well without him. The council of state continued to send him its reports, but in truth there was not very much to say. There was no Parliament during 1556, and although anti-government polemics, both Protestant and secular, continued to appear, there was nothing new in that. Philip himself continued to be the main object of attack, but conspiracies to 'give away the crown' and hand over the kingdom's fortresses to strangers hardly represented creative or original opposition.[17] Moreover, Philip was listening to other voices. His own servants were able to see no reason why he should do anything to gratify a wife who did nothing for him, or spend money and effort in England to no purpose.

In early April, Mary tried again, this time sending no less an envoy than Lord Paget. Federico Badoer, who reported on the mission, believed that Paget had been chosen because of his known favour with the king, which would make it easier for him to be frank. Mary, Badoer believed, was becoming exasperated by Philip's contemptuous neglect of her, and some at least of his own advisers were warning him not to turn her love into hatred.[18] He paid no attention. Either he was completely confident of his ascendancy over his wife, or he did not much care. It was probably confidence at this stage, because there were still cards to be played in England, and he was maintaining a hefty pension list. Mary's health was not yet giving grounds for concern, but he was seriously interested in neutralising Elizabeth by marrying her to his ally Emmanuel Philibert of Savoy. Having failed with Paget, Mary now turned for the last time to the Emperor:

> … the return of the king my husband … I implore your Majesty most humbly for the love of God, do all that is possible to permit it. I see every day the end of one negotiation and the beginning of another …[19]

However, there was no longer any question of permission. Her old friend and protector was a spent force, as she came to recognise, writing for the last time in July: 'I must perforce be satisfied, although to my unspeakable regret.' The French chose to believe that she was infuriated by Philip's behaviour, and had gone around the privy apartments smashing his portraits – but that was probably just wishful thinking.

Both French and Italian reports paint a very gloomy picture of Mary in the summer of 1556. Antoine de Noailles had been declared *persona non grata* for his encouragement of Henry Dudley, and had been replaced as ambassador by his brother Francois, who was neither very close to the court, nor sympathetic to it. Mary was alleged to be living in fear of assassination, her apartment filled with armed men, and only five of her women trusted with access to her. 'She rages against her subjects', he declared,

> for she is utterly confounded by the faithlessness of those whom she most trusted, seeing that the greater part of these miserable creatures [the Dudley conspirators] are kith and kin or favoured servants of the greatest men in the kingdom, even Lords of the Council ...[20]

She was (he had it on good authority) looking ten years older, and sleeping badly. All her time was spent in tears and regrets – and in writing letters to get her husband back. Only Sir Edward Hastings and Sir Anthony Browne were still in favour. All this was greatly exaggerated by an interested party trying to prise apart the Anglo-Habsburg alliance – but it was not invented. Some of the letters we have already noticed, and there were others in the same vein.

On 6 August the privy council also took a most unusual step, and instructed that:

> ... upon consideration of the state of things at this time ... that Mr Controller, Mr Treasurer and Mr Vicechamberlain should tomorrow in the morning call before them the officers of the household and the yeomen of the guard, and other their Majesties ordinary servants under their charges, and to enquire what armour and weapon each of them hath ...[21]

They were then instructed to prepare such armour in order to be mustered before Michaelmas. This would normally have happened only if the monarch had been intending to go to war in person, and is indicative of a high state of tension. Quite what was feared is not apparent. The harvest was again disastrous, the third such in a row and the worst run before the 1590s. Corn riots were inevitable, but they would not normally come anywhere near the court. Similarly the continued burning of Protestants was provoking some angry demonstrations, but these were directed against the bishops, and in no sense threatened the queen. It seems that although Noailles's talk of hysterical collapse and near panic may be wide of the mark, Mary was nevertheless deeply disturbed by the Dudley plot, and remained edgy and depressed for months thereafter. On 10 September she launched yet another epistle at the Emperor, pleading that great – but unspecified – danger would ensue if Philip did not come to remedy matters 'with a firm hand'. 'Consider the miserable plight into which this country has now fallen,' she lamented.[22] This time Charles did not respond, and he probably never received the letter, because he had left for San Yuste, and retirement in all but title, by the 17th.

Philip was still receiving his regular reports from his select council, at least until the end of the summer, but they were mostly concerned with small matters of specific business, and those that have survived would not have given the king any cause for general unease. In any case, he was far too busy to fly to Mary's assistance, even if he had felt inclined to do so. Pope Paul IV was making his hostility increasingly obvious, harrying Imperial supporters within the curia, and appointing blatantly pro-French cardinals to mediate a permanent peace between France and the Empire. Cardinal Pole (who was reasonably impartial) had lost the role of mediator when he became Archbishop of Canterbury, on the reasonable grounds that he now had other things to think about.[23] By July the tension between Brussels and Rome had reached breaking point. Simon Renard (by this time ambassador in France) reported that the pope had mobilised 10,000 men, and was threatening to kill all the Spaniards he could catch. Far from negotiating peace, Paul was doing his best to break the truce that already existed. At the end of June Pole wrote to Philip, begging him to show restraint, but the pope's behaviour was becoming increasingly impossible, and on 6 September the Duke of Alba invaded the Papal States from Naples on Philip's orders. The French immediately came to Paul's assistance and the Truce of Vaucelles collapsed. England was not a party to this conflict, and the French ambassador was not withdrawn, but its impact was nevertheless considerable. Philip was King of England, and the unfortunate Pole sought in vain for some guidance as to how he should conduct himself now that he was (in a sense) the servant of two masters who were at war with each other. The pope at the same time refused to conduct English business on the grounds that, as Philip's wife, Mary was also 'worthy of ecclesiastical censure'.[24] Rather surprisingly, Mary was not particularly distressed by this thought. She was quite capable of distinguishing between her allegiance to the Holy See and the hostile behaviour of a particular pope.

She set out to offer what support she could to her husband, and instructed her archbishop to carry on as normal.

In some ways the conflict seems to have lightened her mood. She was not in any doubt that her first duty was to her husband, and the privy couriers began to move backwards and forwards between them with an alacrity that had not been seen for nearly a year. So far the truce was still holding in the north, but the queen made it clear that if Henry invaded the Low Countries, then England would honour the mutual defence treaty (with Charles V) of 1543. At the beginning of December the Earl of Pembroke was sent across to Calais with reinforcements for the garrison of Calais and its environs (sometimes referred to as 'the Pale'), rumours having been picked up that Henry Dudley had now turned his attentions in that direction. The English population of Calais had for some time included a substantial number of Protestants and fellow travellers. Although there had been relatively little persecution there, Dudley clearly thought that a subversive approach would stand a reasonable chance of success, and he did indeed establish some useful contacts.[25] But he overreached himself and his espionage was detected.

Well before Christmas the English council had realised that it would only be a matter of time before Philip moved to bring England into the war. He was England's king and his honour would require no less. With one or two exceptions they were unenthusiastic, and prepared to marshal an array of arguments against involvement. Mary, on the other hand, was keen. Here was a way in which she could do her duty as a loyal wife without compromising her authority as queen. Here also was a way in which Philip could be persuaded to come back to her.

By Christmas the king was reconciled to the fact that he would have to come to England if the realm were to be persuaded into war. He knew Mary's mind, but did not trust her to be able to overawe her council in the way that he could. He had already demonstrated during his time in England that, in spite of problems of communication, he could knock heads together. The divisions that notoriously afflicted the council, both before his coming and after his departure, were muted during his stay. With all his limitations, he was a man-manager in a sense that Mary was not; but he would have to apply that talent in person if he wanted England in the war.

Before Christmas some of his household servants had begun to appear, and warnings were sent to his English officers to stand by for his coming. Nobody (not even Philip himself) knew when that would happen, but it was now firmly on the agenda. Mary at last began to cheer up, and the court revels over the holiday reflected her mood of anticipation. The New Year gift list that survives from 1557 is comprehensive, and certainly does not appear to reflect a court that was under any sort of a cloud. Twenty-seven peers, 18 bishops, 55 ladies of rank and over 170 other persons either paid their tributes of loyalty or received the queen's bounty – usually both. Elizabeth was one of the principal participants.[26] After what had been in many ways a taxing and distressing year, there must have been comfort for all concerned in this familiar ritual of gift exchange.

The New Year was less than two weeks old when its first crisis struck. The French broke the truce in the north with an attack upon Douai. In some ways this must have been a relief, because a breech had been expected, and such a move was bound to bring Philip's arrival closer. Douai was not English territory, but it was covered by the treaty that Mary had promised to invoke. However, instead of invoking it at once, the queen referred the whole question to her council, and got a very chilling and discouraging response. England was not, in their opinion, bound by the earlier treaties to intervene, because this was the same war that had been going on when the marriage treaty had been drawn up. The Truce of Vaucelles had not constituted a peace settlement, and therefore its breech did not create a new war. England could not, in any case, afford to fight a war, least of all one in which her vital interests were not engaged. Nor had Philip formally requested such intervention, which was true, in spite of his known desire for it. This advice, which survives only as draft *consulta*, or memorandum, probably represents the opinion of the majority of the councillors, because it is known that some – notably Paget – favoured war.[27] Pole, who was not a member of the council, had his own reasons for not wanting to see England and the papacy on opposite sides in a conflict, and he also argued strongly against it. In a sense, none of this mattered, because war and peace were decisions for the monarch to make, and the council could not prevent Mary from doing what she chose; but having asked counsel, she would have been very unwise to ignore it. What this unhelpful attitude did do, however, was to increase the need for Philip's presence – and that was good news to Mary.

By the end of January, the king had decided that he must come. England was strategically important to his plans and had a powerful navy, although its land forces were difficult to mobilise and of doubtful quality. Those who were arguing the poverty of the kingdom's resources after three successive harvest failures, and the consequent malnutrition and disease, had a valid point, but Philip was not expecting to raise large armies or large sums of money. What he wanted were bases and warships. Having made his decision, on 2 February Philip sent Ruy Gomez across as his harbinger, but with instructions not to discuss the war with anyone except Paget. In theory Philip was perfectly entitled to take the kingdom to war if he chose, but if the council could be overridden, Mary could not. He knew that the queen was sympathetic to his position, but he could not be sure that she would defy her own advisers in his interests. Indeed he could not be absolutely confident of his own reception, after such a long separation and in view of the strains that had arisen in their relationship. Would she be (so to speak) waiting behind the door with a rolling pin? In that respect, he need not have worried. Leaving Brussels on 8 March, ten days later he crossed from Calais to Dover and rode straight to join Mary at Greenwich. In spite of everything that had transpired, she was awaiting him with eager anticipation.[28] When they were together his personal ascendancy immediately reasserted itself, and he was quickly reassured that he could count on her support.

The kingdom to which Philip now returned was not quite the same as that which he had quitted eighteen months before. In some respects the situation had improved. Parliament had (somewhat reluctantly) returned the monies collected for the traditional religious levies of 'first fruits and tenths' to the Church, and the clergy stood to gain substantially in the long run. A few monks had even returned to their habit, the Abbey of Westminster having been re-founded in September 1556.[29] The episcopal bench had been strengthened with some new appointments, and the universities had been purged of Protestant remnants.[30] Pole had convened a legatine synod in November 1555, and although it achieved little beyond the expression of good intentions, it was a satisfactory symbol of the Church's recovery of status. In many respects the Church was in good order. Ordinations had recovered from the low point of Edward's reign. The liturgical infrastructure had been put back in place with remarkable ease in most areas. Pole's priorities on order and discipline could be criticised, but he also placed much emphasis on preaching. England's was an ancient Catholic Church, in urgent need of 'calling home again', but it was not a mission field, and missionary orders, like the Jesuits, were not invited to participate.

On the other hand, the persecution was a running sore. Even before Cranmer's death in March 1556, the executions had moved down the social scale. The early victims had mostly been preachers, with the occasional bishop and even the odd (minor) gentleman; but by 1556 they were nearly all weavers, husbandmen (agricultural workers) and serving maids. The crowds that gathered became increasingly hostile, and the bishops increasingly reluctant. Mary drove them on, and a polemical war in print accompanied the burnings. This was a distraction that the Church could have done without, because it merely created a context, a theatre, for truculent defiance. About 800 Protestants fled into exile, and many of them picked up radical notions that they would never have learned at home. Although the Church was steadily gaining in strength and coherence under Pole's guidance, it had come nowhere near destroying its heretics. Instead it gave them a pretext for defiance, which their adroit propagandists succeeded in linking to the general dislike of Spaniards. The fact that Spanish King Philip and the pope were at war made no difference, and in that respect at least nothing had changed.

Consequently, in spite of some positive developments, England was not in a self-confident mood in March 1557. There was much hunger, and an influenza epidemic was reaching serious proportions. There were also persistent rumours about the queen's health – nothing very tangible, but a nagging awareness that she was now forty-two and there was little chance of an heir. Only her life stood between the realm and an unadulterated Spanish kingship – or worse, a contested succession between Philip and Elizabeth. In theory Philip's interest in the kingdom should have come to an end with Mary's death, but nobody expected that to happen, and there was no shortage of pamphleteers willing to play on the anxiety. The City of London, the financial powerhouse of the kingdom, was afflicted by a sullen resentment. Not only was the religious persecution particularly unpopular in that nicodemite[31] environment, but Philip had done his best to sabotage the commercial enterprise of the City by refusing its merchants access to his South American colonies, and by prohibiting their activities on the Guinea coast of Africa. This last prohibition was largely ignored in practice, but the London merchants were claiming, with some justice, that whenever there was a dispute between themselves and the Flemings (which was frequently), the king consistently took the side of the Low Countries men, irrespective of the merits of the case.[32] It seemed obvious where his priorities lay – and his campaign to take England into an unnecessary war confirmed no less.

IO

PHILIP & MARY AT WAR

Philip's second visit to England began auspiciously. Not only was Mary delighted to see him, but his whole arrival had been carefully choreographed. He landed symbolically by barge at Greenwich, having ridden overland from Dover and taken to the water again just a few miles downstream. It was five o'clock on the afternoon of 20 March, and he was greeted with a 32-gun salute, and cries of 'God save the King and Queen'.[1] Every mile of his passage from Calais had been assisted and smoothed by the queen's ships and the queen's servants, and the whole court was mustered to receive him. The following day all the bells of London rang out, and a *Te Deum* was sung in every church – by order of the bishop. On the 23rd the ceremonies continued with a *joyeuse entree*, comprising a ride through the City from Tower Wharf to Whitehall with the sceptre borne before him and all the livery companies in their finery lining the route. All this was for public consumption, not least in Habsburg Europe, where Philip's position in England was regarded as dishonourable.[2] Behind the scenes, difficulties continued. At one level, Englishmen did not love Spaniards any better in 1557 than they had in 1555. As Henry Machyn noted, three shiploads of them arrived with the tide before the sound of rejoicing had died away. These were no doubt the retinues of the courtiers and officials who had accompanied the king, and they seem to have behaved with more discretion than two years before – but they were not welcome.

Although he was extremely active politically, Philip seems to have appeared very little in public on his second visit, after his initial 'shewing' in London. On 23 April – St George's Day – 'the King's grace whent a presessyon at Whytehalle', which was a public appearance of a sort; but Machyn was much more impressed by the 'duke of Muscovy', who turned up on the same occasion with a gorgeously attired (and exotic) retinue.[3] On 10 June the royal couple paid a visit to Hampton Court 'for to hunt and to kyll a grett hartt', but they stayed only a few days and the household remained at Whitehall. On Corpus Christi Day (17 June) they were back at base, and made another procession through the hall and great court, which was open to the public, but hardly ostentatious. Finally, on 30 June, just four days before he would depart England, the king went hunting on his own 'in-to the forest', and wherever that may have been it was certainly not at Whitehall.[4] This time he seems to have succeeded in his mission to kill a stag, although he was reduced to using a gun for the purpose, which was clearly thought to be not quite gentlemanly.

In the political arena, the privy council continued to be deeply divided over the war with France. Paget was in favour, and he was backed by Pembroke, and possibly Shrewsbury, but Pole, Heath and Rochester were vehemently opposed, and they appear to have been supported by Arundel and Winchester. Petre had resigned by this time (possibly over the war issue) and the attitude of his replacement, John Boxall, is not known. On 1 April Mary summoned this council and, in the presence of the king, set out the arguments for war. Two days later they responded with another memorandum. England could not, and should not, become involved in the hostilities.[5]

The council did not, of course, make such decisions; but it looks at this stage as though Philip was preparing to make the best of a bad job. The Count of Feria, who was close to the king, informed the new Venetian envoy, Michiel Surian, that although the king could do what he liked with the English nobility because they were so venal, he would probably settle for money and the use of the fleet, rather than insisting upon a formal declaration of war.[6] Money was what he desperately needed, because he was effectively bankrupt, and credit, whether in Antwerp or Genoa, was costing him 54 per cent. England, however, did not have money – at least not in the quantities that were required. On 12 April Philip confided to the Bishop of Arras that the going was proving tougher than he had expected. Arras pressed him to settle for nothing less than a complete break. As long as there was a French ambassador in England he would continue to stir up trouble and to be a focus for disaffection.[7] Paradoxically one of the king's most effective allies in this conflict was his enemy Pope Paul IV. Because Philip, as King of Spain, was at war with the pope, the conscientious Pole refused to have any direct dealings with him, or to attend council meetings, which deprived the 'peace party' of their most effective and influential spokesman. In early April Paul was contemplating the drastic move of declaring Philip deposed from all his dominions as a rebel against the Holy Church. His own advisers dissuaded him from this, probably on the grounds that he could not make such a sentence effective, and might well make a fool of himself. On 10 April he did, however, revoke all his legates from Philip's lands, including Pole specifically and by name. The cardinal appealed the decision, and his servants effectively ignored it, so it made little difference to his attitude as long as Philip remained in England.[8] Meanwhile Mary's persuasiveness was proving effective. She summoned the members of the privy council one by one and worked on them. It is not clear that anyone specifically changed his mind, but their opposition was much reduced.

What broke this deadlock was a strange raid on the Yorkshire coast by one Thomas Stafford. Stafford was an adventurer with pretensions. His maternal grandmother had been the Countess of Salisbury, and he therefore had a touch of the Plantagenet royal blood. His paternal grandfather had been Edward, Duke of Buckingham, who had died on the scaffold in 1521. He was therefore, in his own eyes, rightful Duke of Buckingham and a claimant to the crown of England. At the beginning of 1557 he was one of those political exiles who besieged the French court, looking for some kind of service or better still, reward.[9] Henry at this time was seriously worried about adding England to his list of declared enemies, and was torn between a desire to make life difficult for Mary and a desire not to do anything that would precipitate a complete break. On 13 January Nicholas Wotton, the English ambassador in France, speculated that the French king might be contemplating using Stafford for some kind of 'great enterprise', but nothing happened and the rumours died down. Then in early April they began again. Talk of war was incessant, and there was a plot of some kind against the town of Guisnes in the Calais Pale. More importantly, an agent of Wotton's had extracted from one of Stafford's servants the information that his master was planning to seize a castle on the English coast. The agent even managed to secure a map of the place, which Wotton sent on to the council with the comment that it looked like Scarborough. 'It is thought,' the ambassador wrote, that 'the French King will not interfere.'[10] On 14 April Wotton reported again that Stafford had left the court, and was gathering arms and men at Rouen. On 23 April he appeared off Scarborough with two ships and somewhere between thirty and a hundred men, 'some French, some English rebels'.

The castle was half ruined, and the small garrison completely surprised. Stafford seized it and issued a lengthy prepared statement to the effect that because she was handing the realm over to foreigners, Mary was no true queen. He proclaimed himself Duke of Buckingham and protector of the realm.[11] No one was interested. In that fairly remote corner of northern England the Spaniards were hardly an issue. By what appears to have been mere chance the Earl of Westmorland was not far off with a force of the local levies that he was on the point of leading to Newcastle for the defence of the border. By the morning of the 24th he knew of the incursion, and by the 28th the intruders had been overpowered and were in custody. The whole farce had lasted just five days, and had posed no threat to anyone.[12] By the 27th the council had been informed, and had issued instructions to the city of Newcastle to fit out four or five ships to go in pursuit of those that had transported Stafford and his men. By the time that they had complied, their quarry had long since disappeared. By the 29th it was known in London that the crisis was over, but even before that Bernardino de Mendoza had decided that the incident would inevitably mean war: 'As for the breach of the truce, the French have spared us the trouble.'[13] He was right: within a week the council had agreed that this was a provocation too far, and acceded to Philip and Mary's demand. Norroy the herald did not bear the queen's defiance to Henry II, the French king, until 1 June, but by then everyone who needed to know was preparing for the conflict.

There are a number of suspicious circumstances about the whole Stafford affair, which proved to be so convenient for the royal desires. Given that it is 200 miles from Scarborough to London, government reaction was incredibly rapid and decisive. It looks almost as though news was being released before it was received. The contrast with the official hesitancy that had initially greeted both Wyatt and Dudley makes this even more remarkable. Even more suspicious is the fact that Jean Ribault, who commanded the French ships, had worked in England in Edward's reign and had been in the service of Lord Paget.[14] Once he had set Stafford ashore, Ribault and his ships simply evaporated. When he discovered what had happened, Henry expressed astonishment and denied involvement of any kind. In the circumstances, he would have been bound to say that but it may well have been true. It is possible (though unprovable) that the money to put this rather pathetic adventure together came not from the French king, but from Philip and Mary, via Paget and Ribault. Stafford, in short, was a dupe, so blinded by his own self-importance and the febrile propaganda of the English exiles that he was quite unable to sense the trap into which he was walking. The council had been warned some time before that Scarborough was the likely target of an attempt, but nobody had told the men on the spot, because it was necessary that the raiders should come ashore in order to declare their treasonable intentions – which they did, right on cue. From the speed of his reaction, however, it looks as though the Earl of Westmorland was expecting the call that came on 24 April. Whether foolishly optimistic or victim in a trap, Stafford, along with John Bradford and a few others, died a traitor's death on 28 May.[15]

So Philip got his war, and some of the military men in England were pleased enough by the prospect of legitimate employment. However, London, which provided most ambassadors with what they could learn of public opinion, was not pleased. As Surian reported in two despatches on 7 and 8 June, they were saying that:

> ... besides the suppression of their trade, on which the kingdom may be said to subsist, they will have to pay constant subsidies for the maintenance of the war. And what weighs more with them than anything else, is to see that all this is being done for the benefit of aliens whom they detest, and most especially the Spaniards.[16]

The reasons officially given for the break – the hostile record of France in relation to the present government, capped by this latest example of bad faith

– were regarded as thin and stale. Philip's honour was satisfied, but only at a price. This is not apparent from any of the surviving documents, but at some point in his final battles with the council he must have agreed to foot the bill for England's war effort. Mary would provide for the defence of her kingdom, including the border against Scotland, and would put her fleet to sea, but if Philip wanted any troops to join his army in the Low Countries, he would have to pay for them himself. Considering how dire Philip's financial straits were in the summer of 1557, he must have set a high value on his honour. London may have been disgruntled, but the military peerage was not the only group to see profit in the war. As we have seen, during his first stay in England, Philip had endeavoured to attract into his service captains and other gentleman-soldiers, many of whom had dubious records of loyalty to the regime. That was even more pronounced now. The three surviving sons of the Duke of Northumberland – Ambrose, Henry and Robert Dudley – together with Lord Braye, Peter Killigrew, Sir Peter Carew, Sir James Croftes, William Winter, and a number of others who had seen the inside of prisons for their opposition to Mary, were all recruited into the king's service.[17] Mary had no control over those whom her husband might recruit for his army, and none of these men enjoyed her favour – or even indulgence.

ENGLAND AT WAR WITH FRANCE, early June (possibly 9th) 1557
AN ACCOUNT OF WHAT THE HERALD FROM ENGLAND DID IN FRANCE
AND THE KING OF FRANCE'S REPLY AT RHEIMS, BY BAGUENOIS,
PRINTER TO THE CARDINAL OF LORRAINE, 1557.

On the 7th June 1557, when the King was in the town of Rheims in Champagne, lodged at the abbey of St Remy, there arrived at the abbey Mr. William [Flower], Norroy King of Arms, from England, wearing a cloak of black cloth, without declaring who or what he was until he reached the door of the King's Council.

He then asked to speak to the Duke of Montmorency, Peer and Constable of France, who had him brought to the Council Chamber … The Constable … asked how he had been so bold as to come without revealing his identity, as he was on such important business; for by so doing he had exposed himself to the danger of being hanged, as he deserved to be. The herald replied that he had landed at Boulogne and continued on his journey, with his escutcheon attached to his breast, without having been asked anything by anybody ... The Constable answered ... that he deserved all the more to be punished ... If he had not had to do with so merciful a king, he would be in danger of losing his life. However the king desired to show his great goodness and clemency, and would forgive him ...

After the herald had made several reverences and had knelt down with his coat of arms on his arm, the King asked him in a loud voice by whom he had been sent, and why. The herald answered that he had been sent by the Queen his mistress, and presented his power, which the King caused to be read publicly. The King then said to him: 'Herald, I see that you have come to declare war on me on behalf of the Queen of England. I accept the declaration, but I wish everyone to know that I have always observed towards her the good faith and amity which obtained between us, as I ever intended to do all my life towards everyone, as far as it lies in my power to do so, as befits a great, honourable and virtuous prince. Now that she picks so unjust a quarrel with me, I hope that God will be pleased to grant me this grace, that she shall gain no more by it than her predecessors did when they attacked mine, or when they recently attacked me. I trust that God will show his might and justice towards him who is the cause of all the evil that lies at the root of this war. I forbid you on your life to speak another word. I act thus because the Queen is woman, for if she were not, I would employ other terms. But you will depart and leave my kingdom as quickly as you can.'

The herald was then led out and accompanied to the English Ambassador's lodging, whither the king, full of generosity as he is, sent him as a present a chain worth 200 crowns, in order that he should speak of what he had seen and heard from the King's mouth, bearing witness in his own country to the King's virtue and generosity which are known to the whole world.

[*Calendar of State Papers, Spanish*, XIII, pp. 294-6. The original ms, a French copy, is at Lille (L.M. 53).]

Perhaps because he had achieved his aims in that direction, Philip does not seem to have indulged in any war games during this second visit. On 3 July 'the King and Queen took their journey towards Dover', staying overnight at Sittingbourne. On the 5th he boarded a ship at Dover, and no one commented upon the emotions of their parting. This time, though, it was final. They were never to meet again. Some time later, Mary was again to declare that she believed herself to be pregnant, so presumably there was nothing too badly wrong with their relationship; but whatever the queen might have liked to think, this had been strictly a business trip for Philip. One part of that business had been the war, and in that matter Philip had got his way; the other had been to persuade or force Elizabeth into marriage, and that had failed.

The relationship between the half-sisters at this time might be likened to an armed truce. Unless or until Mary produced a child, or made some authoritative pronouncement to the contrary, Elizabeth was the heir presumptive, and after the failure of the queen's first 'pregnancy' a group of canny councillors were quietly determined to protect that position – which is why Stephen Gardiner's attempts to get her formally disinherited got nowhere. Philip had also changed his mind. When he had first arrived in England the princess had been under house arrest at Woodstock, and he had regarded her as a serious threat to his interests. Just when his attitude changed is not quite clear, but it was probably early in 1556, when he was becoming convinced that his campaign for a coronation in England was going nowhere, and he had to take stock of the situation in the light of his new responsibilities in Spain. There was no reason to suppose that Mary would die soon, but if she did, what was he to do? The English would not willingly accept any claim by him, and to have imposed himself by force would be unrealistically expensive. If Elizabeth were set aside for any reason, the next heir was Mary Stuart – brought up in France and betrothed to the dauphin, Francis. It would be much better to accept Elizabeth, especially if he could do so in such a way as to create some sense of obligation on her part, and assuage the inveterate hostility of the English. He may have met her fleetingly while she was held at court during Mary's 'confinement', but the idea that he felt any affection for her is romantic fiction. His view of the situation was both cool and self-serving. When the Dudley conspiracy was exposed in March 1556, and fresh opportunities opened up for Elizabeth's enemies to incriminate her with the arrest of her loyal intimate Kate Ashley, Philip instructed (apparently without consulting Mary) that she was not to be molested.[18] Mary knew this, and it did nothing to warm her heart, but there was very little that she could do about it unless Elizabeth blundered – and she was becoming increasingly sure-footed.

An unmarried Elizabeth was, however, from Philip's point of view, uncontrollable, and her actions as queen might be radically unpredictable.

Hence his desire to marry her to the Duke of Savoy, which we have already noticed. Emmanuel Philibert had been dispossessed of his duchy by the French, and had consequently become a loyal Imperialist. He was a good soldier, but more a dependent than an ally, and the prospect of a royal English bride was attractive. He also had the merit of being a good Catholic, which Elizabeth was not. The princess, however, knew perfectly well what Philip was about, and would have none of it. She was twenty-three, and somewhat disingenuously declared herself unready for marriage. Rather surprisingly, Mary was also opposed to the proposed union. The reasons for this are unclear, because it might be thought that a plan to nail her maverick sister down in a safe Catholic marriage would have been very appealing. Privately, however, Mary seems to have convinced herself that Elizabeth's whole claim to royalty was fraudulent. She was, of course, a bastard because Henry had never been married to Anne Boleyn. But it was worse than that. Anne was a convicted whore and adulteress, and Mary seems to have believed that Elizabeth's true father was Mark Smeaton – the court musician who had been executed for alleged adultery with Anne. She is alleged to have remarked upon their close physical resemblance – which was untrue.[19] None of this emerged in public, and our knowledge of it depends upon diplomatic chatter, but the fact remains that Mary opposed her sister's marriage. It is alleged that briefly, soon after his return in March 1557, Philip actually persuaded his wife to accept the idea, but the moment passed and she changed her mind.[20]

The seriousness of Philip's intentions in this respect may be measured by the fact that he recruited two formidable ladies to his team of persuaders, and was followed to England by Christina of Denmark, the widowed Duchess of Lorraine (who had once rejected an advance from Henry VIII), and his own half-sister, Margaret, Duchess of Parma.[21] Whether it was Elizabeth whom they were supposed to persuade, or Mary, or both, is not clear. In any case the campaign failed. Philip could have simply ordered the princess to accompany him on his return to Flanders, and it was widely believed that he intended to do that. Once out of the country, and away from her political supporters, Elizabeth might have found it impossible to sustain her resistance. But a forced marriage of that kind would have been a poor solution. Not only might it be repudiated if the circumstances changed, but it would have deeply offended his

English subjects and reluctant allies. Mary's feelings towards her sister in 1557 can only be deduced, but everyone who commented upon the matter believed them to be very hostile – and heartily reciprocated. 'Although it is dissembled,' wrote Surian, 'it cannot be denied that she displays in many ways the scorn and ill-will she bears her.'[22] Mary was baffled and deeply distressed that so many of her subjects accepted this creature as her natural heir – and even more distressed that her husband was now doing the same. It may have been partly because Philip wanted to secure Elizabeth's marriage as 'the heir of England' that Mary was so deeply opposed to the idea.

In matters religious, there was good and bad news. Although Pope Paul had renewed Cardinal Pole's legatine commission with words of commendation soon after his election, the only positive thing that he had done for the English Church was to issue the papal bull *Praeclara* in June 1555. This had canonically extinguished the religious houses dissolved by Henry VIII, and thus finally put an end to any prospects of their reclaiming property.[23] It was in a sense just a tidying-up operation after the settlement of January, but at least it demonstrated that the new pope, for all his hostility to Philip, had no intention of repudiating the settlement.[24] It also meant that any religious houses established under the existing dispensation in England would be new foundations. There would be no legal continuity. However, the war that had broken out in September 1556 had led to a virtual breakdown of relations with England, and on 9 April Pole was recalled to Rome. It was understood that he was to face investigation upon 'certain charges', by which heresy was generally understood. When Sir Edward Carne, Mary's ambassador in Rome, protested against this decision, Paul was conciliatory. Of course he recognised that England was a special case and needed a legate, but he made no move to reinstate Pole. Perhaps, Carne suggested, a personal appeal from the queen would be in order. On 21 May Philip and Mary duly wrote, protesting the damage that would be done to the English Church by the cardinal's departure, and professing themselves perfectly satisfied with his diligence – and his orthodoxy.[25] Four days later Pole penned his own protest. At about the same time the English council also wrote to the same effect: the English Church was like a convalescent patient, and the pope's action would remove its physician. Paul was unmoved. He had long suspected Pole of unorthodox sympathies, and had strongly resented the advice that the cardinal had recently given him on settling his differences with Philip. The pope had also had enough of humanist intellectuals who favoured reconciliation with the Protestants, and who equivocated over fundamental issues such as justification.[26] On 31 May the cardinal protector of England (and Pole's main contact in the curia), Giovanni Morone, was arrested and sent to the castle of San Angelo. On 14 June the pope repeated his demand for Pole to return to Rome.

At about the same time Paul announced that out of a fatherly concern for the wellbeing of the English Church, he would name a new legate – making an exception to his general rule. The man he named was William Peto. Carne was stunned, and declared openly that he dared not communicate such a decision to England. Peto was an Observant Franciscan who, twenty years earlier, had made a name for himself as a preacher and writer against Henry's divorce and had earned a spell in exile as a result. He had been appointed by the pope to the see of Salisbury in 1543, but had never secured possession. He was personally known to Paul, having spent some time in Rome during his exile, but by 1557 was over eighty and in feeble health.[27] When the Franciscan house at Greenwich was restored in 1556, he had retired there with every intention of spending his last years in prayer and meditation. It may be that the pope, who was an octogenarian himself, did not see age as any handicap, but he should have known that Peto was not up to the job, either physically or mentally. Mary was outraged, regarding such an appointment as little short of an insult, and when the nuncio bearing the news arrived at Calais on 3 or 4 July, he found himself anticipated. Mary refused him admission to the realm.[28] At the same time Peto himself declined the proffered appointment on the grounds of his age and unsuitability. In Rome it was believed that the English schism was about to be renewed, but there was never any question of that, and Paul held back from imposing sanctions. What he did do was studiously ignore English business, whether public or private. Consequently, when Bishop Robert Parfew of Hereford died on 22 September 1557, although a successor was named, he was not installed before Mary herself died. The same happened with Robert King of Oxford and Henry Man of the see of Sodor. Two or three other bishops died in 1558, and none of them was replaced, so the bench was about six or seven short when it came to fight its corner in Elizabeth's Parliament of 1559.

Pole was deeply distressed. Papal authority was one of the sheet anchors of his faith, and if he had been free to choose he would have returned to Rome, and no doubt to incarceration in a papal prison. In the middle of June the Inquisition was known to be examining his activities – a somewhat ironic situation, given that Pole himself was busy persecuting heretics.[29] However, he was not free, and Mary absolutely forbade him to go. This ban was fully endorsed by Philip, who understood and appreciated the stabilising effect that the cardinal had on his wife. Because Pole had appealed against his recall, it has been suggested that there was some uncertainty as to whether the office of legate continued or not, but he himself was in no doubt.[30] His legatine synod, which stood adjourned at the time of his recall, was not reconvened, and although it had made some useful decrees, particularly on the subject of clerical education, it never completed its work, and because Mary died less than two years later its decrees were effectively dead letters. Both Philip and Mary wished him to carry on as though nothing had happened, Mary particularly praising his zeal and application, but that was hardly possible for so conscientious a servant as Pole. What he was able to do, for the time being, was to use his metropolitan authority as Archbishop of Canterbury to maintain the momentum of his reform programme. The Count of Feria's well-known comments about his being 'a dead man', and about the lukewarm never going to heaven, were not only unfair to Pole, but also tell us a good deal more about the count's aggressive evangelical agenda than they do about what was actually going on.[31] He seems to have regarded the country as a mission territory in the same sense as the American colonies.

On 12 September Pope Paul was finally forced out of the war. His resources were quite inadequate to resist Alba's armies, and the French were unable to offer sufficient assistance. The peace was greeted with bonfires and a *Te Deum* in London, but it made very little difference to the pope's attitude to England, and none at all to his perception of Pole. Carne found it increasingly difficult to secure any audience at all, and the only positive result of months of diplomatic pressure was to recover the legatine status of the see of Canterbury. This eased the problems of the Church, and perhaps explains why Pole's servants continued to refer to him as 'legate'; but it was no consolation to the man himself. He continued to remonstrate in letters, and even invoked the intercession of

Cardinal Carlo Carafa, the nuncio in Brussels, and a man for whose personal qualities he can have had little respect. Paul, however, was convinced that the Cardinal of England was a long-standing heretic, and had for years been the mastermind behind a great conspiracy against the Church in which Morone, Priuli, Pate, Flaminio and Vittoria Colonna had all been involved. It was a paranoid and quite unjustified vision, which lent every episode of Pole's career a sinister twist, but, in spite of numerous representations to the contrary, the pope remained implacable.[32] Because Pole was never formally arraigned, we do not know what the actual charges against him may have been, but they seem to have focused on his alleged Lutheran sympathies over justification. As long as Pole remained out of reach in England, however, there was little the pope could do. William Peto died in March 1558, and no attempt was made to replace him. By that time Paul had accepted, although with a very bad grace, that he was not going to get his way over the English mission. From April to June 1558 he was in retreat at the Belvedere. All papal business was hopelessly in arrears, and those in England who had looked expectantly to Rome to infuse new life into the Church were becoming increasingly disillusioned.

In the past, war with France had automatically meant trouble with Scotland, and since Mary Stuart's French mother, Mary of Guise, had been regent north of the Border since 1554, the same was anticipated on this occasion. Mary, however, was not entirely in control of the situation, and the French ascendancy was not popular in Scotland. There is some evidence that the two governments considered themselves to be belligerents, and on 1 August the council in London informed the wardens of the marches that the Scots 'have already entered into wars with us' but nothing happened.[33] Almost at the time of the formal declaration of war, the commissioners for the settlement of the endemic minor disputes of the border were in session. Hearing the news of the breach, the Earl of Westmorland said to his Scottish counterpart, the Earl of Cassilis: 'My lord I think it but folly for us to treat now together, we having broken with France, and ye being French for your lives.' That provoked the unexpected response: 'By the mass, I am no more French than ye are a Spaniard.' Westmorland replied carefully that he was indeed 'a Spaniard' as long as Philip was king, but the point was taken.[34] Although Mary made careful provision for the defence of the north, even resurrecting the earldom of Northumberland for Sir Thomas Percy to that end, and a mobilisation was ordered in Scotland, there was no incursion. Instead, Mary of Guise was soon facing a rebellion that effectively tied her hands.[35] The significance of Scotland in the ensuing conflict was rather different. Having exposed England to the danger of war in the north, the English council was of the opinion that the least that Philip could do as King of Spain was to declare war on Scotland himself. This the king consistently refused to do, to the embarrassment of Feria and the detriment of his relations with England. His Flemish subjects had considerable trading interests in Scottish ports such as Leith, and the only incentive for such a declaration would have been to gratify the English – which he was not inclined to do.

When Philip left England early in July, he was accompanied by an English expeditionary force under the command of the Earl of Pembroke. This was reported to number 10,000, and that may have been its theoretical strength, but the muster rolls disclose only 7,221 actual 'effectives'.[36] Pembroke did not have much experience, but he was high in the king's confidence. His officers were a much more dubious bunch. Many of them were only recently reconciled to the regime, and Surian had probably been right when he wrote that the war was being used as an excuse to get them out of England. On the other hand, they all had something to prove, and that could have its advantages. As soon as they reached Calais, the king pressed on to join his army at the siege of St Quentin. Pembroke, however, did not go with him, because his commission also included a general oversight of Calais and its environs. For several weeks he was occupied there, reorganising and reinforcing the garrisons.

At the beginning of August both Philip and Pembroke were making progress slowly, Philip probably because he wanted his army to take the town before he appeared for a triumphal entry, and Pembroke (apparently) because his artillery train had been delayed and he was reluctant to advance without it. By 10 August he had reached Cambrai. That same morning, the constable of France, advancing incautiously to the relief of St Quentin, was ambushed and routed by the besieging army. This was a thumping victory, which left many French nobles and over 5,000 soldiers as prisoners of war. Philip himself (to his great chagrin) could claim no personal credit as he was still several miles off at the time. The town held out until 27 August, which gave the tardy English time to arrive, but after the defeat of the constable its fall was inevitable. Even so, it did not surrender, but was stormed, the English troops doing something to redeem their reputation by fighting conspicuously well.[37] It would have been ungracious, in the wake of such victories, to criticise his allies publicly, but privately Philip blamed Pembroke severely for the tardiness of his advance.

The French field army having been temporarily destroyed, and the winter not far off, Philip was not interested in further campaigning, but rather in consolidating his hold upon the environs of St Quentin, which embraced several lesser but strategically important towns. The English could now go home. They mustered on 15 September and began to leave piecemeal soon after. By 10 October only 500 were left, and they departed within a few days. The treasurer of the campaign was William Whightman, the receiver of the office of augmentations for south Wales, and it is from notes that he left that we learn that this campaign cost £48,000, the whole of which was found by Philip, £37,000 from his Continental revenues and £11,000, rather mysteriously, from the 'King's moneys in England'. Because of this, Whightman never accounted through the English system, and if his original account now survives, it has not been found.[38]

It was probably the defeat at St Quentin that forced the pope out of the war a few days later, because he now knew that he could expect no further help from Henry. By October 1557, although his finances were in a bigger mess than ever, Philip had every reason to be satisfied. Not only did he have the upper hand both in Italy and the Low Countries, but the anticipated 'second front' from Scotland had not materialised, which eased the pressure for any decisive action there. On 15 August the news of the first victory was greeted in London with *Te Deums*, processions and so forth. The Archdeacon of London (John Harpesfield) preached a 'godly sermon', in the course of which he declared 'how many were taken, and what noblemen they were'.[39]

Perhaps the decisiveness of this victory reconciled some of the doubters to the war. The number of soldiers required had not been enormous, and all those who responded seem to have been volunteers. There was also a certain amount of bonding among the military gentry from which Philip benefited. On the other hand there was a mutiny of unknown seriousness in the fleet, and orders were issued to magistrates in the south-west to round up men who had been pressed to serve and who had then run away.[40] The late summer weather was bad again, and the harvest, although not as disastrous as those of the two preceding years, was again inadequate. It was perhaps inevitable that these acts of God should be blamed by official preachers on the people's faithlessness, but there was good mileage in the counterargument that the Almighty was obviously displeased with the government itself.[41] Moreover, in spite of the fact that Philip had borne the cost of Pembroke's army, the government was swiftly in financial difficulties. By heroic efforts over the previous three years, the crown debt had been reduced from about £180,000 to under £100,000. Now all those gains were to be jettisoned. On a war footing, the fleet alone was costing £70,000–£80,000 a year, to say nothing of the escalating costs at Berwick in the north and at Calais. In September a privy seal loan was launched, which raised nearly £110,000 over six months, but there was plenty of resistance and a procession of gentlemen were hauled before the council for attempting to refuse their assessed contributions. In virtually every case the intimidation seems to have worked – but it did not make the regime any more popular. Moreover the shortage of money betrayed the council into a false economy that it was soon to regret. Having decided that the campaigning season was over for that year, and that in any case the French were in no condition to make any 'attempt', the extra troops who had been sent to Calais and Guisnes in July were withdrawn, leaving the garrisons seriously depleted.

In fact the weakness of France, although real enough in September 1557, did not last very long. Aware that his north-eastern flank was dangerously exposed, Henry decided to cut his losses in Italy and recalled the Duke of Guise to the north. They were both suffering from reputation fatigue, and on the lookout for some feasible counterstroke. By the end of October Philip had mopped up the small towns around St Quentin, and although his field army was in winter quarters, his position there was rightly judged to be too strong to be attacked. There was, however, Calais. Henry had good agents there, and was not short of information about its condition. Most of the fortifications had been extensively repaired during Henry VIII's last war, just over ten years earlier, and although little had been spent on them recently, they were in reasonably good condition. This was not, however, true of the castle, which was less exposed to attack from the landward side, but whose condition was close to ruinous. When he learned in November that the garrison had been reduced, the French king could hardly believe his luck.

As November turned to December, French troops began to filter into Picardy. This was noticed by Philip's spies, but the weather was exceptionally cold, and there was a general reluctance on the Imperial side to believe that any serious campaign was intended. Nevertheless Philip also picked up a warning that the target was Calais, a warning that he duly passed on to London, at least as early as 22 December. Lord Wentworth, the governor of Calais, also had his own independent sources of information, and these convinced him that the French objective was Hesdin – a suspicion that he duly passed on to Philip.[42] He did, in fact, ask for assistance before Christmas, and then withdrew the request, causing considerable confusion. By 27 December the council at Calais was at last convinced that an attack was imminent, and that it did not have sufficient force to defend the whole Calais Pale. If (or when) the attack came they would have to pull all the available troops back to the town itself, and even then would have barely enough to defend it. On the 29th the council in London decided to send the Earl of Rutland to Wentworth's assistance, with whatever force could be immediately available.[43] The country had been for several months in the grip of a serious influenza epidemic, and this meant not only that fit men were hard to find, but also that there was a reluctance to summon them together for fear of spreading the infection. It was not until 2 January that Rutland had enough men to embark a relief expedition, and by then it was too late. Having ignored Philip's earlier warnings, on 31 December Wentworth had finally sent an urgent plea to Philip for assistance. Philip duly despatched 200 arquebusiers, but by the time they reached Calais the town had fallen. Thus ended English control of any part of mainland France.

The French campaign had been meticulously planned by the Duke of Guise and his brother, the Cardinal of Lorraine, and it may well be that Wentworth's complacency was fed by disinformation from the French commanders. Realising that the big threat to their success lay in the last minute arrival of English reinforcements by sea, on 4 January the duke took advantage of the fact that the marshes on the seaward side of Calais were frozen to make a lightning strike to seize Rysbank at the entrance to the harbour. They were only just in time. Rutland's ships arrived the next day, and the earl was minded to force a passage, but his seamen refused to face the fort's guns, which were now in French hands. The fortresses of Guisnes and Hammes were still under English control, but apart from them the Calais Pale was swiftly overrun. On the morning of 7 January, bombardment having breached the walls, Calais itself surrendered and Wentworth and 2,000 of his men became prisoners of war.[44]

The campaign was not over, however, and the first reaction, both in London and Brussels, was to mount a counterattack. On 11 January the Earl of Rutland was again commissioned to lead such an expedition. A treasurer and captains were appointed and forces began to muster. On the 16th the Duke of Savoy announced that he was on his way to the relief of Guisnes. However, the Duke of Guise was too quick at every turn, and was favoured by good fortune. On 10 January the garrison at Hammes mutinied, and that put an end to resistance there. Finally, on the 21st, Guisnes was battered into submission; Lord Grey, its captain, was the only English soldier to emerge with any credit from the whole fiasco. Savoy never reached him, and after a storm had scattered and damaged the English fleet, Rutland's orders were countermanded.

THE FALL OF CALAIS, 1558
MICHIEL SURIAN, VENETIAN AMBASSADOR WITH KING PHILIP, TO THE DOGE AND SENATE, 8 JANUARY.

The French have not attacked Gravelines, as was feared, but remain at Calais, battering it from the castle of Ruysbank, and although at this court Calais is held to be a strong and secure fortress, I nevertheless remember that on my going to see it internally, when I crossed over to England,* I found it very thinly inhabited, most especially by soldiers, and the place being large requires many; nor do I know whether they can put them in at their pleasure, having the sea between them. Besides this, towards the harbour, where the French are now battering it, it seemed to me very weak, as the walls are high in the ancient fashion, and there is no platform,[†] the moat also being small, and it is ill flanked; nor has this ever been remedied because those who have the care of it rely on the opinion current all over the world, that it is an impregnable fortress. It is possible that in other parts it may be more scientifically constructed, and that in this quarter no great care was taken, it seeming secure by reason of its being so very near the sea.

The Earl of Pembroke, Governor of Calais, is not there, and the whole charge of the defence is vested in the Governor of the Town, styled Deputy,[‡] and the soldiers of the garrison are all Englishmen, as they do not trust any other nation; but the moment it was heard in England that the French had taken the castle of Ruysbank, they commenced sending troops to Dover, where the Earl of Pembroke also arrived on his way to Flanders, and at this hour it is heard that he crossed with 5,000 infantry, and landed at Dunkirk, six leagues from Calais.[§]

It has been determined by this side to send the Duke of Savoy towards those frontiers, with an army drafted from several garrisons, including that of St Quentin, about which places it seems that there is nothing to fear, the French now being at a great distance thence, but this might prove to be a second mistake added to the first, which was that of disbanding the army, when the enemy were intent on reinforcing themselves.

Brussels, 8, January

[*Calendar of State Papers, Venetian*, VI, pp. 1415-16. The original MS in Italian, partly in cipher, is in the Vienna Staatsarchiv]

* On 28 March 1557, before the reinforcement of the summer.

† Terrapieno, a mounting for artillery.

‡ Lord Wentworth.

§ This seems to be false information.

'When I am dead and opened you shall find Calais lying in my heart' Mary is famously supposed to have later said, according to John Foxe. But in the long run the loss of Calais was a positive development. Not only was it vastly expensive to maintain, it was also a standing temptation to interfere in France. The days of Anglo-French dynastic states were over, and Calais was a relic. Neither Mary (nor indeed Elizabeth) saw it in that light, but its surrender drew a line under an obsolete system, and encouraged England to look to the Atlantic rather than to Europe for the next phase of its development.[45] At the time, however, it was a subject of anguish and recrimination. Surian, the usually well informed Venetian, had heard nothing of the matter when he wrote on 30 December.[46] Perhaps the warning from Flanders, although issued in Philip's name, did not actually come from him. Whatever the truth, the English instinctively blamed Philip for the loss of their treasure; while he pointed out (with truth) that if the English council had not been so penny-pinching and parsimonious, the crisis need never have arisen. However, there was one explanation upon which both could agree: Calais had been sold out by wicked heretics. A generation earlier, the town had been something of a refuge for various Protestant hues (the 'evangelicals') escaping from the attentions of zealous bishops in England, and there was certainly a Protestant, or crypto-Protestant, element there during Mary's reign.[47] However, there was also a sizeable French population, and as far as the evidence goes it was with them rather than with the Protestants that the various plots against Calais since 1553 had been associated. When he returned from his French prison, Wentworth was charged with treason, not heresy, but it seems that both accusations were mainly intended to save the faces of the council, and to paper over its rift with the king. These accusations also, of course, provided another reason to go on persecuting Protestants. In Rome the 'heretical conspiracy' was naturally believed, one Spanish cardinal writing that: 'The governor of Calais was a great heretic, like all those who were with him there ... so I am not at all surprised at its fall.'[48]

In the immediate aftermath of the disaster, Philip's attitude seems to have been ambivalent. On 25 January Ruy Gomez wrote to the king that the quality of the troops assembled was so poor that there was no point in retaining them. Philip took this information at its face value and ordered them to be disbanded. At the same time, however, he sent Feria across the Channel again to discuss with the council a longer-term plan for a counteroffensive, deploying the whole army of the Netherlands.

This would have been a major commitment, but the English were not keen. They still feared attack from Scotland, they said, and the Danes and the Hanseatic League were reported to be preparing a fleet against them.[49] They would also have to hire mercenaries for the defence of the realm, as the sickness had so depleted their reserves of men. Their whole response (according to Feria) was apologetic:

> ... we do consider that if we should send over an army, we cannot send under
> 20,000 men ... whereof will ask a time, before which time, considering also the
> time that the enemy hath had ... to fortify and victual the place, it is thought that
> the same will be of such strength as we shall not be able alone to recover it.

Such an army would cost £170,000 for five months, which, with all the other expenses of the war, would far outrun the kingdom's resources. The realm was in great poverty; 'the Queen's Majesty's own revenue is scarce able to maintain her estate', and so on. 'We see not,' they concluded, 'how we can possibly (at least for this year) send over an army.'[50] Philip was not pleased.

England's lacklustre war effort was not the only cause of strain between the king and his subjects at this time. The English were bitterly angry about the licences for provisioning Calais, arguing that this was yet another example of Philip putting Flemish interests before their own, and this time as Feria reminded the king on 22 February – they were right. In addition, the English merchants were suffering losses owing to the wartime embargo on their trade with France, while Flemish merchants were being given safe passage. To make matters worse, on 4 February Philip ordered Feria to prohibit, in his name, a proposed London trading voyage to the Portuguese Indies, on the grounds that it was prejudicial to the King of Portugal's subjects, 'which narrowly concern me'. The Londoners were outraged – and ignored the ban. Quarrels between the English traders of the Merchant Adventurers and the Hanseatic League over trading privileges were also endemic. Edward VI's council had cancelled the whole Hanseatic privilege in response to pressure from the Adventurers, but Mary had restored it to please Charles V, whose subjects the Hanseatic merchants mostly were.[51] Early in 1558 there was another deadlock, with the English council supporting the Adventurers and Philip supporting the Hansa. The league's ambassadors spent four fruitless months in England, and frustration was high on all sides.

The low priority that Philip gave to the interests and feelings of his English subjects can be demonstrated over and over again. In February he gave permission for Mary's servants to raise 3,000 German mercenaries for the Scottish Border. They were duly raised in March and April, and paid an advance of about £2,000. Then, when they were on the point of sailing from Gravelines, Philip suddenly announced that he needed them himself, and would pay them henceforth. In fact he disbanded them soon after, blandly informing the English council that he had saved them an unnecessary expense.[52]

During these months Feria was virtually a resident ambassador in England, and his jaundiced reports are one of our main sources of information.

His presence was unfortunate, partly because, as a Spanish grandee, he felt at liberty to speak his mind to the king, and partly because he had no understanding of how English politics operated. Just as Renard had judged the privy council during the first year of the reign by the extent to which it satisfied the Emperor's requirements, so now Feria judged the English government by its responsiveness to his master. 'I am at my wit's end with these people,' he wrote on 10 March, '... they change everything they have decided, and it is impossible to make them see what a state they are in.' 'Numbers,' he wrote on another occasion, 'cause great confusion.'[53] There is no need to take these jeremiads at face value. Attendance at council meetings averaged 13.5 for January and February 1558, but fell away to 9.2 thereafter, and that was not excessive by anyone's standards. Of course the whole council was large – over forty members – but it was organised into a number of standing committees and commissions upon which many councillors served without ever attending the privy council proper at all. From the fact that Feria never mentions it, it would seem that the select council, created by Philip as his link with the privy council from abroad, had virtually ceased to function. Only one letter to it from the king survives, dated 6 April, acknowledging another that does not survive.[54] In a formal sense, it clearly continued, but seems to have become no more than a hat that the inner ring of the privy council donned when it was convenient to do so. By this time Sir Robert Rochester was dead, and had been replaced as controller of the household by Sir Thomas Cornwallis. Cornwallis also seems to have replaced Rochester on the select council, but whether by Philip's appointment or *ex officio* is not clear.

Fearing a French invasion in the wake of the loss of Calais, the council put itself and the country on a war footing. A memorandum to Philip outlining the scheme was enclosed with Feria's despatch of 10 March – not, it will be noted, in any direct communication from the select council. The more vulnerable parts of the country were divided into ten military lieutenancies, each under the command of a nobleman: Devon and Cornwall under the Earl of Bedford, Wiltshire and Somerset under the Earl of Pembroke, and so on. At the same time a council of war and a council of finance were established, adding to the list of standing committees.[55] Philip approved these measures, but seems to have had no part in drafting them.

All in all, Philip was losing interest in England. He had been consistently frustrated in his attempts to become a 'real' king, in spite of the rhetoric that had accompanied his second visit; and the triumph of bringing England into the war had turned to bitterness and recriminations after the loss of Calais. Payments to his English pensioners were months, sometimes years in arrears, and Feria commented as early as February 1558 that none of those noblemen who had previously favoured the king were now prepared to do anything for him. Feria specifically mentioned Paget, whose enthusiasm for the war had evaporated and been replaced with complete disillusionment.[56] The fleet was indeed mobilised, but did not achieve very much beyond some desultory raiding of the Brittany coast. When Philip's trusted adviser Bishop Antoine Perrenot de Granvelle suggested to Lord Admiral Clinton in May that the English fleet was quite capable of landing 5,000 men and causing real damage, Clinton agreed, but showed so little enthusiasm that the bishop commented: 'if this man is the keenest of the Englishmen, the rest must indeed be slack'.[57] Although they were supposed to be allies, it was not safe to place English and Spanish ships in proximity to each other. There was a fray at Plymouth among the seamen, and another at Falmouth involving the townsmen and servants of the Marquis of Verlanga.[58] Only a successful intervention in Kintyre against Scottish interference in Ulster partially redeemed an otherwise futile campaigning season. Part of the problem was that all parties were financially exhausted. By the autumn of 1558 the English crown debt was approaching £300,000, and was costing £30,000–40,000 a year to service. Both Philip and the French king were in much worse conditions, Philip being actually bankrupt and Henry virtually so. It was all very well for Feria and Granvelle to rail at the English for lack of effort – the Continental allies were achieving almost nothing themselves.

Rather surprisingly amid this story of gathering gloom, the Parliament that met from 20 January to 7 March was the least contentious of the whole reign, and it was the only one to be prorogued rather than dissolved.[59] This may have been partly because minds were focused by the reality of war, and by recent setbacks at the hands of the old enemy, France; it may have been because everyone was desperate to get out of London before they were caught by the influenza. The first business, inevitably, was a subsidy for the war. Negotiations ensued. It was pointed out that a substantial loan had only just been raised, and if there were to be an invasion in the summer, everyone would be put to great expense for armour and weapons. Eventually the Commons agreed to one subsidy for 10 June 1558, and a tax of 'one fifteenth' on land for October. For 1559 they would not commit themselves, and Mary had perforce to accept what was offered.[60]

More positively, both Houses were keen to provide for defence in more direct ways, and a number of measures concerning the musters and the possession of weapons passed backwards and forwards between the two Houses, emerging eventually as two statutes (on the Parliament roll, 4 & 5 Philip and Mary, caps 2 and 3). The first of these specified in detail what horses, armour and weapons each citizen was required to produce, in strict accordance with his position in the social hierarchy. The second set out penalties for non-attendance at the musters, by those who had been duly summoned; it also penalised corrupt muster masters, and made desertion (once mustered) a felony. Although these were later claimed to have been sectarian measures, designed to maintain the Catholic ascendancy, there appears to have been no justification for such a view. How effectively the Acts were enforced during the musters of the summer, it is not easy to say, but they remained the basis of the Elizabethan domestic military system for nearly twenty years.[61] An attempt was also made to recover debts owed to the crown through the sequestration of real estate, but this ran into great difficulties and was eventually abandoned on the queen's orders just a few days before the session ended.

There was no reason why the loss of Calais should have made any difference to the Church, except in so far as it contributed to a growing sense of malaise. 'I am told,' Feria wrote in February, 'that since the fall of Calais, not one third as many Englishmen go to mass as went before ...'[62] This need not be taken too seriously because Feria, as we have seen, believed that Pole's whole strategy was mistaken and ineffectual, but it was indicative of the struggle that the regime was having to maintain its credibility at a time when misfortune was naturally interpreted as evidence of divine disapproval. Meanwhile, the heretics were continuing to make their way to Smithfield.

The xxii day of December [1557] was burned in Smithfield one Sir John Ruff, a friar and a Scot, and a woman, for heresy ...[63]

The financial demands of war also pressed hard on the Church. Pole was well aware of the extent to which various dioceses, and indeed the Church as an institution, had benefited from Mary's generosity, and he was insistent that clerical taxation should be voted by convocation, and paid in full. But it was a struggle, and rumours that Pole had made a personal fortune of £100,000 out of his position were very wide of the mark. He did have an income of about £3,000 a year, but to maintain his status as archbishop, even when he had ceased to be papal legate, that was by no means too much – and would not have been considered such. However, he seems to have been careless about distinguishing between his private money, the money attached to his various offices, and the funds of the Church as a whole – such as the dues of 'first fruits and tenths'. After his death this left his secretary, Priuli, with a great deal of disentangling to do, and although there is no reason to doubt the cardinal's financial integrity, he certainly gave hostages to fortune.[64]

In some ways the Church (the burnings excepted) was still doing well in the last nine months of Mary's reign, a period that saw the publication of Thomas Watson's *Wholesome and Catholic Doctrine*, one of the most effective pastoral works of the reign. There is still some evidence of a recovering piety among ordinary people, not least in bequests to parish churches and refounded religious houses. But the shadow of papal disfavour continued to hang over the whole enterprise.[65]

II

MARY & ELIZABETH

When Philip left England for the second and last time in July 1557, Mary was left pretty much to her own devices. Charles V had retreated to San Yuste, the pope was hostile, and her old and faithful servant Robert Rochester died in November. Her great personal props and supports in this isolation were Susan Clarencius, another old and faithful servant, and her cousin Reginald Pole.

Susan Clarencius is not very visible after Mary's marriage, except in so far as she received a number of small but lucrative rewards in the form of lands, wardships and rectories (allowing her to draw the tithes from certain parishes). She inveigled a coach and horses out of the Venetian ambassador, in return no doubt for the favour of access,[1] and can be glimpsed taking money off Sir William Petre while she entertained him at cards as he waited in the privy chamber to be received. She exchanged New Year gifts with Mary in 1557, but that list was governed by the strictest protocol and tells us nothing of Mary's degree of intimacy with her servants. More revealing perhaps is the fact that she was able to write to the Countess of Bedford with news of her husband's 'valiantness' on campaign with the king before any official despatch had mentioned him. On 25 July 1558, St James' Day (and the anniversary of the royal marriage), she even took delivery of a consignment of flags and other images intended for a court celebration of the saint.[2] These may well have been displayed in a public procession of some kind, but the relevant pages of Henry Machyn's diary are missing and no other chronicler mentions it. As evidence of a close relationship, this does not amount to much, but we have John Foxe's testimony to the fact that she was 'most familiar' with the queen, and was one of those who attended her on her deathbed.

In a sense Pole is much more visible because of his ecclesiastical authority, but the evidence of his personal relations with Mary is virtually all oblique or circumstantial. Philip thought highly of Pole's influence over his wife, but was never explicit about how that influence was exercised. There are occasional references to his good offices as a councillor, usually in a clerical context, but he appears to have played almost no part in the secular government, which was the queen's main preoccupation.[3] Pole lived at Lambeth Palace, just over the river from Whitehall, so it is not surprising that his comings and goings to the court attracted little attention. On 15 July 1557 Henry Machyn noted that 'the Queen's grace dined at Lambeth with my lord cardinal Pole' on the eve of one of her regular moves to Richmond, which suggests that visits in that direction were not common.[4] On St Andrew's Day in the same year he accompanied Mary from St James' to Whitehall, where after mass Sir Thomas Tresham was created master of the Order of St John in England, 'and iiii knights of Rodes made'. It was on this occasion, after dinner, that Pole notably preached in the presence of 'all [the] juges and bysshopes'.[5]

However, this was all in the way of ecclesiastical duty, and does not tell us much about their personal relationship. When Mary made her will on 30 March 1558, she named Pole as the chief executor (leaving him £1,000 for his pains), a role that should probably be seen as that of a trusted friend rather than an *ex officio* function of the Archbishop of Canterbury.[6] When Pole made his own will on 4 October, he requested his executors 'to inform the Queen concerning this will, and to entreat her to show me the same favour when I am dead as she did in all my affairs while I was alive', which is correct but hardly effusive.[7] Neither left any 'memorial' to the other, as Mary very conspicuously did to Philip, and this suggests a close professional association rather than warm personal friendship. Whether the cardinal ever acted as the queen's confessor we do not know.

When Mary returned to London after Philip's departure, she seems to have retreated into her shell. Apart from the state opening of Parliament on 20 January 1558, and the relevant high mass, there are almost no mentions of her appearance, and the revels accounts tell a similar story. They show no sign of activity at all between June and December 1557, and the total Christmas expenditure amounted to £36 4s 0d.[8] Nothing at all seems to have been spent on props or new costumes, which suggests a very low level of activity, and no originality whatsoever. 'Masks, plays and other pastimes' are mentioned, but nothing is specified, and there is no reference to anything being created for the occasion. For Candlemas in the same year the costs were even more modest: £18 2s 0d. In fact the last entertainment of the reign for which any description survives was a 'great mask' of Almains (i.e. Germans), pilgrims and Irishmen, which took place at Whitehall on 25 April 1557; in other words, while Philip was still in England. This seems to have accounted for a large part of the £151 17s 7d spent in that financial year.[9] Mary seems to have lacked all enthusiasm for such capers, although the fact that she again believed herself to be pregnant early in 1558 may offer a partial explanation. When the king was away, no one else was in a position to act as cheer leader for the regime, and the royal magnificence was veiled. On New Year's Eve 1558 'there came a lord of misrule from Westminster' into London with a suitable retinue, but there is no certainty that this had any connection with the court.[10]

When Giacomo Soranzo, the Venetian ambassador, left England for another posting in May 1557, he wrote (as was customary) a full description of England for the benefit of his successor, and this contained a detailed description of Mary herself.[11] This offers as much evidence as we are likely to obtain about her appearance and main characteristics, but of course Soranzo had no access to her private person, and did not apparently know anyone who had. 'She is of low rather than middling stature,' he commenced, but clean limbed and with 'no part of her body deformed'. Her frame was spare and delicate, unlike either her father or her mother who (apparently) had run to fat in middle age. Where young Mary had been considered a beauty, her present wrinkles were caused more by anxiety than by age, although the effect was to make her look older than her real years (forty-one at this point). 'Her aspect,' he continued, 'is very grave' (*nel resto molto grave*), with eyes so piercing that they inspired fear in anyone who was scrutinised by them. He admitted that this was slightly deceptive, as she was very short-sighted and had to hold any book or document close to her face in order to be able to read it. Her 'piercing eyes' may therefore have been rather less perceptive than Soranzo was willing to admit. Indeed it is unlikely that she could see anything very clearly at a distance of more than a few feet. Spectacles were not unknown as a remedy for such a deficiency by this time, but either her physicians did not wish to advise them, or the queen herself was averse to the idea – a touch of vanity perhaps. Her voice, with which he must have been very familiar, was rough and loud, 'almost like a man's', and audible at a considerable distance. She was, he concluded, a 'seemly woman, never to be loathed for ugliness', which, given the courtly world within which he was operating, was rather less than enthusiastic.

Her mind, he went on, was quick. She was able to comprehend 'whatever is intelligible to others'. In case this should also seem to be faint praise, he makes clear that the 'others' referred to were male, and that this constituted 'a marvellous gift for a woman'. She understood five languages, he wrote (somewhat optimistically), and spoke English, Latin, French and Spanish. Italian she understood but did not speak. Mary's competence in Spanish is somewhat controversial, because other contemporary opinions do not agree with the Venetian in this respect, and it is unclear what she got from her mother and what from Philip.[12] It is also probable that he got it by hearsay as he did not speak Spanish himself, and his conversations with the queen were conducted in Latin. The fact that her intelligent responses 'surprised everyone' is more a comment on the times than on the queen, because there is plenty of evidence that Mary was (and always had been) an intelligent and highly educated woman.

For the sharpness of her political perceptions, on the other hand, there is less supporting evidence, because her judgement was so often derailed by her conscience – a matter upon which Soranzo did not see fit to comment. The stubbornness which we know from earlier episodes and other evidence was one of her defining characteristics, and Soranzo glossed it as courage in 1557. She would never 'display or commit any act of cowardice or pusillanimity', showing thereby a 'wonderful grandeur and dignity' becoming a princess of such a noble house. He then went on to expatiate upon the magnificent determination with which she had defended the true faith against the machinations of her brother's councillors.

A lot of this is fairly predictable, but the ambassador also writes of her more humdrum qualities, and in so doing gives some insight into her daily routine and habits at this time. She was expert, he noted, in 'woman's work' – that is embroidery and needlework of every kind. She was an accomplished musician, playing expertly upon the clavichord and the lute to a level that astonished professional musicians, although, he notes, 'now she plays rarely'. In some respects she was 'much like other women', being sudden and passionate. She was also mean over small things – a vice not altogether becoming in a bounteous queen – which may have reflected some dissatisfaction with his own parting gift, although he nowhere hints at that.

Above all, according to Soranzo, Mary was exceptionally pious. Few women in the world, royal or otherwise, were more assiduous in their prayers than she was, 'never choosing to suspend them for any impediment whatsoever'. She regularly kept the canonical hours with her chaplains, either in a public church, or in her chapel or closet, and meticulously observed all the feasts and fasts of the Church, 'precisely like a nun and a religious' (*apunto come una monaca et una religiosa*).

Soranzo clearly intended to be thorough, so what he does not say is as significant as what he does. Nowhere does he commend her love of learning, or suggest that she patronised either artists or scholars – let alone scientists, as her father had done. Indeed her difficulties with reading may well have curtailed any tendencies that she had in that direction. Nor does he say anything about her application to business, which had been elaborated upon by earlier commentators. Soranzo had been in England for some time, so his observations did not only describe the Mary of early 1557, and it may well be that he was taking her industriousness for granted. On the other hand perhaps, as with her music, she was applying herself less rigorously. If that was the case, it was not because she was indulging in dancing or revelry. Neither aspect of court life merits a mention in the Venetian report, and that is probably because they were not considered noteworthy – even while Philip was present. Making due allowance for the conventions within which he was operating, Soranzo's portrait of the mature queen is that of a very sober, very pious woman, of masculine intelligence but faded beauty, who no longer allowed herself the smallest indulgence, even in the music that she had once embraced so wholeheartedly.

In her younger days Mary had gambled enthusiastically, wagering money, horses and even meals on bowling, the turn of a card or the fall of a dice.[13] This continued after her accession, and there are several references to 'passdice', but by 1557 such frivolities seem to have been put behind her. Not only does Soranzo not mention them, but there is no other evidence to suggest that the habit continued. There was, of course, plenty of gambling going on within the court, but either Mary was unaware of it, or turned a blind eye. Bored courtiers had to do something while they waited on her pleasure, and presumably it was better (and safer) than flirting. Mary had once been a keen hunter, and had flown her hawks with enthusiasm as a girl. Now the kennels and the toils were dutifully maintained, but no one pretended that the queen was very interested. She accompanied Philip on the first occasion when he went after the great buck in June 1557, but the second (and successful) expedition he made on his own.

Nowadays we would describe Mary during the last two years of her life as stressed and tense, unable (seemingly) to relax, or to enjoy those modest pleasures in which she had once been seen to indulge. Yet there was a softer side to her. She did not pray or ply her needle alone, and the women who were close to her and shared her waking hours (when she was not closeted with councillors or ambassadors) became deeply attached to her. Jane the Fool still haunted the presence chamber like an amiable ghost, still presumably plying her trade (whatever exactly that may have been) and still receiving medication for her periodic ailments.[14] Mary may have been depressive, or perhaps her health was declining long before anyone thought fit to comment upon it, but there is a distinct lack of animation about her after Philip's second departure. She seems to have suffered from periodic fits of bitterness, and it was commented that separation was doubly grievous to 'a woman naturally tender' – not a description that we can recognise from Soranzo, but probably just as close to the truth. This bitterness is particularly apparent in her hostile relations with Elizabeth, whom she claimed was not only a dissembler and a heretic (which she was), but also the 'illegitimate child of a criminal'.[15] Her own childlessness may well have been the affliction that preyed most on Mary's mind, because this most pious of queens was singularly short on cheerful resignation, but her calculated antagonism to her sister did nothing to alleviate the situation.

Shortly after Mary's death, the chief gentleman of her privy chamber, John Norris, drew up a memorandum for the guidance of his successor.[16] Norris had been described by Edward Underhill as a 'great papist', and he withdrew into private life on Elizabeth's accession, but his guidelines offer a valuable insight into the workings of the privy chamber over which he had presided. Norris might be described as a 'master of ceremonies'. He even claimed to have had full control over the celebrations at the time of Mary's wedding, a claim that the lord chamberlain would surely have challenged – if he had ever found out about it. Most of Norris's document records the protocol that had been observed in Henry VIII's time at the various festal days of the Church. For example:

> Also it is to be knowen that the king offrith one Christenmas daie xxs; that is to saie on noble to be hadd out of the comptinghouse and to be delyvred by the treasorer of householde and two nobles to be delyveryd from the treasorer of the kinges chamber for the tyme being ...[17]

There is no certainty that Mary followed these elaborate routines, but given the general conservativism of the court it is very probable that she did. Also, if these practices had been superseded, Norris would surely have mentioned it, since his intention was to provide guidance for the future.

In spite of its importance, Norris's position had one major drawback from our point of view – he had no access to the inner sanctum, which was female territory. When the queen retreated to her bedchamber, no man could go beyond the door. To the privy chamber itself, a total of nine men had access: three gentlemen, three gentlemen ushers (who included Norris) and three grooms. No other man could even go so far unless specifically summoned, so that no councillor (not even Reginald Pole) could intrude upon the queen's presence uninvited. Consequently, although we have some patchy evidence of the conduct of ordinary business, we have absolutely no idea of what happened 'beyond the door'. It seems likely that Mary used these privy chamber gentlemen as a protection when she was in low spirits. There is some evidence for that in the aftermath of her first false pregnancy, and rather more in the spring of 1558, when she was recovering from the second (see below).

Henry VII had followed earlier custom in that he dined in the great hall on formal occasions, when the whole court would have been in attendance. At other times he ate in the great chamber, where his principal officers 'kept their tables' and only the chamber servants had access.[18] His son virtually abandoned the great hall, keeping his 'Board of State' in the great chamber, and other meals in the privy chamber – a practice that Edward VI seems to have maintained. In the latter part of her reign Mary seems to have retreated entirely. According to Norris:

> There (the Privy Chamber) her meal was set and one of the ordinary servants without did go for it when he was commanded by a gentleman usher and brought it to the door and there the ladies and gentlemen did fetch it …[19]

Presumably the privy chamber gentlemen waited at table, but there is no suggestion that anyone other than the occasional invited guest would have shared the queen's meal. Not even the privy chamber servants dined 'within', unless they were on duty. The rest of the privy chamber dined 'with mistress Clarencius in her Chamber', or in another chamber set aside for the purpose. Susan Clarencius regularly received two 'messes', which would have fed about a dozen people, and the off-duty grooms another mess between them. There is no suggestion that 'bouge of court' (the right to be fed at the monarch's expense) was much reduced by these measures, so presumably the head officers continued to keep their tables in the great chamber, and the ordinary servants ate either in the hall, or, more likely, took their rations to their own quarters.[20] Meals as public spectacles, or as 'bonding sessions' between the monarch and the court, were not on the agenda by this time.

It is possible that this regime was intended as an economy measure, because the meals consumed in the privy chamber would have come from the queen's kitchen and been of superior quality to those produced from the great kitchen. There was considerable competition to be fed from the queen's kitchen, and if the monarch was dining in public in the great chamber, then the whole lot was upgraded. With Mary 'in retreat' only the privy chamber would have been so privileged. It is perhaps relevant that the household expenditure for 1557–8 was no more than £36,208, which was the lowest for over a decade, and lower than Elizabeth ever achieved.[21]

By this time, Mary seems to have had no expensive tastes; even her extravagant and rather indiscriminate dress sense is no longer commented upon. As became a sober matron, she had no flamboyant favourites, clamouring for expensive rewards. Those who did particularly well out of her regime, like Sir Thomas Cornwallis or the Earl of Northumberland, did so for clearly identified political or administrative reasons.[22] Apart from the opening of Parliament, the only royal event recorded by Henry Machyn in the first half of 1558 was Mary's removal from Whitehall to Greenwich on 10 March 'for to keep Easter'.

Shortly afterwards, Mary made her will. There appears to have been no particular crisis in her health at this point, but the occasion was her second phantom pregnancy. She began her will thus: 'Thinking myself to be with child in lawful marriage', and proceeded to set her affairs in order.[23] Since Philip had left early in July 1557, she should have been nearing her due date by the end of March, and her condition should have been obvious to all. Mysteriously, no commentator says anything about it. During her first phantom pregnancy early in 1555 everyone had remarked upon her changing body shape, her physicians' opinions were regularly quoted, and there was a general air of expectancy throughout Europe. Elaborate preparations had been made, nursery staff appointed, and proclamations drafted announcing the happy event. This time there was nothing.

The conclusion must be that it was all happening in Mary's own mind. She had confided her hope to Philip as early as January, explaining the long delay by saying that, after her earlier disappointment, this time she wanted to be quite sure.[24] He had responded with suitable congratulations, but the fact is that he seems not to have believed her – which is hardly surprising. He may have last slept with her on the eve of his departure, but perhaps had his own reasons for knowing that the condition was a fiction. The news leaked out, but caused hardly a ripple of interest. The Cardinal of Lorraine could not keep a straight face, observing that this time they would not have so long to wait, as it had been more than six months since her husband had left her.[25] She must, presumably, have confided in her own ladies, but they kept their counsel, and in fact her conviction probably worried them a good deal. Equally worrying to her councillors, if they were aware of her will, would have been the fact that, amid all the detailed provisions for interment, pious statements and a long list of specific bequests, there was no provision for the succession, save in the requirement that 'the issue of my body that shall succeed me in the Imperial Crowne of this Realm' should be no impediment to the execution of her will.[26] Against such invincible optimism, or self-deception, there was for the time being no remedy.

By May it was clear – even to Mary – that nothing was going to happen. Unsurprisingly, she was noted to be weak and melancholy, but how far this affected her participation in the government is uncertain. The conduct of the war (in so far as there was any) was in the hands of her council, and although there is no shortage of formal documents issued in her name, there is no clear evidence that she did anything other than give her consent. Signet letters continued to be issued on a variety of subjects, but the surviving copies do not bear her signature.[27] By the end of July the person most likely to comment, the Count of Feria, had returned to Philip, being replaced by the anonymous Alonso de Cordoba. This represented a downgrading of the mission, and presumably indicates that Philip saw no immediate crisis upon the horizon. It was to be another three months before it became clear that he had been too complacent.

With the benefit of hindsight there is a fin de siecle air about the year 1557–8, but it may not have seemed that way at the time. In fact Mary managed quite well on her own, because after his second departure Philip was not sufficiently interested to interfere. By the summer of 1558 his English pensions were anything up to two years in arrears, and there are no signs that the reorganisation of household officers that took place at Christmas 1557 owed anything to his influence.[28] Mary had made all her big decisions, and had set in place an administrative machine that worked with commendable efficiency. On the other hand, there are some signs that she was losing touch with reality. Her second phantom pregnancy provides some evidence of that, as does her determination to settle the succession only on her own offspring, in which nobody else now believed. It may also be significant that the religious persecution, which she was so instrumental in driving, increasingly turned into mass incinerations of six or seven offenders at a time. The careful examinations and macabre theatre that characterised most of the burnings, down to and including Cranmer's in March 1556, were increasingly abandoned in favour of these more general executions. Mary had no intention of giving up on this campaign, but it seems to have become more and more mechanical.

ELIZABETH THE HEIR

On 19 June 1558 Philip sent a special courier to England to inquire about his wife's health. 'She has not written to me for some days past,' he wrote to Feria, 'and I cannot help being anxious.' He had been expected in England for several weeks – or at least Mary had been expecting him. Ships had been put on standby to escort him, but he had not come. The excuses were the same as usual, and on the 23rd Feria reported that the queen was bearing her disappointment patiently.[1] Her health seemed to be a little better than it had been of late, and he referred somewhat dismissively to 'her usual ailments'. She had reacted badly to the disappointment over her second phantom pregnancy, and for several weeks was reputed to be weak and sleeping badly, so it was probably this familiar state of depression to which the ambassador was referring. There was, however, a lack of animation about her, and in particular her enthusiasm for the war seemed to have waned. This Feria blamed on the malign influence of certain councillors. He may have had Pole in mind, but he did not name him. With the benefit of hindsight it looks as though Mary had entered into a slow but terminal decline from the early summer, but it did not seem that way to contemporaries. Mary had suffered from menstrual problems, and from fits of lassitude and depression, for as long as anyone could remember. These fits had tended to alternate with periods of intense application, anger and determination. Her physicians manifested no particular alarm, and the general expectation seems to have been that this disorder would pass, as the others had. Philip's anxiety was probably as much diplomatic as caring, because the royal couple were in the middle of another quarrel over Elizabeth.[2]

Although no longer in the diplomatic front line, at some point, probably in the spring of 1557, Simon Renard had written to Philip about the English succession. In this undated memorandum he had pointed out that, undesirable as she might be for many reasons, Elizabeth was the best bet if (or when) Mary succumbed to one or other of her illnesses. It was therefore essential to bring her under control, because left to her own devices she would marry an Englishman, restore the heretical Church and align her foreign policy with France.[3] Philip did not need this advice, because he had already come to the same conclusion, but his persuasions had failed in 1557. In the spring of 1558, he returned to the charge. Perhaps Mary's second phantom pregnancy had set the alarm bells ringing, but something prompted him in March or April to revive the project to marry Elizabeth to the Duke of Savoy. Mary became angry and distressed – any mention of Elizabeth seems to have upset her. In April an embassy arrived from Gustavus Vasa of Sweden, seeking the princess for his son and heir, Eric. There was no chance that Mary would have consented to her sister's marriage with a Lutheran, and in any case the ambassador misbehaved by going straight to Elizabeth's residence at Ashridge without the queen's permission. Mary was extremely annoyed, not least, it would seem, because the incident put her half-sister firmly back on the agenda.[4]

An exchange of letters with Philip seems to have followed. Only one of these now survives, but it gives an indication of the progress of the negotiation. Mary offered to put the whole question of the succession before Parliament. This may have been stalling, because Parliament had recently been prorogued and there were no immediate plans to recall it; however, it was a perfectly proper suggestion. There were good precedents for a legislative answer to English succession problems, but what she may have had in mind was the repeal of the 1544 Act, under which Elizabeth was the heir. The condition that had been attached to that status was that she should marry with the consent of the council. Whether Mary had it in mind to impose some other condition, or to change the order altogether, we do not know. The suggestion apparently angered Philip, who replied that if Parliament altered the succession he would hold her to blame. In the one surviving letter, Mary responded:

> I beseech you in all humility to put off the business until your return ... For otherwise your highness will be angry against me, and that will be worse than death to me, for I have already begun to taste your anger all too often, to my great sorrow.[5]

She had, she continued, already discussed her conscience in this matter with Friar Alphonus (one of the king's confessors), who had left her more confused than before. She had believed for twenty-four years that Elizabeth was a bastard, and she was not going to change now. Only if Philip and Savoy both came to England could she see any hope of resolving the matter – although how their presence would achieve that, she did not explain.

Meanwhile Feria was visiting Elizabeth at Ashridge. As the king's confidential agent he did not need permission to do this, and how often he went before he returned to the Continent in July we do not know. Such visits are referred to occasionally in his reports, but he never committed to writing the substance of their discussions – merely saying that they were 'satisfactory'.[6] Elizabeth was expressing a total unwillingness to marry at all, so it is unlikely that he elicited any signs of a change of mind. Probably his satisfaction derived from the fact that the princess was showing a proper gratitude for Philip's support, and a willingness to continue good relations if (or when) she should become queen. There is no sign of a thaw in relations between the sisters. In February Elizabeth visited her London residence at Somerset House 'with a great company of lords and noble men and noble women'. She stayed just over a week, paying a brief and chilly visit to the court, but then returned to the country with a similar retinue.[7] The point can hardly have been missed. Between Philip's recognition and her own domestic support, the princess was now very much the second person in the kingdom, and too strong to be touched, even if Mary had had the will to do so.

The war ground on. The Duke of Guise inflicted a sharp defeat on Philip's forces at Thionville in June, but the king redeemed the position by taking Gravelines at the beginning of July. Philip had ordered the English fleet to support this operation, only to find that it had been deployed for the defence of Alderney on the queen's orders. His reaction is not recorded, and may have been muted by the fact that a squadron under vice admiral John Malen did turn up while the battle was in progress and successfully bombarded the French positions.[8] At the end of July, Lord Clinton landed 7,000 men near the port of Brest, but was unable to take it and withdrew after a few days, his stores having run out and his Flemish allies having departed. It was unsuccessful, but hardly a disaster, and the English fleet maintained control of the English Channel in an unheralded but effective way throughout the summer, at the same time maintaining a squadron off the Firth of Forth. They got little enough thanks from Philip, who measured everything by battles in the Low Countries, but they effectively prevented French troop movements by sea in a manner that no one else could have done. There is little sign of strategic coordination, but the French fleet offered no effective challenge. With both sides approaching financial exhaustion, there was talk of peace as early as May 1558, but the sparring continued throughout the summer as each side hoped for a tactical advantage. Only in September was Henry finally manoeuvred into requesting formal negotiations, which then commenced at Cercamp.[9] The English participated, but had almost no leverage, because Mary was by that time extremely sick, and Philip had no intention of putting himself out for allies with whom he remained extremely dissatisfied.

About the middle of August, Mary developed a fever. This was unusual for her, and may indicate that she had contracted a mild version of the influenza that was still raging among her subjects. However, Pole reported to Philip that she was taking good care of herself, and by the following month the symptoms had disappeared. Optimism, however, was premature. By the end of September the queen was ill again, with what was described as a 'dropsy', and this time her condition soon began to give rise to serious anxiety. Her attendants were saying that only a visit from Philip would restore her to health, but unfortunately the king could not come. His own father, the Emperor, died at San Yuste on 21 September, and although he had long since handed over all his responsibilities, Charles remained in theory Holy Roman Emperor, and his funeral rites would be elaborate and prolonged.[10] Philip could hardly absent himself at such a time. Moreover the peace negotiations had finally opened on 8 October and required close attention, particularly as one of the main sticking points was Calais.

There was probably also another consideration in the king's mind. If he should be in England when the queen died, his honour would require him to claim a continued role especially as he had (albeit secretly) repudiated the limitations of the marriage treaty that forbade him to do any such thing. However, he had no desire to do so, having decided that he would accept Elizabeth and cut his losses in England.

Philip therefore resolved to send back the Count of Feria, who was well known to Mary, ostensibly to commiserate with her on her illness, but in fact to keep a watching brief and, if Mary should die, to ensure that Elizabeth succeeded without any impediment. On 28 October the queen added a codicil to her will, finally acknowledging that there was unlikely to be any 'fruit of her body', and confirming that the succession was to go to the next heir by law. She carefully avoided naming Elizabeth, although her meaning was clear enough.[11] A few days later she sent a message to her half-sister, acknowledging Elizabeth's right, and requesting only that her debts be paid and that the Church be maintained. As far as we know Elizabeth did not respond, and the two did not meet, but Mary had done the one thing necessary to ensure a peaceful succession.

On 9 November, Feria reached the English court. The queen, he reported, was glad to see him, and particularly to receive news of her husband, but too weak to read the letters that he had brought with him. 'There is ... no hope of her life,' he wrote, 'but on the contrary each hour I think that they will come to inform me of her death, so rapidly does her condition deteriorate from one day to the next.'[12] He wrote these words on 14 November, and by the time that Philip received them, Feria's prediction had been fulfilled. As she grew weaker, Mary seems not to have wanted to talk about Philip, but confided to those about her that she had had a vision of angels 'like little children', and is alleged to have said that 'Calais' would be found written on her heart. During her final illness she received the sacrament more than once, and each time an improvement in her condition was imaginatively attributed to its efficacy. Finally, on 17 November, she received the 'viaticum,' the holy communion for the dying, made the responses, and then slipped into a coma. The exact moment of her passing was not even noticed by those present – a peaceful end, they said, as a reward for a noble and virtuous life.

John Foxe, who claimed to have his information from Rees Mansell, a gentleman of Mary's privy chamber, who was present, took a rather more detached view.

MARY'S DEATH, 1558

Touching the manner of whose death, some say she died of a tympany,* some by her much sighing before her death, supposed she died of thought & sorrow. Whereupon her council seeing her sighing, & desirous to know the cause to the end that they might better minister the more ready consolation unto her, feared, as they said, that she took that thought for the King's Majesty her husband, which was gone from her. To whom she answering again: Indeed (said she) that might be one cause, but that is not the greatest wound that piercest my oppressed mind: but what that was she would not express to them.

   Albeit afterwards she opened the matter more plainly to Mr. Rise and Mistress Clarencius (if it be true that they told me which heard it of Mr. Rise himself) who then being most familiar with her, & most bold about her, told her that they feared that she took thought for King Philip's departing from her. Not that only (said she), but when I am dead and opened, you shall find Calais lying in my heart. And here an end of Queen Mary, and of her persecution.

[John Foxe, *Acts and Monuments* (1583), p. 2098.]

* A swelling of the abdomen, probably a tumour.

The various stories do not entirely agree, and that is hardly surprising. Nor were her epitaphs consistent. To those close to her, and to the loyal ballad makers of London, she was a loving and generous mistress:

> She never closed her ear to hear
> The righteous man distressed,
> Nor never spared her hand to help,
> Where wrong or power oppressed.[13]

To Pope Paul IV she was a wayward and difficult daughter, whose passing he did not much regret, while to John Foxe she had been the dupe of evil priests:

Of which Queen this truly may be affirmed and left in story for a perpetual memorial or epitaph for all kings and queens that shall succeed her to be noted, that before her never was read in story of any King or Queen of England since the time of King Lucius, under whom in time of peace, by hanging, heading, burning, and prisoning, so much Christian blood, so many Englishmen's lives, were spilled within this realm, as under the said Queen Mary ...

No contemporary view was entirely fair, but one or two things are clear. Mary's death stopped the religious persecution dead in its tracks, and left her councillors staring apprehensively into an uncertain future. 'These councillors,' Feria wrote, 'are extremely frightened of what Madame Elizabeth will do with them. They have received me well, but somewhat as they would a man who came with bulls from a dead Pope.'[14] Cardinal Pole, he reported, was also in a very frail condition with a quartan ague (which was almost certainly influenza) and likely to die. A few hours after Mary's death, in an uncanny confluence of events, that prediction too was fulfilled. Circumstances had conspired to give Elizabeth an extremely easy ride.

Even if Philip had been more deeply attached to Mary than he was, there would have been little that he could have done in November 1558. 'The Queen my wife is dead,' he wrote when the news reached him, adding: 'I felt a reasonable regret.' In translation this probably sounds more callous than it was intended, but in truth the emotion in their relationship had been all on her side, and his main reaction was probably one of relief.[15] He was only thirty-one, and after a decent interval would be free to marry again. Not only was this a useful diplomatic asset, he also urgently needed more children. He instructed Feria to secure (if possible) the jewels that Mary had bequeathed to him in her will, and to represent him with suitable dignity at her obsequies, but he had many other things to occupy his mind. The negotiations at Cercamp were temporarily stalled by the news from England, because it remained to be seen what stand the new government would make over Calais. From Henry's point of view, anyone would be an improvement on Mary, so although he toyed with the idea, he did not push the chances of his own preferred candidate, Mary Stuart of Scotland. He did not share Renard's conviction that Elizabeth was bound to be pro-French, but her position was so strong that any intervention would be tantamount to self-harm. Philip would apply whatever pressure he could to ensure that the new queen maintained her sister's policies, but he was not over-sanguine, and indeed Elizabeth was an unknown quantity on the international scene.

At the same time Philip was in the middle of a full-blown row with his uncle Ferdinand, the new Emperor.[16] Philip had been trying for some months to persuade Ferdinand to give him *de facto* control over the Imperial lands in Italy, on the reasonable grounds that he was in a position to defend them, while the Emperor was not. Ferdinand refused to compromise his honour and in November, just about the time of Mary's death, Philip annexed the key strategic territories of Bari and Rossano.[17]

This was in direct contravention of his treaty obligations, and the Emperor was mortally offended. There was however (as Philip had no doubt calculated) nothing that he could do about it. In fact the king's position in Italy was now overwhelmingly strong, but he did not see it that way, being acutely aware of the extent of anti-Spanish feeling in places like Naples, and uncertain of alliances that he had no sound reasons to doubt. It was to be some years before these anxieties subsided, as both France and the Empire became weaker after 1560.

Although Mary was still alive when Feria reported on 14 November, and the ambassador was scrupulously respectful of that fact, his main concern was with Elizabeth, and with what kind of a queen she would make. She was, he noted, both clever and vain; schooled in her father's ways of doing business; and surrounded by heretics. He was particularly concerned that, in spite of her assurances of continued friendship, her attitude to him was more distant, and she was refusing to concede any debt of gratitude to Philip for the strength of her position. He visited her after going to court, probably at Brockett Hall, near Hatfield, and noted that, although she had received him well, his reception was not as joyful as it had been earlier – that is, back in June.[18] They enjoyed a convivial dinner, and afterwards she talked to him privately, accompanied only by two or three of her ladies 'who spoke only English' and who would not be able to understand what was said. Feria does not mention the language used, but it was probably French or Italian. His own despatch was written in Spanish, but it is not clear that Elizabeth had that tongue sufficiently. She teased him over Philip's attempts to marry her to the Duke of Savoy, 'laughing a great deal', and he responded rather stiffly that the king had never intended anything against her honour. She then went on to discomfort him further by observing that her sister had lost her subjects' affection by marrying a foreigner, to which he had replied, punctiliously but untruthfully, that on the contrary Philip had been much loved. She was grateful for Philip's support, but set no particular store by it, placing all her confidence in the English people, who were, she was convinced, 'all on her side'. This, Feria concluded ruefully, 'is undoubtedly true'. It must have been a difficult interview, because even by his own account she seems to have been playing him like a fish.

The rest of his despatch is filled with speculation about who would be in, and out, of favour under the regime that was now impending. Paget, Petre and Mason he expected to be particularly favoured, although Paget had now become 'a complete rogue' and was temporarily out of action with influenza.[19] Clinton and Nicholas Wotton he also expected to be well placed, and observed that the latter was a man worth cultivating. He had it on good authority that William Cecil would be secretary. 'He is said to be an able and virtuous man, but a heretic.' The Earl of Arundel would not be in favour, and the idea that Elizabeth might marry him was a joke. Elizabeth's particular bile was reserved for Secretary Boxall and Cardinal Pole.[20] The latter was so disliked that Feria feared for his safety. The heir to the throne was fiercely indignant about her imprisonment, and about the way in which she had been dealt with by her sister's government, and was not likely to be in a forgiving mood towards those whom she held to have been responsible. In his judgement she was very unlikely to continue in 'the true religion', but genuinely wanted peace and was perfectly prepared to continue the treaty of alliance with Philip – although she would now do so on her own terms.

FERIA'S DESPATCH CONCERNING ELIZABETH, 14 November 1558

I arrived here on Wednesday, the ninth of this month, at lunchtime and found the Queen our lady's health to be just as Dr Nunez* describes in his letter to your Majesty. There is, therefore, no hope of her life, but on the contrary each hour I think that they will come to inform me of her death, so rapidly does her condition deteriorate from one day to the next. She was happy to see me, since I brought her news of your Majesty, and to receive the letter, although she was unable to read it. In view of this I felt that there was no time to waste on other matters and sent word to the council to assemble as I wished to talk to them on your Majesty's behalf. This I proceeded to do, and they all came, except the earl of Pembroke and Paget, who is ill. I gave them your Majesty's letter, and spoke to them as your Majesty had instructed me about the peace negotiations. I also declared your Majesty's will on the question of the succession to the kingdom, and told them how pleased your Majesty would be to hear of their good offices with Madame Elizabeth on this matter, reminding them how your Majesty had sought to have this done much earlier, as they all well knew. I stressed this point, giving them to understand – without actually saying so openly – that they were to blame for the delay, because Mason was there[†] and he is greatly favoured by Madame Elizabeth and would report to her all that had passed between us ... As for the other matters I had no further comments to make until I had seen what their commissioners would negotiate with the French. These councillors are extremely frightened of what Madame Elizabeth will do with them. They have received me well, but somewhat as they would a man who came with bulls from a dead pope.

The day after I arrived, I went to a house belonging to a gentleman some twenty three miles from here, where Madame Elizabeth is staying.[‡] I arrived there some time before she might wish to dine, and she received me well, although not as joyfully as she did last time. She asked me to dine with her and the wife of Admiral Clinton who was there when I arrived was also invited. During the meal we laughed and enjoyed ourselves a great deal. After dinner she rose and told me that should I desire to speak with her I might now do so, for she was giving orders that only two or three women who could speak no other language than English should remain in the room ... I gave her to understand that it was your Majesty who had procured her recent recognition as the queen's sister and successor, and not the Queen or the council, and that this was something your Majesty had been trying to secure for some time, as she no doubt realised, for it was common knowledge in the whole kingdom; and I condemned the Queen and the council severely ... She was very open with me on many points, much more than I would have expected, and although it is difficult to judge a person one has known for as short a time as I have known this woman, I shall tell your Majesty what I have been able to gather. She is a very vain and clever woman. She must have been thoroughly schooled in the manner in which her father conducted his affairs, and I am very much afraid that she will not be well disposed in matters of religion, for I see her inclined to govern through men who are believed to be heretics, and I am told that all the women around her definitely are. Apart from this it is evident that she is highly indignant about what has been done to her during the Queen's lifetime. She puts great store by the people, and is very confident that they are all on her side – which is certainly true …

Of the councillors, she is on good terms with the Chancellor,§ Paget, Petre,** and in particular with Mason, whom I understand will be one of the most favoured … she is on good terms with Dr. Wotton [and] with admiral Clinton … She joked with me about what had been said of her marriage with the earl of Arundel.†† She does not get on with him, nor with Pembroke, nor the bishop of Ely – according to what she told me. With the Lord Chamberlain, with the Controller,‡‡ and with Boxall her relations are worse, and with the cardinal worst of all …

I have been told (although not directly by her, as was the case with those I have already mentioned) of certain others with whom she is on very good terms. They are, the Earl of Bedford, Lord Robert, Throgmorton (one who went everywhere with the aforesaid earl during the last war) Peter Carew, and Harrington (the man behind King Edward's uncle – the admiral who was later beheaded – he is reputed to be very able and devilish). I have been told for certain that Cecil, who was King Edward's secretary, will also be secretary to Madame Elizabeth. He is said to be an able and virtuous man, but a heretic …

Last night they administered extreme unction to the queen our lady and today she is better, although there is little hope of her life. Our Lord etc., From London, 14th November 1558.

[*Camden Miscellany*, xxviii (1984), pp. 319-37. Original in Spanish. Copy in AGS, Seccion de Estado, legajos 811-12.]

* Luis Nunez, a Portuguese practising in the Netherlands, sent over with Feria at the request of Alonso de Córdoba.

† Sir John Mason (1503–66). A privy councillor from April 1551, reappointed by Mary in July 1553. Treasurer of the chamber in October 1557, and retained by Elizabeth in that position.

‡ Probably Brockett Hall, the home of Sir John Brockett, who was one of her Hatfield tenants.

§ Nicholas Heath, Archbishop of York.

** Sir William Petre (1505?–72). Principal secretary from 1543 to 1557; Joined Elizabeth's council on 24 November 1558.

†† Henry Fitzalan (1511?–80). Lord steward to both Mary and Elizabeth. Apparently he took his matrimonial chances seriously, and provided lavish entertainments for Elizabeth during her summer progress in 1559.

‡‡ Thomas Thirlby (1506?–70), Bishop of Ely; Edward, Lord Hastings of Loughborough (1519?–72), lord chamberlain; Sir Thomas Cornwallis (1519–1604), controller.

Mary had died surrounded by her loyal familiars, and one of her last thoughts was for the young Jane Dormer, who many years later recorded one of the versions of the queen's death.[21] Jane was betrothed to no less a person than Feria himself, and the queen had delayed their nuptials in the hope of being able to attend. Now that would be impossible, and she expressed her sorrow for having stood in their way. By virtue of this relationship, the ambassador seems to have considered himself an honorary Englishman, but no one else shared this view, and in the light of his generally low opinion of his wife's countrymen, that is hardly surprising. Feria and Jane Dormer were eventually married in December, after Mary had been laid to rest, and they remained in England until the following April, by which time Jane was already pregnant with their first child.[22] As Duchess of Feria she long outlived her husband, dying in about 1610, but she never returned to England and her contacts with her English kindred faded away.

The old queen lay in state at St James' for nearly a month, in accordance with the standard practice, and all the protocols were strictly observed, but Feria found himself distressed by the tone of the comments that he was picking up. In spite of his friendly relations with Elizabeth, he now had only the access of a normal ambassador, and Jane neither had, nor would have wished to have, any place in the new establishment. Nevertheless he understood that the new queen's councillors were being sharply critical of Mary for having sent large sums of money out of the country (which was not true), and he even found himself accused of having spirited away 200,000 ducats (£70,000), which was even less true.[23]

Someone close to the new queen was concerned to undermine her predecessor's reputation, and this came long before there was any question of a religious issue. A memorandum of ways 'in which the realm has suffered great damage' survives among the state papers in the hand of Mr Secretary Cecil, and he may well have been the source of these rumours.[24]

Mary was finally buried on 14 December in King Henry VII's chapel at Westminster Abbey, attended, as she would have wished, by Abbot John Feckenham and his monks. The full traditional rites were observed, and the funeral sermon was preached by John White, Bishop of Winchester. His text he took from the words of Solomon, '*laudavi mortuus magis quam viventes*' [let us praise the dead rather than the living], to which the privy council took exception, but in truth his sermon had nothing to say of the living, being a pure panegyric in the traditional style:

> She was king's daughter, she was a king's sister, she was king's wife; she was a queen and by the same title a king also ... What she suffered in each of these degrees before and since she came to the Crown, I will not chronicle; only this I say, howsoever it pleased God to will her patience to be exercised in the world, she had in all estates the fear of God in her heart.[25]

The ceremonies were not spared. They lasted two days and cost £7,763, approximately the cost of a large warship.

Before the grave was filled, as was customary, Mary's officers broke their wands of office and cast them on top of the coffin. For most of them, this was no mere symbolic act – it marked the end of their public careers. Of the senior officers of the household only the lord great chamberlain (the Earl of Oxford, who hardly ever appeared), the lord steward (the Earl of Arundel) and the treasurer of the chamber (Sir John Mason) were reappointed. The lord chamberlain (Lord Hastings), the vice chamberlain (Sir Henry Bedingfield), the master of the horse (Sir Henry Jerningham) and the comptroller (Sir Robert Freston) all retired into private life.[26] Sir Thomas Cheney, the treasurer of the household, died, and all the ladies of Mary's privy chamber returned to their families. As Feria had feared, the new privy chamber was a hotbed of Protestantism as the queen sought congenial companions. Kate Ashley, banished for suspected heresy in 1556, was back in her quasi-maternal role as principal gentlewoman, supported by members of the Boleyn, Dudley and Cecil families. Susan Clarencius, Mary's long-serving mistress of the wardrobe, went with the Ferias to Spain, and died there in about 1564.[27] The whole climate of the court was changed, foreshadowing the changes that were to take place in both Church and state. The new court was highly educated and overwhelmingly secular; predominantly, but not entirely, Protestant; and almost exclusively English.

Elizabeth was proclaimed the same morning that her sister died, and the Parliament, which had reconvened on 5 November, was immediately dissolved.

> The same day [17 November] between xi and xii afore noon, the Lady Elizabeth was proclaimed Queen Elizabeth, Queen of England, France and Ireland, and defender of the faith, by divers heralds of arms and trumpeters ... [and] ... at afternoon all the churches in London did ring, and at night [they] did make bonfires, and set tables in the street, and did eat and drink and make merry for the new Queen Elizabeth, Queen Mary's sister ...[28]

London, which had endured an uneasy relationship with the old queen, and had been even more uneasy with Philip, was looking for better times. In the country at large there was relief that the succession had been unchallenged, and relief to see the back of King Philip, but Mary herself was mourned in many places. Even the Protestant tirade that appears to have been delivered in York on 24 November (the day the news reached that city), and that was published soon after, mourned the passing of 'a Lady that of her own inclination wished all for the best'. It was not, the author asserted mendaciously, the queen who had been responsible for the wicked persecution, but her 'spiritual council' – the Catholic clergy.[29] Mary had been weak, easily led – both by her bishops and her husband – and, above all, not really English. This had been a constant theme of alehouse gossip throughout the reign: 'She loves another realm better than this'; she would let Philip 'put out Englishmen' from the government and so on. By no means all these mutterers were Protestants. Many of them, when challenged, claimed to be loyal Catholics.

In contrast Elizabeth was not merely her father's daughter, but (as she described herself) 'mere English'. Here was a queen who would not only get rid of pernicious Spanish influences and restore the country's autonomy, but would also restore its pride and self-respect. She was, declared the York pamphleteer, 'a prince of no mingled blood, of Spaniard or stranger, but born mere English here amongst us'.[30] Even the diarist Henry Machyn, who was cautious and preferred the old ways, caught something of the euphoria of the moment. There was 'such shooting of guns as never was heard afore' when the queen processed through the City to the Tower on 28 November.[31]

Thanks to Philip, and to Mary's timely, albeit painfully reluctant, surrender in the matter of the succession, there had been so sign of a challenge. The French remained silent, and Margaret Clifford, who had once been Mary's preferred choice as successor, was confined to the role of chief mourner at her funeral. Elizabeth's supporters, who had been quietly mobilising their retinues against the possibility of trouble, equally quietly disbanded them. The queen was dead – Long live the queen!

Unlike Mary at a similar stage, Elizabeth preferred to keep the courts of Europe guessing about her intentions on all major issues. What was she going to do about the war? Her marriage? The Church? The signals were mixed, but seemed to indicate continuity rather than the reverse. She renewed the commission of the negotiators at Cercamp, and made it clear that she had no intention of surrendering on the issue of Calais; she reaffirmed her intention not to marry, at least for the time being; she insisted upon maintaining the status quo in public worship. About half of her new privy council had served Mary in the same capacity. Paul IV waited for a dutiful communication from his new daughter. However, those with rather sharper eyes, like Feria, saw the situation rather differently. The only senior officer of state to be reappointed was the lord treasurer, the Marquis of Winchester. Heath did not receive the great seal, nor Paget the privy seal. Instead Nicholas Bacon became lord keeper, and the privy seal remained vacant. Mass continued to be celebrated in the Chapel Royal, and there was no repetition of the iconoclastic enthusiasm of 1547; but those imprisoned for heresy and awaiting trial began to be released, and Protestant sermons were again heard at Paul's Cross.[32] The accommodating George Carew took over as Dean of the Chapel Royal from

William Hutchenson, and some of the more optimistic Protestant exiles began to return. Whereas Mary and Gardiner had encouraged Catholics to ignore the ecclesiastical laws that were in place at her accession, and had restored deprived bishops with only the most perfunctory of process, Elizabeth insisted that all existing laws should be obeyed unless (or until) they were changed. At twenty-five she had an advantage of twelve years' youth over her half-sister at the time of her accession, and could afford to be more procrastinating about marriage. In due course the succession would become an issue – but not yet.

Feria had been about two-thirds right in his predictions. He was wrong about Arundel, who retained his post, and most conspicuously about Paget, who continued to bombard the council with unsolicited advice but never regained a place on it. He was also wrong, although less obviously, about Pembroke, Throgmorton and Carew. He was probably right about Pole, but the latter's death made that unprovable, and conspicuously right about William Cecil and Robert Dudley. The latter was not immediately the focus for gossip that he later became, but he was promptly appointed to the prestigious position of master of the horse.[33] This was not a surprise. Elizabeth had known him for a number of years; at one time he had even loaned her money, and they had shared the disfavour and mistrust of Mary as well as the (slightly clandestine) favour of Philip. He was also safely married to Amy, the daughter of Sir John Robsart of Norfolk. So no one saw anything scandalous about his appointment to a position that carried with it – and required – a great deal of unsupervised access to his mistress.

Sir William Cecil was a quite different proposition. He was an experienced politician, having already served one term as secretary of state during the regency of the Duke of Northumberland (Robert Dudley's father) between 1550 and 1553. He had lost this position at Mary's accession, and had maintained a low profile throughout the reign, but he had continued to serve as Elizabeth's receiver general, a position to which he had first been appointed in about 1549, when he had also been secretary to the then lord protector, the Duke of Somerset. When Elizabeth named him as principal secretary at Hatfield on 20 November 1558, the new queen is alleged to have given him a prophetic charge:

... you shall be of my Privy Council and content yourself to take pains for me and my realm. This judgement I have of you, that you will not be corrupted by any manner of gift, and that you will be faithful to the state, and that without respect of my private judgement, you will give me that counsel that you think best.[34]

The source of this statement is a copy, and it is not known just when it was written, but its iconic significance is immense. It is the foundation stone of one of the great political partnerships of English history. Mary had no Cecil. Nor, in all probability, would she have known how to use him if she had found such a person, because when it mattered, her own private judgement was too strong to be gainsaid.

Elizabeth was not lacking in conviction, either about her position as queen or about her faith. The prayers and other personal memoranda that she committed to paper make her Protestantism abundantly clear,[35] but she also distinguished – in a way that Mary was unable to do – between matters fundamental and *adiaphora*, matters indifferent. On the former she would accept the guidance of her clergy, and on the latter she would please herself. The pope was pointedly omitted from the list of European sovereigns who were formally notified of her accession, and Sir Edward Carne was recalled from Rome. He declined to come, preferring to stay in Italy, but that was not the point; his diplomatic status with the Holy See had come to an end. That in itself was not decisive. Elizabeth might have been intending to send some other representative, and by the time that it was clear that she would not, Parliament had created a new religious settlement in England.

By Christmas 1558 it was becoming clear that those who feared for the future of Mary's Church were fully justified. By then it was too late to argue about Elizabeth's right to the throne, and in any case they had no plausible alternative. The best that they could hope to do was to muster sufficient strength in Parliament to deter the queen from whatever changes she may have had in mind. Had Cardinal Pole still been alive he might have orchestrated a more coherent resistance, although given the ambiguous nature of his own relations with Rome that cannot be assumed. As it was, the leadership of the Church fell to Archbishop Heath of York, a conciliatory man who was as convinced of Elizabeth's right to the throne as the most militant Protestant. Elizabeth, however, was a pragmatist, and what mattered most to her was the securing of a broad popular base for her authority. Whatever her intentions, and however strong her personal faith, she would not seek to impose a settlement in defiance of the wishes of Parliament – and therein lay the Catholic hope.

13

THE ENGLAND OF THE TWO QUEENS

Elizabeth, it soon transpired, had a taste for political theatre. Her coronation was fixed for 15 January 1559, and the *joyeuse entrée* into London that traditionally preceded a coronation was a splendid opportunity. All the pageants had been carefully designed in consultation with the revels office, so the appearance of presentations of 'The seat of worthy governance', a 'Decayed commonwealth', and 'Deborah taking council with the judges of Israel' were not coincidental.[1] Elizabeth milked the situation hard:

> To all that wished her Grace well she gave Hearty Thanks, and to such as bade God save her Grace, she said again God save them all, and thanked with all her heart. So that, on either side there was nothing but gladness, nothing but prayer, nothing but comfort ...

Admittedly this account comes from Richard Mulcaster's official narrative, but it was the kind of interactive performance of which Mary would have been quite incapable. A little later in the proceedings she was presented with an English bible, and 'as soon as she had received the book, kissed it, and with both her hands held up the same, and so laid it upon her breast'. The Protestant iconography was plain for all to see. The pageant of Deborah was even more explicit. The child who presented it started with:

> Jabin, of Canaan king, had long by force of arms,

Oppressed the Israelites; which for God's people went;
But GOD minding at last, for to redress their harms
The worthy DEBORAH as judge among them sent.[2]

The implication could hardly have been clearer. The City, with the queen's connivance and approval, was petitioning for a new start, no less than a revolution in Church and State. 'Time,' she said at the presentation of one pageant, 'hath brought me hither.' The reference to Mary's motto, that Truth is the daughter of Time, was also quite explicit. When, at a solemn High Mass, the queen walked out at the rite of Elevation, the gesture was both clear and characteristic. At the coronation mass itself there was no Elevation, on the queen's instructions, and Elizabeth herself communicated in both kinds. The mass was permitted because it was in accordance with the existing law – but its core symbolism was rejected.[3]

No one who had witnessed any part of this ceremonial can therefore have been surprised by the bills that were introduced into the Parliament that met on 23 January. Two of these are relevant in this context: one restoring the royal supremacy over the Church, and the second restoring the Protestant Church order of Edward VI. The first of these passed the House of Commons without any controversy. In the House of Lords it was solidly opposed by the bench of bishops, led by Archbishop Heath, who spoke strongly and cogently against it.[4] However, the bishops numbered only fifteen in a House of about fifty peers, and although they attracted some lay support, it was nothing like enough to defeat the bill. The uniformity bill also passed the Commons with only a few dissenting voices, but this time it was a different story in the Lords. The bishops were again solidly opposed, as was to be expected, and they attracted considerable lay support. Deadlock or a government defeat seemed likely when the assembly adjourned for Easter. There was considerable speculation about what would happen next. Some believed that the queen had achieved her real objective with the passage of the supremacy bill, and would be content with that – at least for the time being. Others, who knew her commitment better, looked forward to a renewed struggle after the recess. Meanwhile, the convocations, the clerical assemblies that met alongside Parliament, had in a sense cut off her retreat. They had unanimously and unequivocally reasserted a full Catholic position.[5] This had no force in law as against the decisions of the Parliament proper, but it did mean that there was no prospect of being able to find a bench of bishops for a restored Henrician Church. Consequently, although the laity would probably have been happy with such a solution, from the queen's point of view there was no point in settling for supremacy without uniformity.

What actually happened savours of sharp practice. On the initiative of the council (which probably means Cecil), a disputation was arranged between the existing establishment and the challenging reformers. This was a common tactic, which had been used all over Europe when issues of the faith were in question. Heath was perfectly willing to accept such a trial of strength, probably thinking that he and his colleagues held the trump cards. However, for reasons that have never been satisfactorily explained, two of the Catholic disputants, both of them bishops, ignored the procedural rules that had been laid down and agreed by both sides. When they persisted in their refusal to conform, they were imprisoned for contempt.[6] The disputation ended inconclusively, but when Parliament reconvened, two of the fifteen bishops were missing. Seizing the opportunity, Bacon pushed the uniformity bill to a division in the Lords, and won by a single vote. So when Parliament was dissolved on 8 May, a new religious settlement came into force. The heresy laws disappeared, and with them both the papal authority and the Catholic faith. Within six months all but one of the surviving bishops of Mary's reign had been deprived of their sees, and a new Protestant bench was in place, of whom fourteen had been in exile under Mary.[7]

This was Mary's most critical defeat: worse than her childlessness; worse even than her failure to prevent Elizabeth's accession. John Foxe hailed it as the providential vindication of all that the persecuted Protestants had stood for, and in a sense he was right. Mary's ecclesiastical restoration, although it appeared to be so popular, had yet failed to win hearts and minds where it actually mattered most, among the political elite that represented the realm in Parliament. In the House of Commons, which was the more truly representative body, although not the more powerful, only a handful of voices were raised in defence of the status quo; and in the House of Lords no more than a dozen lay peers stood with the bishops on the strongest part of their agenda.

Why did the restored Catholic Church fail to strike root where it mattered most? One reason, which particularly affected the peers, was that the new settlement was clearly Elizabeth's will, just as the old one had been Mary's will. It required both courage and conviction to stand against that will in so public a forum. The Protestant settlement had gone by default partly for that reason in 1553, although Mary had been forced to bargain hard for the return of the papacy. The persecution had also been widely unpopular. Too often it gave the impression of being selectively vindictive and amenable to private agendas. Englishmen were not necessarily heretics at heart, but they did not hate heresy, nor associate it with political subversion in the way that the council sought to persuade them. Sixteenth-century men and women were not squeamish about public executions, and often cheered the demise of felons and traitors, but they did not see heresy as a threat in the same way. Finally, and perhaps most importantly, the Catholic Church became associated with 'foreign tyranny'. Henrician propaganda against the papacy had been more effective than anyone realised, and if anyone had asked the man in the street for his religious preference at any time between 1547 and 1560 he would have said 'religion as King Henry left it'. This was the Old Faith with an English face, and had a resonance that neither the Roman nor the Protestant regimes had. Those who wrote in defence of the Catholic restoration were (for the most part) dutiful or even enthusiastic about the pope,[8] but that did not represent general opinion. Most English people – and that included the governing elite – thought of the pope as an interfering foreigner who took money out of the country and did very little in return.

Worse still for Mary's popularity was the Spanish connection. Why Spaniards should have been so unpopular is a difficult question, bearing in mind that 90 per cent of Englishmen had never met one, and the French, not the Spanish, were the 'ancient enemy'. London was a special case, because it was so open to influences from Germany and the Low Countries. In spite of the formal courtesies that had greeted his visit there in 1549, Philip had not gone down well with the northern Netherlanders, who contrasted his insular Spanishness with his father's cosmopolitanism. In Holland and Zeeland Spaniards were regarded as aloof, arrogant – and tyrannical if they were given a chance.

These attitudes travelled readily across the North Sea. There were also old resentments over how English merchants had been treated in Spain after Henry had repudiated Catherine of Aragon – what Renard called 'merchants' quarrels'.[9] However, London was not England, and it may well be that foreign observers (upon whom we are so heavily dependent for our information) were too strongly influenced by attitudes in the capital. Philip's favourable reception at Winchester would suggest that. Here it is probable that the elite were more fearful than the population at large: fearful of losing lands and offices to intrusive foreigners; fearful of losing places and influence at court; fearful (quite unrealistically) of being coerced by a Spanish Inquisition; and perhaps above all, fearful of seeing the common law subverted. These fears, picked up and amplified by a few strident propagandists, must have filtered down through society in the course of the reign, strengthened no doubt by powerful – although extremely vague – fears of a foreign king on principle.

So Philip got the blame for an unpopular persecution, which was quite unfair; for an unpopular war, which was fair enough; for the loss of Calais; and for everything else that had gone wrong. The fact that he was at daggers drawn with the pope after 1555 made no difference at all, and his bad relations with the merchants of London (who had a lot of contacts) undoubtedly made the situation worse. As a result of feelings so generated, which were often inarticulate but none the less strong for all that, the Old Religion lost something of its Englishness – it became contaminated by both Rome and Spain. As a result Protestantism, which had appeared to be a German or Swiss intrusion under Edward VI, began to acquire patriotic credentials. It would be wrong to exaggerate this tendency, and it could easily have been irrelevant if things had worked out differently in 1559. But as it was, it not only helped to get Elizabeth's Acts of Supremacy and Uniformity through their critical stages in Parliament, but it also helped to make them enforceable afterwards.

The true legacy of Mary's major project, therefore, the restored Catholic Church, was not a long-term Catholic establishment, but rather an energetic Catholic opposition and lingering hatred, bitterness and suspicion. It is often said that Mary's only mistake was to die relatively young. Had she survived even a few more years, the shadows of influenza and of war would have retreated, the Church would have settled down, and Elizabeth would have become so accustomed to dissembling that she would have forgotten where her real faith lay.[10] Philip, despairing of offspring, would have contrived to annul his marriage and the realm would have been freed from his contaminating presence. Mary, returned to the status of *femme seule*, would have been the main beneficiary.

Like all such historical speculations, however, this makes a number of assumptions. If Philip had succeeded in annulling his marriage, which is by no means certain, could Mary have survived the trauma and humiliation? Emotionally she never ceased to be dependent upon her husband, and the strains that that induced were never resolved. Even if her health had been more robust than it was, could she have lived with the thought that she had loved, and slept with, a man who was not really her husband? Similarly, there is an assumption that the Protestant opposition would simply have withered away in time. There is absolutely no sign of that happening. The active leadership within England had been largely eliminated by 1558, but the constant stream of ordinary men and women who were prepared to die for their faith showed no sign of drying up. The leadership abroad was also becoming increasingly radical. Men such as Cranmer and Ridley had been loyal upholders of the royal supremacy, and advocates of non-resistance – that had been part of their problem in facing a royal commission – but the likes of Christopher Goodman and John Ponet had no time for non-resistance. If a ruler was 'ungodly' (that is, Catholic) he or she should be overthrown, by force if necessary.[11] Given the powerful suspicions that lingered on among the lay peers and gentry about the return of 'sacerdotalism', priestly power – suspicions that were reflected in the parliamentary votes of 1559 – it is by no means certain that the Church could have gone on enjoying its restored authority and prestige unchallenged. If Philip had remained king, there could well have been another Elizabethan rebellion, which might have succeeded. If Philip had ceased to be king, and Mary had survived, there could well have been religious civil war on the French model. We do not know; but it is not safe to argue that if Mary had lived another twenty years England would have enjoyed a comfortable and safe Catholic future, at least into the following century, and perhaps longer.

Mary's reign was a failure in terms of her own aims and priorities. Not all this was the queen's fault. She could not be blamed for harvest failures, bad weather, influenza or her own childlessness and early death. However, she did make mistakes, some of which were serious, and the idea that she was simply a victim of misfortune at the time, and of a malign Protestant historiography after her death, is no more satisfactory than the legend of Bloody Mary.[12]

In the first place Mary did not deal wisely with her council. Once she was settled in power she should have dropped most, if not all, of the 'Framlingham council'. They were loyal to her, and she liked them, but they were not of adequate experience and ability to run the country. She should also have made up her mind sooner and more steadfastly about whom she was going to trust. Dithering about this not only sent out uncertain signals, but also opened the way for the plausible and selfserving Simon Renard to establish a confidential influence that should never have been tolerated. She should also have been more willing to knock heads together when her councillors fell out, as they were bound to do. As it was she left that to Philip, and the divisions reappeared as soon as he had left. These weaknesses were partly the result of inexperience, and partly of a lack of self-confidence. She expected her council to give consensual, if not unanimous, advice on all important issues – and of course it did not do so. This left her vulnerable to suggestions from people like Renard that her council was not competent, or even that some of its members were disloyal, when in fact it was simply behaving like a normal Tudor council. The privy council (unlike a modern cabinet) had no collective responsibility. Each member was sworn individually to give advice in accordance with his own conscience and judgement, so of course there were differences of opinion on most issues. Elizabeth (who had no more experience than Mary when she came to the throne) understood that perfectly well, and she preferred divided counsels because they increased her freedom of action.[13] Mary, like any monarch, relied more on some councillors than others, and when the 'inner ring' was formalised into the select council, this seems to have worked reasonably well at a political level – but that was Philip's initiative rather than the queen's. The Marian council worked best at an administrative level, when its members sat on sub-committees and special commissions. This was a system that emerged when Paget took over as lord privy seal at the beginning of 1556, and how much Mary herself was involved in its planning we do not know. One of the few occasions upon which the council did give the queen consensual advice on a political issue was over the declaration of war in 1557, and she ended by rejecting it.

Mary's second mistake was her marriage. This error arose very largely from the weakness of her independent judgement, because she virtually referred the most crucial decision of her life to her cousin, the Emperor Charles V, who had not the slightest right to interfere. Because it suited his own agenda, he advanced the suit of his own son Philip, conveniently a widower. There were sound arguments in favour of such a match: he was of the most royal blood in Europe, a good Catholic and of great resources. Also, because of the circumstances, his father was prepared to concede generous terms, limiting Philip's authority in England and guaranteeing the country's autonomy. At the same time there were sound arguments against, which were brushed aside. Philip was heir to his father's Spanish empire, and would soon have little enough time to be King of England. He was also purely Spanish in upbringing, outlook and language; he could be expected to have no knowledge of England or its ways. The English were deeply distrustful of any foreign king, and Philip was not the right person to allay those fears. They did not trust him to observe the marriage treaty willingly – and they were right. Also, because of the way in which her decision was reached, Mary did not consult her own council until after it had been made – an omission that, in the eyes of some hostile commentators, invalidated the whole marriage.[14] In the event Philip did observe the marriage treaty, although not willingly, and did not do much lasting harm – or good – in England. At a personal level the marriage failed, but that was hardly Mary's fault. She gained no children and very little emotional support, in return for a high level of investment and commitment on her own part. Philip's Spanishness not only offended his English subjects, it caused them to remember that Mary was herself half Spanish, and that was not good for the images of either of them.

Mary's third mistake, although perhaps an unavoidable one, was to allow Philip to push through the reconciliation with Rome. Most Englishmen regarded the papacy with indifference, but Philip's role in ending the schism gave the Church a foreign face that it could have done without. Furthermore, it was the restoration of Roman jurisdiction that opened the way for a persecution of quite unprecedented severity. As a policy, this also turned out to be a mistake, although it probably did not deserve the prominence that it later achieved. If Mary had been prepared to wait, to put through the reconciliation on her own authority and in her own time, and if she had been less militantly coercive, the whole future of the Catholic Church might have been different. In taking the course that she did, Mary not only misjudged the climate of opinion in England, she put her own conscience ahead of the political needs of the realm. She was perfectly entitled to do that, but it was not wise. Mary's conscience was a curse. It worked positively in impelling her to claim the throne in July 1553, but it deceived her into believing that God had given her the crown with a divine mission to restore the True Faith in all particulars. It also blinded her to the consciences of others, and made her quite unable to see that men and women might have genuine convictions that differed from her own.[15] Heretics were in her eyes simply criminals who had broken the laws of God, and upon whom the infliction of punishment was a religious duty.

When Mary's conscience spoke to her clearly, it made her strong and implacable, but it seriously impaired her judgement. When her conscience was not engaged, Mary was a gentle, humane creature, much loved by those who knew her well. She was also inclined to be indecisive, and was sometimes blandly disregarded, both by her husband and her council. She complained on one occasion that she spent all her time shouting at her councillors, to no effect. When Elizabeth threw a tantrum, everyone within earshot quaked.

Another weakness, although it was hardly a mistake, was her lack of image consciousness. Mary was absolutely convinced of her own royalty, but at a loss to know how to express it. As far as she was concerned, royalty was a masculine thing, expressed through war games and military prowess. The only images open to a woman were those of virgin or of wife, and both (particularly the latter) were images of dependence rather than authority.[16] She could dress magnificently, and carefully choreograph her appearances with Philip to emphasise her independence, but none of this was satisfactory. She hardly understood the concept of Englishness, and, unlike her dazzling sister, she kept her sexuality private and regarded her femininity as a crippling disadvantage in a ruler. So Mary never worked out how to present herself, and her surviving portraits reflect that. In these she is a grim, once handsome woman, magnificently but rather indiscriminately clad. There is no mystery and no power. When the need arose, she could speak powerfully and persuasively in public, as she demonstrated at the Guildhall in January 1554 when threatened by Wyatt's rebellion, but the kind of interaction with the crowd at which Elizabeth excelled was quite outside her repertoire. Mary knew how to be pious in public, but exploited it very little, never processing to shrines in the manner of her mother, nor making public offerings in the manner of her father. By contrast, Philip was very image conscious, but in the most conventional manner. His war games have to be seen in that context, because his image of a king was as a warrior. His imagery was heraldic and very Habsburg,[17] so that he took little trouble to present himself as an English king, even if he had known how to do so – which manifestly he did not. The contrast with the intense theatricality of Elizabeth is startling. Where Mary hid her sexuality (as it were) under a bushel, Elizabeth set hers upon a hill. Elizabeth was equally royal, but also beautiful, mysterious and manipulative. She had all the armoury for controlling men that her sister so conspicuously lacked, and it did not need a forty-five-year reign to demonstrate the difference. Even if she had lived a lot longer, and been more successful than she was, Mary would never have made the impact upon history that Elizabeth did – she was just a very different kind of woman.

In emphasising Mary's weaknesses and mistakes, however, we must remember that there was another side to her reign. In some respects it was a period of very positive development, although not, probably, in the way that Mary would have wanted. Most importantly, she was forced to confront the gender of the crown. There had never been a ruling queen in England. The much-discussed Matilda in the 1140s had claimed the throne, and fought a civil war to obtain it, but she had never been generally accepted, much less crowned. Consequently, although there was no Salic law[18] to prevent it, such a succession was not an issue that had ever been seriously discussed. Kings were soldiers, lawgivers, defenders of the realm and righters of wrongs. Queens were consorts, sealers of alliances, fertile (if you were lucky), pious and (again if you were lucky) submissive. Sometimes in practice queens were termagants or courtesans, but that was never their image. Now for the first time England had a sovereign lady. As long as she was unmarried this did not present too much of a problem. The common law was familiar with the idea of the *femme seule* – the virgin or widow who controlled her own property and ran her life as she thought best. But suppose she married? By the common law the property of the *femme couvert* (i.e. married woman) passed to her husband in full ownership for the duration of his life. Did this apply to the crown? As we have seen, the issue was resolved by statute. No gender limitations applied to the royal authority, and the queen, married or unmarried, was also the king.[19] This created terrible problems of conscience for Mary, as she struggled to be both a dutiful wife and a queen, but it laid down a principle for the future from which several ruling queens benefited – not the least of whom was Elizabeth I. And without benefiting from so many of Mary's unintentional lessons, good and bad, concerning the exercise of queenly power in a male world, would Elizabeth's reign and image then have taken the shapes they did? Might one of the virgin queen's marriage negotiations have actually been realised, had the spectre of Mary's unpopular Spanish marriage not always been lurking? These are psychological speculations, of course, but ones justified by the context.

The other beneficiary was Parliament, whose right to legislate on all such issues was confirmed. Parliament gained in many ways from Mary's reign. In the beginning, her successful bid for the crown established the validity of Henry's 1544 succession act, which had been challenged by Edward's 'Device'. The queen herself scarcely perceived this, because she thought of herself as the heir by inviolable hereditary right, but both her council and her Parliament thought of her as the heir by law. Even more significantly, she repealed both her brother's and her father's ecclesiastical laws. Logically, she should have regarded all such statutes as concerning matters beyond the scope of mere laws and simply ignored them. Pole advised her to do just that, but in this case her conscience did not speak unequivocally, and she allowed the advice of her council to prevail. By this means it became accepted on both sides of the religious divide that the lawful way to make a religious settlement for England was in Parliament. Consequently no challenge of principle was mounted against the Acts of Supremacy and Uniformity in 1559. As we have seen, Mary fought a long and hard rearguard action against accepting Elizabeth as her successor, but in the end she faced reality: if she wanted to insist on some other successor, the country would be faced with civil war. Rather than run that risk, she yielded and acknowledged her half-sister, thereby again confirming the order laid down in 1544. By the time that the next succession crisis occurred in the 1590s events had made the Act of Succession obsolete, and it was ignored without any danger to the authority of Parliament, but that would not have been the case in 1558.

In many respects, Mary governed well. The early Elizabethan myth that Mary's successor had inherited a kingdom feeble, rudderless and in chaos was far from the truth. In spite of the harvest failures caused by bad weather, and the resulting hardship, there was no repetition of the outbursts of 1549. Nor, in spite of the constant alarms and frequent plots, were there any significant rebellions, apart from that of Sir Thomas Wyatt. The country was religiously divided, but in spite of some claims to the contrary the Protestant minority (perhaps 10 per cent of the population, very unevenly spread) had as yet mounted no political challenge. That may not have continued, given the radical ideas that were becoming current, but it had not happened when Mary died. The courts all functioned normally, and apart from one misguided attempt to impose martial law on hostile pamphleteers, no special measures were deemed to be necessary.[20] The memorandum addressed to Elizabeth that described the King of France as 'bestriding the realm, with one foot in Scotland and the other in Calais; was alarmist exaggeration. There were French forces in Scotland, but they were scarcely a threat, being tied down by domestic rebellion. The garrison of Berwick, warned by the example of Calais, was at full strength and the borders were effectively organised for defence.[21] Militarily, England looked weak, because mobilisation had been sporadic and half hearted, but the system of lieutenancies, creating regional military commanders, was potentially strong, and the navy was fully deployed. The idea that Mary neglected the navy until activated by Philip is mistaken. Philip was sufficiently interested in the English navy to keep copies of ship lists in his archive at Simancas, but Mary had never neglected it, as the treasurer's accounts demonstrate conclusively.[22] London was discontented because Philip sided consistently with its competitors, and Mary did nothing to redress the balance, but it was during this period (in 1555) that the north-eastern voyages of the previous reign bore fruit in the form of the Muscovy Company, and the newly discovered enterprise of the City was scarcely checked by the king's hostility. That might have happened in due course, but Philip's attitude made little difference in the short term.

Financially, the reign ended on a low note because of the war, but the English debt never went out of control (as Philip's did), and, thanks to the efficiency of Thomas Gresham, English credit in Antwerp remained sound. At the time of her death, and after eighteen months of war, Mary owed about £300,000, mostly in Antwerp. This cost more than £40,000 a year to service, but because credit was sound and because repayments could be recycled through the Merchant Adventurers that was bearable.[23] Whether this would have continued, given the rising levels of discontent in the City, we do not know, but it lasted Mary's lifetime and was quickly picked up by her sister – whose relations with London were much more positive. One of the grouses that Elizabeth's council had against her predecessor was that she had returned much-needed revenue to the Church. This was true up to a point. The traditional Church dues of 'first fruits' had been returned, or rather set off against the remaining monastic pensions, but in fact Mary never carried out her expressed intention of returning all ecclesiastical lands still in the hands of the crown. She went on selling them for her own benefit, as her predecessors had done, and as Elizabeth was to continue to do. The new queen ignored her predecessor's will, so the only crown revenues that remained in Church hands had been the endowments of the half dozen or so religious houses that had been founded, a matter of some £3,500 a year. As we have seen, the early months of the new reign were full of rumours of financial impropriety and extravagance, involving Philip, Feria, Cardinal Pole and the Church in general. There was hardly any fire to justify all this smoke. Philip had put far more money into England than he had taken out of it, and the re-endowment of the Church had been at a very modest level.

In a way the Church had been another success story. This fact has been concealed partly by high-profile stories of the persecution, and partly by the fact that its achievement was largely dismantled after Mary's death. There was insufficient time for Pole to do much about improving the quality of the existing clergy, but the universities were overhauled, seminaries decreed (although never established), and several effective manuals of pastoral guidance published.[24] There was strong emphasis upon discipline and the sacraments, but neither preaching nor instruction were neglected. Traditional lay piety recovered strongly, but allegiance to the papacy remained weak, and restored English

Catholicism continued to show several idiosyncratic traits derived from its Henrician and Edwardian past rather than the Counter-Reformation. Pole and his Spanish helpers were keenly aware of the new devotional fashions and theological emphases that were sweeping the Continent, but transmitted these ideas to the English Church only very incompletely.[25] What English Catholics yearned for was an 'English face' to the Church, but circumstances largely conspired to deprive them of this. As a result, the majority slipped easily into the new conformity when it was offered to them after 1559, and the main legacy of Pole's strenuous efforts lay in the large number of dedicated Catholic intellectuals who abandoned Oxford and Cambridge for the Continent in the early 1560s. For many years Catholic survivalism continued to haunt the Elizabethan Church, as conservative clergy and laity conspired to circumvent the law, but it was not from that quarter that the dangerous challenge began to come after 1570. The seminary and Jesuit missions that then began were theologically sophisticated, pastorally committed, and politically subversive. They were also the result of the intellectual exodus, and hence of Pole's rigorous policies. At the end of the day, their political nature brought about their failure because most Englishmen, however conservative their views, preferred to give their allegiance to their own crown rather than to a distant Italian, even if he did claim to be the Vicar of Christ.

If Mary's failure can be attributed to a single factor, it was that she and her regime were seen as insufficiently English. This was ironic, as she had never set foot outside England, but the combination of a Spanish mother, a Spanish husband, a cardinal archbishop who had spent twenty years in Italy, the allegiance to a foreign pope and dependence upon an Imperial protector was all simply too much for her insular subjects. They were accustomed to rulers who had defied Europe, in arms or in faith, and had no desire for the safety of a Habsburg embrace and a Universal Church. Elizabeth, it soon transpired, was much more to their taste, and she was so concerned to distance herself from Mary that there has been a general failure to recognise how much she owed to her predecessor. It is time that England's first queen was better appreciated.

NOTES

Full author names and publication dates are given for the first citation of a book or article; thereafter, short references are used.

Abbreviations used in these Notes:

APC Acts of the Privy Council.

BL British Library.

Cal. Span. Calendar of State Papers, Spanish.

Cal. Ven. Calendar of State Papers, Venetian.

L &P Letters and Papers ... of the Reign of Henry VIII.

ODNB Oxford Dictionary of National Biography.

SP State Papers (at the National Archives).

TNA The National Archives.

INTRODUCTION

1. Andrea C. Gasten, 'The Kingship of Philip and Mary', in Wim de Groot (ed.) *The Seventh Window* (2005), pp. 215-25.

1 THE CHILD

1. They had married in 1468, when they were the heirs to their respective kingdoms. J. H. Hillgarth, *The Spanish Kingdoms, 1250–1516* (2 Vols, 1978).

2. For a full discussion of these celebrations and their significance, see Sydney Anglo, *Spectacle, Pageantry and Early Tudor Policy* (1969), pp. 98-103.

3. It was the consummation that created the blood relationship, not the ceremony of marriage, which constituted only a bar of 'public honesty'. Perhaps by oversight, this lesser impediment was not dispensed.

4. Garrett Mattingly, *Catherine of Aragon* (1942), pp. 57-9. In spite of its age, this is still the best biography of Catherine.

5. Edward Hall, *The Union of the two noble and Illustre families Yorke and Lancaster*, ed. Henry Ellis (1809), [*Chronicle*] p. 519.

6. *Cal. Span.*, ii, 164. J. J. Scarisbrick, *Henry VIII* (1968), p. 51.

7. BL Harleian MS 3504, f. 232.

8. This treaty was finally concluded in August 1521. BL Cotton MS Galba B VII, f 102. *L&P*, iii, 1508.

9. *L&P*, ii, 3802. D. Loades, *Mary Tudor: A Life* (1989), pp. 346-7.

10. *L&P*, iii, 970.

11. Mattingly, *Catherine of Aragon*, pp. 140-1.

12. *De institutione foeminae christinae* contained a preface clarifying Vives's intentions. 'Let her be given pleasure in stories which teach the art of life ... stories which tend to some commendation of virtue and detestation of vice.' Maria Dowling, *Humanism in the Age of Henry VIII* (1987), p. 225.

13. Loades, *Mary Tudor*, pp. 20-1.

14. G. R. Elton, *The Tudor Constitution* (1982), pp. 202-3. S. J. Gunn, *Early Tudor Government, 1485–1558* (1995).

15. Although Mary is referred to as princess, there was no official creation for Wales between 1504 (Henry) and 1610 (Henry Stuart). A creation was planned for Edward in 1547, but was overtaken by Henry VIII's death.

16. W. R. B. Robinson, 'Princess Mary's Itinerary in the Marches of Wales, 1525–1527: A Provisional Record', *Historical Research*, 71 (1998), pp. 233-52.

17. Ibid, pp. 248-9.

18. A parliamentary subsidy had been granted in 1523, and resistance to this new imposition proved unbreakable. Henry's confidence in Wolsey was severely shaken in consequence. G. W. Bernard, *War, Taxation, and Rebellion in Early Tudor England* (1986).

19. Robert Wakefield is the scholar who is alleged to have convinced the king of this important interpretation. E. Surtz and V Murphy (eds), *The Divorce Tracts of Henry VIII* (1988), p. xiii.

20. Andre Chastel (trans. Beth Archer), *The Sack of Rome, 1527* (1983).

21. Loades, *Mary Tudor*, p. 45.

2 DISRUPTION

1. This was the so-called 'Levirate', which required a man to take the widow of his deceased brother in marriage in order to protect her. Henry claimed that this was 'ambiguous'. Surtz and Murphy, *The Divorce Tracts of Henry VIII*, p. xiii.

2. Scarisbrick, *Henry VIII*, pp. 198-240.

3. Loades, *Mary Tudor*, p. 55.

4. For a full discussion of the pros and (mostly) cons of Wolsey's dismissal, see Peter Gwynn, *The King's Cardinal: The Rise and Fall of Thomas Wolsey* (1990, pp. 587-98.

5. An account of some of these sharp exchanges is given in Eric Ives, *Anne Boleyn* (1986), pp. 154-5, drawing mainly on *Cal. Ven.*, 1527–33.

6. Loades, *Mary Tudor*, p. 61. Augustino Scarpellino to the Duke of Milan, 16 December 1530. *Cal. Ven.*, 1527–33, p. 642.

7. Beverley Murphy, *The Bastard Prince* (2001), pp. 107-8.

8. N. H. Nicolas, *The Privy Purse Expenses of Henry VIII* (1827), p.146.

9. Loades, *Mary Tudor*, pp. 78-9. Mattingly, *Catherine of Aragon*, pp. 292-3.

10. The implications of this claim, and its rejection, are discussed by Scarisbrick, *Henry VIII*, pp. 261-73.

11. *L&P*, VII, 296. Ives, *Anne Boleyn*, pp. 246-8.

12. These charges were based on the fiction that Wolsey had exercised his jurisdiction without royal licence. The convocations paid the king £118,000 for their discharge. TNA KB29/162, r.12. Scarisbrick, *Henry VIII*, pp. 274-5.

13. In order to secure a settlement in England, Henry had to be sure of his control over his own clergy. Scarisbrick, 'The Pardon of the Clergy, 1531', *Cambridge Historical Journal*, XII (1956) pp. 25 ff.

14. *The Manner of the Triumph at Calais and Boulogne* (1532), printed in A. F. Pollard, *Tudor Tracts* (1903), pp. 1-8. This describes 'My Lady Mary' as following 'My Lady Marquess of Pembroke' in one of the dances. Pollard identifies this lady as Mary Boleyn – but the intention was obviously to give the impression that the king's daughter had been present.

15. Diarmaid MacCulloch, *Thomas Cranmer* (1996), pp. 69-76.

16. *The Noble Triumphant Coronation of Queen Anne* (1533). Pollard, *Tudor Tracts*, pp. 11-35.

17. *Letters and Papers*, VII, 1208.

18. Giustinian to the Signory,13 March 1533, *Cal. Ven.*, *1527–33*, p. 863.
19. Loades, *Mary Tudor*, p. 72.
20. BL Harleian MS 6807, f. 7.
21. *L&P*, VI, 1186. Loades, *Mary Tudor*, pp. 74-5.
22. BL Arundel MS 151, f 194. *L&P*, VI, 1126.
23. Loades, *Mary Tudor*, p. 78.

3 TRAUMA
1. *L&P*, VII, 296. Ives, *Anne Boleyn*, pp. 247-8.
2. For a more detailed account of some of these abrasive encounters see Eric Ives, *The Life and Death of Anne Boleyn* (2004), pp. 197-9.
3. Expenses of the Princess Elizabeth's Household, 25 March 1535. *L&P*, VIII, 440.
4. Loades, *Mary Tudor*, pp. 82-3.
5. *L&P*, VII, 1206 and 1336. Despatches of 30 September and 31 October 1534.
6. Ibid., IX, 596.
7. Loades, *Mary Tudor*, pp. 86-7.
8. Statute 25 Henry VIII, cap. 22. *Statutes of the Realm*, III, pp. 471-4.
9. She claimed that Mary's 'ennuy' had cleared up completely after a visit from her father as early as 1529 – which is directly contradicted by the evidence of the accounts. Marillac to Francis I, 12 October 1541. *L&P*, XVI, 1253.
10. Ives, *Life and Death of Anne Boleyn*, pp. 194-5.
11. Mattingly, *Catherine of Aragon*, p. 309.
12. David Loades, *Henry VIII and His Queens* (1997) pp. 90-1.
13. Ives, *Life and Death of Anne Boleyn*, pp. 296-8.
14. For a full account of this thesis, see Retha M. Warnicke, *The Rise and Fall of Anne Boleyn* (1989), and for a refutation, Ives, *Life and Death of Anne Boleyn*, pp. 296-7.
15. *Cal. Span.*,1536–38, p.137.
16. Ives, *Life and Death of Anne Boleyn*, pp. 326-7.
17. For a full list of the sources describing Anne's execution, see ibid., pp. 419-20.
18. Loades, *Mary Tudor*, p. 98. Even Chapuys admitted that there were murmurings in London about the manner (and speed) of Anne's despatch.
19. MacCulloch, *Thomas Cranmer*, pp.158-9.
20. There is a portrait of Jane by Hans Holbein in the Kunsthistorisches Museum, Vienna, which has been frequently reproduced.
21. Loades, *Mary Tudor*, pp. 98-9.
22. Ibid., p. 99.
23. *L&P*, X, 968.
24. BL Cotton MS Otho C.X, f. 278. *L&P*, X, 1022.
25. Loades, *Mary Tudor*, p. 101.
26. Ibid. None of the documents surviving from this crisis are precisely dated, so the timetable is reconstructed.
27. Chapuys to the Emperor, 1 July 1536. *L&P*, XI, 7.
28. Mary to Cromwell, probably 30 June 1536. *L&P*, X, 1186. For Susan Clarencius see *ODNB*.
29. BL Cotton MS Vespasian C. XIV, f. 246. Loades, *Mary Tudor*, p. 106.
30. Ibid., p.104.

4 RESTITUTION
1. *L&P*, XI, 132. Ives, *Life and Death of Anne Boleyn*, p. 198.
2. There are many discussions of the Pilgrimage of Grace, and of the Pilgrims' attitude towards Mary. The most recent is R. W. Hoyle, *The Pilgrimage of Grace and the Politics of the 1530s* (2001), especially p. 347.
3. Thomas F. Mayer, *Reginald Pole: Prince and Prophet* (2000), pp. 62-78.
4. When asked to adjudicate the rival claims of the Duke of York and Prince Edward in 1460, the House of Lords had declared that they had no competence 'in so high a mystery'.

5. Loades, *Mary Tudor*, p. 110. *L&P*, XII, 445.
6. *The Privy Purse Expenses of the Princess Mary*, ed. F. E. Madden (1831), p.1.
7. *L&P*, XII, 637, 1314.
8. *The State Papers of King Henry VIII*, (1830–52), I, pt. ii, p. 551.
9. Edward Hall, *Chronicle*, ed. H. Ellis (1809), p. 825.
10. *L&P*, XIV, 655. Loades, *Mary Tudor*, p.115.
11. Retha M. Warnicke, *The Marrying of Anne of Cleves* (2000), p. 174.
12. Hazel Pierce, *Margaret Pole, Countess of Salisbury, 1473–1541. Loyalty, Lineage and Leadership* (2003), pp. 115-40. Dr Pierce concludes that the evidence against the Poles and the Courtenays, although not strong enough for any modern court, was sufficient to force the king to act.
13. Loades, *Mary Tudor*, p. 116.
14. Ibid.
15. Chapuys to the Queen of Hungary, 17 December 1542. *L&P*, XVII, 1212.
16. There is a portrait attributed to Wilhelm Scrots in London's National Portrait Gallery, which is the only authentic likeness. Loades, *Henry VIII and His Queens* (2000), pp. 137-8.
17. Catherine's *Lamentations of a Sinner*, which was not published until 1548, is unambiguously Protestant in places. However, nothing so revealing was published in Henry's lifetime. By the time that it appeared, Mary had left the queen dowager's household.
18. Nicholas Udall, *Paraphrases of Erasmus* (London, 1548); preface to Luke.
19. The only source for the story of the conspiracy against Catherine is John Foxe, *Acts and Monuments* (edition 1583), pp. 1,242-4. For a discussion of its provenance, and of the possible role of Stephen Gardiner, see G. Redworth, *In Defence of the Church Catholic. The Life of Stephen Gardiner* (1990), pp. 232-7.
20. Statute 35 Henry VIII, c.1.
21. Scarisbrick, *Henry VIII*, p. 448.
22. Loades, *Mary Tudor*, pp. 123-5.
23. Marillac to Francis I, 27 December 1539 *L&P*, XIV, 744.
24. *L&P*, XVII, 371.
25. For a full discussion of Pole's views, and of his role in the Council of Trent, see Mayer, *Reginald Pole*.
26. *L&P*, XXI, 802.

5 THE KING'S SISTER

1. *L&P*, XXI, 675, 684. Scarisbrick, *Henry VIII*, p. 495. Neither Catherine nor Mary had been admitted to his chamber since Christmas.
2. T. Rymer, *Foedera* (1704-35), XV, p. 117.
3. W. K. Jordan, *Edward VI: The Young King* (1968), pp. 52-3.
4. Charles returned the greetings that were sent to him in the name of the new king, without acknowledging his title, writing to Van der Delft: 'We want no further than this with regard to the young king, in order to avoid saying anything which might prejudice the right that our cousin the Princess might advance to the throne.' *Cal. Span.*, IX, p. 38.
5. The Act of Succession (35 Henry VIII, c.1) had specified that the king's will should be 'signed with his most gracious hand', whereas in fact it had been stamped. This was a fully recognised method of authenticating documents when the king was incapacitated, but it was challenged by Maitland of Lethington in 1566 in the interest of Mary Queen of Scots. G. Burnet, *The Historie of the Reformation of the Church of England* (1679), I, p. 267. See also E. W. Ives, 'Henry VIII's Will: A Forensic Conundrum', *Historical Journal*, 35 (1992), pp. 779-804.
6. College of Arms MSS, I, 7, f. 29. J. G. Nichols (ed.), *The Literary Remains of King Edward VI* (1857), I, p. lxxvii.
7. *APC*, II, p. 16.
8. TNA SP10/1, no. 11. This is a rough draft, with proposed grants of land also inserted.
9. TNA SP10/6, no. 14. Deposition of William Parr, Marquis of Northampton, January 1549.
10. Van der Delft to the Emperor, to July 1547. *Cal. Span.*, IX, p. 123.

11. *Calendar of the Patent Rolls, Edward VI*, II, p. 20.

12. TNA SP10/6, no. 10. Deposition of John Fowler, January 1549.

13. *APC*, II, pp. 84, 86, 92, 100, 120, 122, 141. Loades, *Mary Tudor*, pp. 138-9.

14. *APC*, II, pp. 63-4,13 March 1547. Jordan, *Edward VI*, pp. 72-3.

15. A J. Slavin, 'The Fall of Lord Chancellor Wriothesley: A Study in the Politics of Conspiracy', *Albion*, 7 (1975) pp. 265-85. Loades, *John Dudley, Duke of Northumberland* (1996) pp. 92-5.

16. Burnet, *Historie of the Reformation*, II, p. 115, reproduces the text of the protector's letter.

17. Ibid. Gardiner's views on the same subject can be seen in letters that he wrote from the Fleet Prison between 14 October and 4 December 1547. J. A. Muller (ed.), *The Letters of Stephen Gardiner* (1933), pp. 379-428.

18. Loades, *Mary Tudor*, pp. 144-5.

19. Van der Delft to the Emperor, 16 June 1547. *Cal. Span.*, IX, p. 100.

20. For a full discussion of the failure of the protector's policy in Scotland, see M. L. Bush, *The Government Policy of Protector Somerset* (1975), pp. 32-40.

21. TNA SP10/6, no. 21.

22. TNA SP10/6, nos. 7-22. Depositions taken relating to the charges against the lord admiral.

23. G. W. Bernard, 'The Downfall of Sir Thomas Seymour', in G. W. Bernard (ed.), *The Tudor Nobility* (1992), pp. 212-40.

24. He had been sent to the Tower in June 1548, having preached before the king on the 29th. He remained there until released by Mary in August 1553, having been deprived of his bishopric in 1552. J. A. Muller, *Letters*, p. 439. Redworth, *In Defence of the Church Catholic*, pp. 285-90.

25. *APC*, II, p. 291.

26. Mary to the council, 22 June 1549. Loades, *Mary Tudor*, p. 146. She did not claim that her conscience was superior to the law, but that the law was defective owing to some (fictitious) pressure that had been applied to Parliament.

27. Emperor to Van der Delft, to May 1549. *Cal. Span.*, IX, p. 375.

28. Jordan, *Edward VI*, pp. 206-9. *Cal. Span.*, IX, pp. 406-8, 19 July 1549.

29. Bush, *Government Policy of Protector Somerset*, pp. 73-83. Ethan Shagan, 'Protector Somerset and the 1549 Rebellions: New Sources and New Perspectives', *English Historical Review*, 114 (1999) pp. 34-63. Shagan, *Popular Politics and the English Reformation* (2003), pp. 270-305.

30. Loades, *Mary Tudor*, p. 149.

31. For a full discussion of the circumstances of Somerset's fall in October 1549, see Loades, *John Dudley*, pp. 130-39.

32. Dale Hoak, *The King's Council in the Reign of Edward VI* (1976), pp. 54-61.

33. BL Add. MS 48126, ff. 15-16. H. James 'The Aftermath of the 1549 Coup, and the Earl of Warwick's Intentions', *Historical Research*, 62 (1989), pp. 91-7.

34. BL Add. MS 48126, f 16. Loades, *John Dudley*, p. 145. There has always been some doubt about the reality of this 'plot', which rests upon the evidence of a single source, but Van der Delft, writing on 19 December, noticed the change of atmosphere in the council. *Cal. Span.*, IX, p. 489.

35. Van der Delft to the Emperor, 14 January and 18 March 1550. *Cal. Span.*, X, pp. 6, 40.

36. W. K. Jordan, *Edward VI: The Threshold of Power* (1970), pp. 120-22.

37. Van der Delft to the Emperor, 2 May 1550. *Cal. Span.*, X, 80.

38. *Cal. Span.*, X, pp. 124-35. Charles had approved the plan on 21 June.

39. Dubois report, ibid., p. 127.

40. Loades, *Mary Tudor*, pp. 156-7. Rochester had, apparently, been consulting astrologers who had told him that the king would die within the next year – hence his anxiety about the succession.

41. W. K. Jordan (ed.), *The Chronicle and Political Papers of King Edward VI* (1966), p. 40.

42. Conversation between Bassefontaine and St Mauris, 28 July 1550. *Cal. Span.*, X, p. 145. This appears to be the first mention of a marriage between Philip and Mary. At this point he was twenty-three and she was thirty-four.

43. *APC*, III, p. 171.

44. John Foxe, *Acts and Monuments of the English Martyrs* (1583), pp. 1,335-7.

45. Scheyfve to Mary, January/February 1551. *Cal. Span.*, X, p. 428.

46. Jordan, *Chronicle and Political Papers of Edward VI*, p. 55.

47. Loades, *Mary Tudor*, p.163.

48. Dudley did not take the title of protector, partly because it was discredited by Somerset's incumbency, but more, it would seem, because he was anxious to promote the view that the king himself was making decisions. This can be seen not only in his dealings with Mary, but also in the 'political papers' that Edward was encouraged to prepare. It is still uncertain whether there was any reality behind this façade. Loades, *John Dudley*, pp. 180-229.

49. *APC*, III, p. 336.

50. '... my father made the more part of you almost from nothing.' This was true, but not really relevant. *APC*, III, p. 347.

51. Ibid. To the modern observer Mary's flamboyant obstinacy, together with her behaviour under pressure, suggests a degree of mental instability – but no one suggested that at the time.

52. *Cal. Span.*, X, p. 377.

53. Ibid.

54. Jordan, *Chronicle and Political Papers of Edward VI*, pp. 89-91. Loades, *Mary Tudor*, pp. 168-9.

55. Fourteen was the minimum age of co-habitation within marriage (for a boy), and kings of France came of age at fourteen. The age had no particular significance in English law.

56. When he was himself under sentence of death in 1553, Northumberland confessed that many of the charges against his rival had been fabricated. BL Harley MS 787, f. 61.

57. Loades, *Mary Tudor*, p. 169.

58. Statute 5 & 6 Edward VI, c.1. *Statutes of the Realm*, IV, pp. 130-31. Redworth, *In Defence of the Church Catholic*, p. 286.

59. Inner Temple, Petyt MS xlvii, f. 316. Printed and edited in J. G. Nichols, *Literary Remains of King Edward VI* (1857), ii, pp. 571-2. Jane was the eldest granddaughter of Henry's younger sister, Mary – known as 'the French Queen'.

60. *Cal. Span.*, XI, pp. 8-9, 17 February 1553 Henry Machyn, *The Diary of Henry Machyn*, ed. J. G. Nichols (1848), pp. 30-31.

61. BL Lansdowne MS 3, no. 23.

62. Loades, *John Dudley*, p. 239.

63. E.g. *Cal. Span.*, XI, p. 50. '... the sputum which he brings up is livid, black fetid and full of carbon; it smells beyond measure ...'

64. Inner Temple, Petyt MS xlvii, f. 316.

65. The Emperor's instructions to messieurs de Courrieres, de Tholouse and Simon Renard (his special envoys) are calendared in *Cal. Span.*, XI, pp. 60-5.

66. Ibid.

6 MARY THE QUEEN

1. Noailles to Henry II, 28 June 1553. Cited by E. H. Harbison, *Rival Ambassadors at the Court of Queen Mary* (1940), p. 43. A recent and highly detailed account of the events of this crisis, makes a case for the legitimacy of Jane's claim, but admits that few outside the council accepted it at the time. Eric Ives, *Lady Jane Grey: a Tudor Mystery* (2009).

2. Ambassadors to the Emperor, 13 July 1553. *Cal. Span.*, XI, pp. 72-80.

3. 'The Vita Mariae Reginae of Robert Wingfield of Brantham', ed. D. MacCulloch, *Camden Miscellany*, 28 (1984), pp. 203/251. Loades, *John Dudley*, p. 259.

4. 'Vita Mariae', pp. 203/252.

5. Ibid., pp. 205/253.

6. Loades, *John Dudley*, p. 259. This information was given out in the general letter announcing Jane's accession.

7. *Historical Manuscripts Commission*, Molyneux MSS, p. 609. Ives, *Lady Jane Grey*, pp. 191-2.

8. Machyn, *Diary*, pp. 35-6.

9. 'Vita Mariae', pp. 206/254-5.

10. Ibid., pp. 210/259.

11. *Cal. Span.*, XI, pp. 84-6. Harbison, *Rival Ambassadors*, pp. 49-50.

12. 'Vita Mariae', pp. 206/255. There are several discussions of the formation of Mary's council: Loades, *The Reign of Mary Tudor* (1991), pp. 18-24; A. Weikel, 'The Marian Council Revisited', in J. Loach and R. Tittler (eds), *The Mid-Tudor Polity*, 1540–1560 (1980), pp. 52-73; D. E. Hoak, 'Two Revolutions in Tudor Government: The Formation and Organization of Mary I's Privy Council', in C. Coleman and D. Starkey (eds), *Revolution Reassessed* (1987), pp. 87-116.

13. Arundel had been dismissed from office and from the council following the supposed plot against the Earl of Warwick (as Dudley then was) in December 1549. He had been harassed again, imprisoned and fined for his supposed involvement in Somerset's 'treason' in 1552. His fine was remitted and he was recalled to the council only in early June 1553. Loades, *John Dudley*, p. 262.

14. J. G. Nichols (ed.), *The Chronicle of Queen Jane* (Camden Society, 1850), p. 10. Machyn, *Diary*, p. 37.

15. BL Lansdowne MS 3, f. 26. The story of large scale desertions from Northumberland's force before his final arrival in Cambridge is rejected by Ives, who claims that they only took place after the Duke had given up his campaign. Ives, *Lady Jane Grey*, p. 205.

16. Loades, *John Dudley*, pp. 264-5. R. Tittler and S. L. Battey, 'The Local Community and the Crown in 1553: The Accession of Mary Tudor Revisited', *Bulletin of the Institute of Historical Research*, 136 (1984), pp. 131-40.

17. None of these men had ever served on the council before, or occupied anything more than local offices. Loades, *Reign of Mary*, pp. 18-24.

18. *Chronicle of Queen Jane*, p. 14.

19. Ambassadors to the Emperor, 16 August 1553. *Cal. Span.*, XI, p. 172.

20. Loades, *Mary Tudor*, pp. 193-4.

21. *Chronicle of Queen Jane*, pp. 53-6.

22. Ambassadors to the Emperor, 2 August, 8 August, 31 August (*Cal. Span.*, XI, pp. 129-34, 155-8, 374-5), etc.

23. Renard to the Bishop of Arras, 9 September 1553. *Cal. Span.*, XI, pp. 227-8.

24. P. L. Hughes and J. F Larkin (eds), *Tudor Royal Proclamations*, II (1969), pp. 5-8.

25. 1 Mary, sess. 2, c.1. J. Loach, *Parliament and the Crown in the Reign of Mary Tudor* (1986), pp. 78-9.

26. Pole to Mary, 2 October 1553. *Cal. Ven.*, V p. 419. Loades, *Reign of Mary*, p. 69.

27. *Cal. Span.*, XI, p. 60.

28. Cardinal Reginald Pole was also mentioned as a possibility in some quarters, as he was only in deacon's orders, and could therefore have been dispensed to marry. This would have been to resurrect an old idea, but in 1553 neither Pole nor Mary showed any interest in it. Loades, *Reign of Mary*, pp. 59-60.

29. Renard to the Emperor, 31 October 1553. *Cal. Span.*, XI, p. 328. She felt, she said, 'inspired by God'.

30. M. J. Rodriguez-Salgado, *The Changing Face of Empire* (1988), pp. 82-5, considers Imperial attitudes to the marriage.

31. Loach, *Parliament and the Crown*, pp. 79-80.

32. David Loades, *Two Tudor Conspiracies* (1965), pp. 12-24.

33. M. R. Thorpe, 'Religion and the Rebellion of Sir Thomas Wyatt', *Church History*, 47 (1978), pp. 363-80.

34. Harbison, *Rival Ambassadors*, explores this involvement thoroughly in chapters 4 and 5.

35. Renard to the Emperor, 18 January 1554. *Cal. Span.*, XII, p. 34.

36. Noailles to Montmorency, 12 January 1554, cited by Harbison, *Rival Ambassadors*, p. 119.

37. TNA SP11 /3, no. 18 (i). Testimony of Sir Anthony Norton.

38. J. Proctor, *The History of Wyats Rebellion* (1554), reprinted in A. F. Pollard, *Tudor Tracts* (1903), pp. 229-30.

39. 'And touching the marriage, her Highness affirmed that nothing was done herein by herself alone, but with consent and advisement of the whole Council upon deliberate consultation ...' Proctor, *History*, p. 239. There is no evidence of any such consultation until after the decision had been made.

40. *The Chronicle of Queen Jane*, p. 49. The author was not overly sympathetic to the

Notes

government.

41. Rodriguez Salgado, *The Changing Face of Empire*, pp. 82-5.
42. *The Chronicle of Queen Jane*, p. 54.
43. Ibid., pp. 73-4.
44. 178 out of nearly 30,000. G. R. Elton, *Policy and Police* (1972), p. 389.

7 MARRIAGE

1. AGS Patronato Real, 7. A secret instrument *ad cautelam* is enclosed with the copy of the marriage treaty preserved at Simancas. *Cal. Span.*, XII, p. 4.
2. Rodriguez Salgado, *The Changing Face of Empire*, pp. 85-8.
3. Renard to the Bishop of Arras, 7 January 1554. *Cal. Span.*, XII, p. 15.
4. For a discussion of the position of the *femme couvert* and her property rights, see *The Lawes Resolution of Womens Rights, or the Lawes Provision for Woemen*, by 'E.T.' (London, 1632).
5. Loach, *Parliament and the Crown*, pp. 96-7.
6. Commendone had come on behalf of Geronimo Dandino, papal legate in the Low Countries, the previous September. For a general consideration of the progress of the religious reaction, see E. Duffy and D. Loades (eds), *The Church of Mary Tudor* (2006).
7. Loades, *Reign of Mary*, pp. 124-6.
8. *Cal. Span.*, XII, p. 216. *Loach, Parliament and the Crown*, pp. 97-9.
9. Ibid., p. 98.
10. *Cal. Span.*, XII, p. 251.
11. Renard to the Emperor, 13 May 1554 *Cal. Span.*, XII, pp. 250-4.
12. Thomas F. Mayer, *Reginald Pole, Prince and Prophet* (2000), pp. 60-1.
13. TNA SP11/4, no. 10.
14. *Cal. Span.*, XII, pp. 297-9.
15. Ambassadors to the Emperor, 22–25 May 1554. *Cal. Span.*, XII, p. 258.
16. 'The officers appointed for his Highness's service have been living at Southampton at great expense for a long time, and are now beginning to leave that place, speaking strangely of his Highness.' Renard to the Emperor, 9 July 1554. *Cal. Span.*, XII, p. 309.
17. Loades, *Mary Tudor*, p. 223.
18. 'John Elder's Letter, describing the arrival and marriage of King Philip …', *Chronicle of Queen Jane*, Appendix X, pp. 139-40.
19. Ibid., p. 140.
20. Ruy Gomez (Philip's secretary) to Francisco de Eraso, 27 July 1554, commenting on Mary's appearance and demeanour during the wedding service. He also added that she had kept her eyes fixed on the sacrament throughout, and was 'a perfect saint'. *Cal. Span.*, XIII, p. 2.
21. In Spanish, '*Que yo no quiero amores, / en Ingalterra, / pues otros mejores / tengo yo in mi tierra …*', Fernando Diaz-Plaja (ed.), *La Historia de Espana en sus Documentos* (1958), p. 149.
22. *The Chronicle of Queen Jane*, Appendix XI. 'The Marriage of Queen Mary and King Philip' (the official heralds' account).
23. Ibid.
24. *The Chronicle of Queen Jane*, p. 170. Edward Underhill's account.
25. *Tres Cartas de to sucedido en el viaje de su Alteza in Inglaterra* (1877), Primera Carta, p. 111.
26. Ibid.
27. *Tres Cartas*, Tercera Carta, p. 102.
28. *Cal. Span.*, XIII, p. 11.
29. Loades, *Mary Tudor*, p. 177.

8 A WOMAN'S PROBLEMS

1. Judith M. Richards, 'Mary Tudor as "Sole Quene"? Gendering Tudor Monarchy', *Historical Journal*, 40 (1997) pp. 895-924.
2. *Cal. Span.*, XIII, p. 11.
3. Glyn Redworth, '"Matters impertinent to women"; male and female monarchy under Philip and Mary', *English Historical Review*, 112 (1997), pp. 597-613.

279

4. S. Anglo, *Spectacle, Pageantry and Early Tudor Policy* (1969), pp. 56-98. The pageants offered on that occasion had been a *tour de force* of humanist imagination.

5. 'John Elder's Letter', *Chronicle of Queen Jane*, p. 146. See also Anglo, *Spectacle*, pp. 327-38.

6. 'The ambassador,' he wrote, 'gets everything in a muddle. However, I do not blame him, but rather the person who sent a man of his small attainments to conduct so capital an affair as this match, instead of entrusting it to a Spaniard.' Renard was a Franc-Comptois, and the dig is at Antoine de Perrenot, Bishop of Arras. 23 August 1554. *Cal. Span.*, XIII, p. 35.

7. Ibid., p. 33.

8. Machyn, *Diary*, pp. 69, 72.

9. Archivo General de Simancas, CMC la E, legajo 1184.

10. Redworth, '"Matters impertinent"'. Mary had instructed the select council that they were to 'tell the king the whole state of the realm', but they seem to have used their judgement in interpreting that.

11. For a discussion of Philip's impact on the court during 1554-5, see D. Loades, *Intrigue and Treason: The Tudor Court 1547-58* (2004), pp. 178-213.

12. *Cal. Span.*, XIII, p. 28.

13. William Forrest, *A Newe Ballad of the Marigolde* (1554).

14. *Cal. Ven.*, VI, p. 10. A memorandum on developments concerning Church property.

15. *Cal. Span.*, XIII, pp. 63-4. Loades, *Mary Tudor*, p. 236. For a full discussion of this negotiation, see Rodriguez Salgado, *The Changing Face of Empire*, p. 97.

16. *Cal. Span.*, XIII, pp. 92-5.

17. House of Lords Records Office, Original Act, 1 & 2 Philip and Mary, c.18. Loach, *Parliament and the Crown*, p. 106.

18. The text of Pole's address is preserved in Biblioteca Vaticana, Rome, MS Vat. Lat. 5968, which is available on microfilm. A translation was printed by J. Collier, *An Ecclesiastical History of Great Britain* (1714), II, pp. 372-3.

19. Donato Rullo to Cardinal Seripando, 1 December 1554. Carlo de Frede, *La Restaurazione Cattolica in Inghilterra sotto Maria Tudor* (Naples, 1971) p. 57.

20. *Cal. Span.*, XIII, p. 117.

21. Feckenham had urged that, no matter what the dispensation might say, the possessioners were in conscience bound to surrender their gains. He was interviewed by an embarrassed council on 29 November. *Cal. Span.*, XIII, p. 108. *APC*, V, p. 85.

22. Priuli had no knowledge of English law, and sometimes missed the point of the discussions. BL Add. MS 41577, ff. 161-6. Loach, *Parliament and the Crown*, pp. 109-111.

23. 1 & 2 Philip and Mary, c. 8. Loach, *Parliament and the Crown*, p. 111.

24. Loades, *Reign of Mary*, pp. 167-8.

25. Machyn, *Diary*, p. 76.

26. Ibid., p. 80.

27. Ibid., p. 79.

28. Loades, *Mary Tudor*, p. 248.

29. *Cal. Span.*, XIII, pp. 165-6.

30. Loades, *Mary Tudor*, p. 249.

31. Machyn, *Diary*, p. 81.

32. Ibid., p. 82. Renard to Philip, 5 February 1555, wrote: 'Some of the onlookers wept, others prayed God to give him strength ... not to recant ... others threatening the bishops ...' *Cal. Span.*, XIII, p. 138.

33. D. Loades, 'The Marian Episcopate', in Duffy and Loades, *The Church of Mary Tudor*, pp. 33-56.

34. The submission of John Barret, Norwich's leading evangelical preacher under Edward VI, took all the stuffing out of Protestant resistance in Norwich. Ralph Houlbrooke, 'The Clergy, the Church Courts and the Marian Restoration in Norwich', ibid., pp. 124-48.

35. *The Displaying of the Protestants* (1556), p. 51.

36. Jose Ignacio Tellecehea Idigoras (trans. Ronald Truman), 'Fray Bartolome Carranza: A Spanish Dominican in the England of Mary Tudor', in J. Edwards and R. Truman (eds), *Reforming*

Catholicism in the England of Mary Tudor: The Achievement of Fray Bartolome Carranza (2005), pp. 21-32.

37. See (for example) Patrick Collinson, 'The Persecution in Kent', in Duffy and Loades, *The Church of Mary Tudor*, pp. 309-33.

38. *A Short Treatise of Politike Power* (1556), f. E v.

39. Thomas F. Mayer, 'The Success of Cardinal Pole's Final Legation', in Duffy and Loades, *The Church of Mary Tudor*, pp. 149-75.

40. Machyn, *Diary*, p. 86.

41. John Foxe, *Acts and Monuments* (1583), p. 1,597. Foxe claimed to have been told this story 'by the woman herself'. Her son was called Timothy.

42. Federico Badoer to the Doge and Senate, 21 July 1555. *Cal. Ven.*,VI, pp. 138-9. According to Badoer several members of the council wrote at the same time, distancing themselves from her instruction.

43. One contemporary report states that she had been delivered of a shapeless mass of flesh, which would suggest a tumour, but there is no proper corroboration. Her physicians seem to have expressed no opinion.

44. Rodriguez Salgado, *The Changing Face of Empire*, pp. 92-3, 101.

45. Machyn, *Diary*, p. 93. The English gentlemen stayed only to witness the handover of power on 25 September and then returned home.

9 MARY ALONE

1. Redworth, '"Matters Impertinent"'.

2. Redworth says, on Spanish authority, that Mary discussed some matters of state with the select council rather than the privy council, but is not clear what these matters were. Probably the reference is to Philip's Continental affairs in so far as these affected England.

3. Rodriguez Salgado, *The Changing Face of Empire*, p. 101.

4. Loach, *Parliament and the Crown*, pp. 129-58. It was during this session that some members held illicit meetings with the French ambassador to discuss oppositional tactics, and the Commons rejected a government measure for the recall of religious refugees.

5. *A Machiavellian Treatise by Stephen Gardiner*, trans. and ed. P. S. Donaldson (1975). On Gardiner's authorship, see also D. Fenlon in *Historical Journal*, 19 (1976), p. 4; to which Donaldson replied in the same journal, 23 (1980), pp. 1-16.

6. Redworth, '"Matters Impertinent"'.

7 Loades, *Mary Tudor*, pp. 258-9.

8. Typical, although unusually explicit, was John Bradford's *Copy of a letter ... sent to the Earls of Arundel, Derby, Shrewsbury and Pembroke* (1556).

9. Rodriguez Salgado, *The Changing Face of Empire*, pp. 149-51.

10. Loades, *Two Tudor Conspiracies*, pp. 176-27. Henry was the second son of John Sutton de Dudley, and the younger brother of Edmund Sutton, 4th Baron Dudley. He is always called by the name of his brother's title.

11. TNA SP11/7, no. 47. Third confession of Thomas White, 30 March 1556.

12. D. Loades, *The Tudor Navy* (1992), pp. 164-5.

13. There are several lists of 'suspect persons' in the State Papers, e.g. TNA SP11/7, nos. 23, 24, 25.

14. *Cal. Ven.*,VI, p. 285.

15. Pole to Philip, 5 October 1555. *Cal. Ven.*, VI, pp. 205-6. Renard was not replaced for the obvious reason that Philip's servants were seen to be discharging his function, but Renard had always been the Emperor's ambassador, not the king's.

16. For a full discussion of Cranmer's fate and its implications, see Diarmaid MacCulloch, *Thomas Cranmer* (1996), pp. 573-91.

17. Bradford, *Copy of a letter*. Other works in a similar vein include *A Supplication to the Queen's Majesty* (1555) and *A Warning for England* (1555).

18. *Cal. Ven.*,VI, pp. 401-2.

19. *Cal. Span.*, XIII, p. 260.

20. R. A. de Vertot, *Les ambassados de Mss de Noailles* (1743) V pp. 361-3.
21. *APC*, V p. 320.
22. *Cal. Span.*, XIII, p. 276.
23. Mayer, 'The Success of Cardinal Pole's Final Legation'.
24. *Cal. Ven.*, VI, p. 880.
25. Nicholas Wotton to the queen, 20 and 29 October 1556. *Calendar of State Papers, Foreign*, II, pp. 267-73.
26. The list is printed as Appendix 2 in Loades, *Mary Tudor*, pp. 358-69.
27. *Cal. Span.*, XIII, pp. 286-7.
28. Loades, *Mary Tudor*, p. 273.
29. C. S. Knighton, 'Westminster Abbey Restored', in *The Church of Mary Tudor*, pp. 77-123.
30. Loades, 'The Marian Episcopate'.
31. Secret Protestants – after Nicodemus, who came to Christ at night.
32. BL Lansdowne MS 170, f 129. Loades, *Reign of Mary*, pp. 186-8.

10 PHILIP & MARY AT WAR

1. Machyn, *Diary*, p. 129.
2. I am indebted to Corinna Streckfuss of Christ Church, Oxford, for several important points relating to Philip's image in contemporary Habsburg propaganda.
3. Machyn, *Diary*, p. 133. This Russian, who had returned with Richard Chancellor, and narrowly survived shipwreck in Scotland, was Ossip Nepeja, but Machyn had no means of knowing that.
4. Ibid., p. 141. The 'forest' was probably Windsor Great Park. It was just before this that Sir James Granado had been killed in a riding accident while showing off a horse at St James'. Mary had apparently witnessed the accident.
5. Francois de Noailles to Montmorency, 5 April 1557. Harbison, *Rival Ambassadors*, p. 324. A Latin version was also prepared for Philip. BL Sloane MS 1786.
6. Surian to the doge and senate, 3 April. *Cal.Ven.*, VI, 1, 004. Feria had apparently told Surian that 'it is in His Majesty's power to make the country wage war against France when and in what manner he chooses'. This was theoretically correct, but not practicable, as Philip himself realised.
7. Loades, *Reign of Mary*, p. 191.
8. For a discussion of the circumstances of this revocation, see Mayer, *Reginald Pole*, pp. 312-14.
9. Loades, *Two Tudor Conspiracies*, pp. 151-75.
10. Notes by Wotton, April 1557. TNA SP69/10/587.
11. Strype, *Ecclesiastical* Memorials, III, ii, p. 515, prints the full text of the proclamation.
12. Loades, *Reign of Mary*, pp. 305-6.
13. *Cal. Span.*, XIII, 290-1.
14. Loades, *Mary Tudor*, p. 278. On Ribault and his activities, see G. Lefèvre-Pontalis, *Correspondance Politique de Odet de Selve*, pp. 218-23; also Harbison, *Rival Ambassadors*, pp. 283-5.
15. Strype, *Ecclesiastical Memorials*, III, ii, pp. 67-9. TNA KB8/37.
16. These despatches contain a full account of Norroy the herald's mission to the French king. *Cal. Ven.*, VI, 1,148-51.
17. C. S. L. Davies, 'England and the French War, 157-9', in Loach and Tittler, *The Mid-Tudor Polity*. BL MS Stowe 571, ff 77-132.
18. Loades, *Elizabeth I*, pp. 116-17.
19. *Cal. Span.*, XI, 393. *Cal. Ven.*, VI, 1058. Henry Clifford, *The Life of Jane Dormer, Duchess of Feria*, ed. J. Stevenson (1887), pp. 79-80.
20. This was according to a report written by Michel Surian long after the event. *Cal. Ven.*, VI, 1537. Fresnada, the king's confessor, was credited with this brief breakthrough.
21. *Cal. Ven.*, VI, 1024.
22. Loades, *Mary Tudor*, p. 289.
23. On the bull *Praeclara*, see M. C. Knowles, *The Religious Orders in England, III, The Tudor Age*, pp. 423-6.
24. This could not be assumed, as Paul had already withdrawn similar concessions made elsewhere.

In this case Pole's 'special case' representations were successful.

25. Philip and Mary to Paul IV, 21 May 1557. Strype, *Ecclesiastical Memorials*, III, ii, pp. 474-6.

26. For a full discussion of Paul's views on heresy, particularly in respect of Pole, see Dermot Fenlon, *Heresy and Obedience in Tridentine Italy* (1972).

27. *ODNB*.

28. TNA SP69/11/637. *Ecclesiastical Memorials*, III, ii, p. 37.

29. *Cal. Ven.*, VI, 1161, 1166. Mayer, *Reginald Pole*, pp. 307-15.

30. Mayer, ibid., pp. 316-20.

31. Feria to Philip, 10 March 1558. *Cal. Span.*, XIII, 366-9. Mayer, 'Cardinal Pole's Final Legation', in Duffy and Loades, *The Church of Mary Tudor*, pp. 149-75.

32. Bernardo Navagero to the doge and senate, 14 August 1557. *Cal. Ven.*, VI, 1428. Navagero also understood that Mary was insisting that if any charges were to be proffered against Pole, they should be heard in England – as had been done with Cranmer.

33. *APC*, VI, p.137.

34. *Calendar of State Papers relating to Scotland* (1898), I, 416.

35. Susan Brigden, *New Worlds, Lost Worlds* (2000), p. 218. Loades, *Reign of Mary*, p. 311.

36. BL Stowe MS 571, ff 77-132.

37. Juan de Pinedo to Fransisco de Vargas, 2 September 1557. *Cal. Span.*, XIII, 317.

38. BL Stowe MS 571. This information is included in a note written on the document some years later by Richard Beale, then clerk of the council, saying that he had had it from Robert Davys, who had been Whightman's assistant, 'so the whole charge was borne by King Philip' (f. 78).

39. Machyn, *Diary*, p.147.

40. *APC*, VI, pp. 141-2. A shortage of victuals appears to have been responsible.

41. Loades, *Reign of Mary*, pp. 376-8.

42. Ibid., p. 317. For a full discussion of these events see David Potter, 'The Duc de Guise and the Fall of Calais', *English Historical Review*, 98 (1983), pp. 481-512.

43. TNA SP69/11/699.

44. Loades, *Reign of Mary*, p. 317.

45. David Loades, *England's Maritime Empire, 1490–1690* (2000), pp. 83-5.

46. *Cal. Ven.*, VI, 1,396-7.

47. P. Morgan, 'The Government of Calais, 1485–1558' (Oxford University DPhil, 1967).

48. The Cardinal of Siguenza to the princess dowager of Portugal, 29 January 1558. *Cal. Span.*, XIII, 346-7.

49. Philip to Feria, 31 January 1558. *Cal. Span.*, XIII, 347. Feria to Philip, 2 February 1558, ibid., 349-51. For the possible influence of sickness upon this reluctance, see F. J. Fisher, 'Influenza and Inflation in Tudor England', *Economic History Review*, 2nd Series, 18 (1965).

50. BL Cotton MS, Titus B II, f. 59. Printed in G. Burnet, *The History of the Reformation in England* (1681), II, pp. 324-5.

51. Loades, *Reign of Mary*, pp. 144-8.

52. Feria to Philip, 5 July 1558. *Cal. Span.*, XIII, 402-3.

53. Feria to Philip, to March 1558. *Cal. Span.*, XIII, 366-8. It is clear that Feria's hostile and suspicious attitude made a difficult situation worse, as he never troubled to conceal his contempt.

54. TNA SP11/14, no. 3. *Cal. Span.*, XIII, 416-7.

55. *Cal. Span.*, XIII, 369. Loades, *Reign of Mary*, p. 324.

56. Loades, 'Philip II and the Government of England', in Claire Cross, David Loades and J. J. Scarisbrick (eds), *Law and Government under the Tudors* (1988), pp. 177-94.

57. Arras to Feria, 26 May 1558. *Cal. Span.*, XIII, 388.

58. *APC*, VI, p. 303,13 April 1558. Ruy Gomez to the queen, 26 July 1558. TNA SP69/13/811 (English copy).

59. Loach, *Parliament and the Crown*, pp. 159-72.

60. Ibid., p. 161. 4 & 5 Philip and Mary, c.16.

61. L. O. Boynton, *The Elizabethan Militia, 1558–1638* (1967).

62. Feria to Philip, 2 February 1558. *Cal. Span.*, XIII, 351.

63. Machyn, *Diary*, p. 161.
64. TNA SP11/11/57. Loades, *Reign of Mary*, p. 375. Mayer, *Reginald Pole*, pp. 320-1.
65. For a recent and favourable assessment of the church at the end of Mary's reign, see Eamon Duffy, *Fires of Faith; Catholic England under Mary Tudor* (2009), pp. 171-187.

11 MARY & ELIZABETH
1. For example the manors of Chingford, Runwell and Rivenhall in Essex, granted in March 1555. *Calendar of the Patent Rolls, Philip and Mary*, I, p. 225. It was Giovanni Michieli from whom she obtained the coach. J. A. Rowley Williams, 'Image and Reality: The Lives of Aristocratic Women in Early Tudor England' (University of Wales PhD, 1998),p. 232.
2. TNA LC9/52/21.
3. Mayer, *Reginald Pole*, pp. 302-55.
4. Machyn, *Diary*, p. 143.
5. Ibid., p. 159. For a full discussion of this sermon and its significance, see Eamon Duffy, 'Cardinal Pole Preaching: St Andrew's Day 1557', in Duffy and Loades, *The Church of Mary Tudor*, pp. 176-200.
6. Loades, *Mary Tudor*, pp. 370-1.
7. TNA SP11/14, no. 1.
8. A. Feuillerat, *Documents Relating to the Office of the Revels in the Reigns of Edward VI and Mary* (1914), p. 335.
9. Ibid., pp. 225-31. For a fuller discussion of this see Loades, *Intrigue and Treason* (2004), p. 225.
10. Machyn, *Diary*, p. 162.
11. *Cal. Ven.*, VI (ii), ii May 1557, p. 1,054.
12. Michieli had earlier said that she understood Spanish, but did not speak it. Loades, *Mary Tudor*, p. 225.
13. Loades, *Intrigue and Treason*, pp. 217-18.
14. Ibid., p. 226. Jane appears to have been an 'innocent', that is an adult with the mental age of a child. She had been in Mary's service for many years. John Southworth, *Fools and, Jesters at the English Court* (1998), pp. 100-6.
15. Loades, *Mary Tudor*, pp. 302-3.
16. BL Add. MS 710009.
17. Ibid., f. 15v. Extracts from the document, edited by Fiona Kisby, were published in Ian Archer *et al.* (eds), *Religion, Politics and Society in Sixteenth Century England*, Camden Society (2003), pp. 18-35.
18. Loades, *Intrigue and Treason*, pp. 222-3.
19. BL Add. MS 710009, ff. 31-2.
20. David Loades, *The Tudor Court* (1986), pp. 63-4. William Cecil later made strenuous efforts to stamp out this 'room service'.
21. TNA E351/1795.
22. On Cornwallis, see R. C. Braddock, 'The Rewards of Office Holding in Tudor England', *Journal of British Studies*, 14 (1975) pp. 29-47.
23. Loades, *Mary Tudor*, pp. 370-80.
24. Surian to the doge and senate, 15 January 1558, *Cal. Ven.*, VI (ii) p. 1427. Philip to Pole, 21 January, *Cal. Span.*, XIII , p. 340.
25. Loades, *Mary Tudor*, p. 302.
26. Ibid., p. 377.
27. TNA SP11/13, nos. 51, 52, 54, 55, etc.
28. Machyn, *Diary*, pp. 161-2. Sir Edward Hastings (master of the horse) became lord chamberlain, Sir Thomas Cornwallis controller, Sir Henry Jerningham master of the horse, and Sir Henry Bedingfield vice chamberlain and captain of the guard.

12 ELIZABETH THE HEIR
1. *Cal. Span.*, XIII, 398. Loades, *Reign of Mary*, p. 333.
2. Feria to Philip, I May 1558. *Cal. Span.*, XIII, 378-80.

3. Notes in Renard's hand for a letter to Philip (it is not certain that it was ever sent), dated in the *Calendar* 'March ? 1558', but apparently written before the author knew of Thomas Stafford's execution on 28 May 1557. *Cal. Span.*, XIII, 272-3.

4. Loades, *Mary Tudor*, p. 303.

5. BL Cotton MS Titus B.II, f. 109. Strype, *Ecclesiastical Memorials*, III, ii, p. 418.

6. Feria to Philip, 23 June 1558. *Cal. Span.*, XIII, 399-400.

7. Machyn, *Diary*, pp. 166-7.

8. T. Glasgow, 'The Navy in the French Wars of Mary and Elizabeth, 1557–59', *Mariners Mirror*, 53 (1967), pp. 321-42; 54 (1968), pp. 23-37.

9. Rodriguez Salgado, *The Changing Face of Empire*, pp. 306-7.

10. Extracts from *A Journal of the Travels of Philip II* by Jean Vandenesse, printed as an appendix to *Cal. Span.*, XIII.

11. Loades, *Mary Tudor*, pp. 380-3.

12. 'The Count of Feria's Despatch to Philip II of 14 November 1558', ed. M. J. Rodriguez Salgado and Simon Adams, *Camden Miscellany*, XXVIII (1984) pp. 319/28.

13. *An epitaphe upon the death of Quene Marie*, Society of Antiquaries, Broadsheet 46. Foxe, *Acts and Monuments*, p. 2,098.

14. 'Feria's despatch', pp. 320/29.

15. Philip to the princess dowager of Portugal, 4 December 1558. *Cal. Span.*, XIII, 440. The letter was written in haste, and mainly about other matters.

16. Rodriguez Salgado, *The Changing Face of Empire*, pp. 166-7.

17. Ibid.

18. 'Feria's despatch', pp. 320 /29 and note.

19. Ibid., pp. 25/35. Paget had refused to see Feria privately.

20. In fact Elizabeth had no particular animus against Boxall, who was a relative nonentity. He was a clerical pluralist on a grand scale, but of the second rank, being warden of New College, Winchester, Archdeacon of Ely and Dean of Peterborough. He became a principal secretary in December 1556.

21. Her story was written down by her servant, Henry Clifford, appearing in 1887 as *The Life of Jane Dormer* (cited above).

22. *Cal. Ven.*, VII, p. 93. Rowley Williams, 'Image and Reality', p. 237.

23. Feria to Philip, 21 November 1558. *Cal. Span., Elizabeth*, I, pp. 1-4.

24. TNA SP12/1, no. 57.

25. Strype, *Ecclesiastical Memorials*, III, pp. 536-50.

26. Loades, *Intrigue and Treason*, pp. 250-5.

27. Rowley Williams, 'Image and Reality', p. 243.

28. Machyn, *Diary*, p. 178. For a discussion of Machyn's attitude to Elizabeth (and other things), see Gary G. Gibbs, 'Marking the Days: Henry Machyn's Manuscript and the Mid-Tudor Era', in Duffy and Loades, *The Church of Mary Tudor*, pp. 281-308.

29. *A Speciall grace, appointed to have been said after a banket at Yorke ... in November 1558* (RSTC 7599). BL MS Royal 17. C. III.

30. Ibid.

31. Machyn, *Diary*, p. 180.

32. These sermons were not officially encouraged, and were banned by proclamation, but not until 27 December. Hughes and Larkin, *Tudor Royal Proclamations*, II, pp. 102-3.

33. *Intrigue and Treason*, p. 271. Machyn, *Diary*, p. 180.

34. TNA SP12/1, no. 7. L. S. Marcus, Janel Mueller and M. B. Rose, *Elizabeth I. Collected Works* (2000), p. 51.

35. Ibid., pp. 135-50. W. P. Haugaard, 'Elizabeth Tudor's Book of Devotions: A Neglected Clue to the Queen's Life and Character', *Sixteenth Century Journal*, 12 (1981), pp. 79-105.

13 THE ENGLAND OF THE TWO QUEENS

1. *The Passage of our most dread Sovereign Lady, Queen Elizabeth, through the City of London* ... (1559), in A. F Pollard, *Tudor Tracts*, pp. 367-95.

2. Ibid., p. 387.

3. Perhaps suspecting her intention, none of the senior bishops of the Church would agree to crown her. It was left to the relatively junior Owen Oglethorpe of Carlisle to perform the ceremony. D. E. Hoak, 'The Coronations of Edward VI, Mary I and Elizabeth I, and the Transformation of Tudor Monarchy', in C. S. Knighton and Richard Mortimer (eds), *Westminster Abbey Reformed* (2003), pp. 114-51.

4. *Proceedings in the Parliaments of Elizabeth I: 1558–1581*, ed. T. E. Hartley (1981), pp. 12-17.

5. D. Wilkins, *Concilia Magnae Brittaniae et Hiberniae* (1737), IV, p. 179; translated in Philip Hughes, *Rome and the Counter-Reformation in England* (1942), pp. 138-9.

6. J. Strype, *Annals of the Reformation* (1725), I, pp. 73-81.

7. *Handbook of British Chronology*, pp. 227-83. Loades, *Elizabeth I*, p. 137 and note.

8. Lucy Wooding, 'The Marian Restoration and the Mass', in Duffy and Loades, *The Church of Mary Tudor*, pp. 227-57.

9. This friction had culminated in the so-called 'Reneger incident' in 1545 when Robert Reneger of Southampton became so exasperated by the attitude of the authorities at San Lucar that he seized an incoming Indiaman worth many thousands of ducats, for which he was mildly reprimanded by the council. G. Connell Smith, *The Forerunners of Drake* (1954) p. 141. TNA SPI/200, ff. 95-6.

10. Elizabeth Russell, 'Mary Tudor and Mr Jorkins', *Historical Research*, 63 (1990), pp. 263-76.

11. Christopher Goodman, *How Superior Powers ought to be Obeyed* (1558). John Ponet, *A Short Treatise of Politic Power* (1556). For a brief consideration of these views, see J. W. Allen, *A History of Political Thought in the Sixteenth Century* (1928), pp. 116-24.

12. Loades, Mary Tudor, pp. 315-45.

13. Wallace MacCaffrey, *The Shaping of the Elizabethan Regime, 1558–1572* (1968).

14. John Bradford, in his *Copy of a Letter*, pointed out that Henry's will had settled the succession on Mary on the condition that she married with the consent of the council. The council did consent – but after the event.

15. Loades, 'The Personal Religion of Mary I', in Duffy and Loades, *The Church of Mary Tudor*, pp. 1-32.

16. Richards, 'Mary Tudor as "Sole Quene"'.

17. Juan Rafael de la Cuandra Blanco, 'King Philip of Spain as Soloman the Second', in de Groot, *The Seventh Window*, pp. 169-80. Pole had also compared Philip to Solomon in his rebuilding of the temple of the Church in England – a task that had been denied to 'David' (Charles V).

18. This was the law, the origin of which was attributed to the Salian Franks, that forbade any woman to inherit the throne of France, or to transmit such a claim.

19. Statute 1 Mary, sess. 3, c. 1. See above.

20. Proclamation of 6 June 1558. Hughes and Larkin, *Tudor Royal Proclamations*, II, p. 90. There is no evidence of it being invoked.

21. P. S. Boscher, 'Politics, Administration and Diplomacy: The Anglo-Scottish Border 1550–1560' (University of Durham PhD, 1985).

22. TNA E351/2195-8.

23. Loades, *Reign of Mary*, pp. 348-51.

24. Claire Cross, 'The English Universities, 1553–58', in Duffy and Loades, *The Church of Mary Tudor*, pp. 57-76.

25. John Edwards, 'Spanish Religious Influence in Marian England', in ibid., pp. 201-26.

BIBLIOGRAPHY

MANUSCRIPTS
The National Archives
E351/1795
KB8/37
KB29/161
LC9/52
SP½oo
SP10/1
SP11/3,/4,/7,/13,/14,/57
SP12/1
SP69/10
The British Library
Add. 48126, 710009
Arundel 151
Cotton Galba B.VII
Cotton Otho C.X
Cotton Titus B.II
Cotton Vespasian C.XIV
Harley 787, 3504, 6807
Lansdowne 3, 170
Stowe 1786

CALENDARS, GUIDES AND WORKS OF REFERENCE

Acts of the Privy Council, ed. J. Dasent (1890–1907).

Calendar of the Patent Rolls, Edward VI and Philip and Mary (1924–1939).

Calendar of State Papers, Domestic, Edward VI, ed C. S. Knighton (1992).

Calendar of State Papers, Domestic, Mary, ed. C. S. Knighton (1998).

Calendar of State Papers, Foreign, 1553–1558, ed. W. B. Turnbull (1861).

Calendar of State Papers relating to Scotland, ed. J. Bain et al. (1898–1952).

Calendar of State Papers, Spanish, 1485–1558, ed. Royall Tyler et al (1862–1954); *1558–1603*, ed. M. A. S. Hume (1892–1899).

Calendar of State Papers, Venetian, ed, Rawdon Brown et al. (1864–1898).

Elton, G. R., *The Tudor Constitution* (1982).

Hughes, P. L, and J. F. Larkin, *Tudor Royal Proclamations* (1964–1969).

Letters and Papers, Foreign and Domestic, of the Reign of Henry VIII, ed. J. Gairdner et al. (1862–1932).

The Oxford Dictionary of National Biography (2004).

Rymer, T., *Foedera, Conventiones etc.* (1704–1735).

Statutes of the Realm, ed. A. Luders et al. (1810–1828).

CONTEMPORARY PRINTED WORKS, AND MODERN EDITIONS

An Epitaph upon the Death of Queene Marie (1558).

A Special Grace appointed to have been said after a banket at York (1558).

Bradford, J., *The Copye of a letter sent to [the Earls of Arundel, Derby, Shrewsbury and Pembroke]* (1556).

ET, *The Lawes Resolution of Womens Rights, or the Lawes Provision for Women* (1632).

Forrest, William, *A Newe Ballade of the Marigolde* (1554).

Foxe, John, *The Acts and Monuments of the English Martyrs* (1583).

Goodman, Christopher, *How Superior Powers ought to be Obeyed* (1558).

Hall, Edward, *The union of the two noble and illustre houses of York and Lancaster* (1545), ed. H. Ellis (1809).

Huggarde, Miles, *The Displaying of the Protestants* (1556).

Ponet, John, *A Shorte Treatise of Politike Power* (1556).

Proctor, J., *The Historie of Wiatt's Rebellion* (1554) in Pollard, *Tudor Tracts*.

Surtz, E, and Virginia Murphy ed., *The Divorce Tracts of Henry VIII* (1988).
The Manner of the Triumph at Calais and Boulogne (1532) in A. F. Pollard, *Tudor Tracts* (1903).
Udall, Nicholas, *The Paraphrases of Erasmus* (1548).

EDITIONS OF DOCUMENTS
Adams, S., and M-J. Rodriguez Salgado, 'The Count of Feria's despatch ... of 14th November 1558', *Camden Miscellany*, 28, 1984.
Clifford, Henry, *The Life of Jane Dormer, Duchess of Feria*, ed. J. Stevenson (1887).
Diaz-Plaja, Fernando, *La Historia de Espana en sus Documentos* (1958).
Donaldson, P. S., *A Machiavellian Treatise by Stephen Gardiner* (1975).
Feuillerat, A., *Documents Relating to the Office of the Revels in the Reigns of Edward VI and Mary* (1914).
Hartley, T. E., *Proceedings in the Parliament of Elizabeth I, 1558–1581* (1981).
Historical Manuscripts Commission, Molyneux Papers at Loseley.
Jordan, W. K., *The Chronicle and Political Papers of King Edward VI* (1966).
MacCulloch, D., 'The Vita Mariae Angliae Reginae of Robert Wingfield of Brantham', *Camden Miscellany*, 28, 1984.
Madden, F. E., *The Privy Purse Expenses of the Princess Mary* (1831).
Muller, J. A., *The Letters of Stephen Gardiner* (1933).
Nicolas, N. H., *The Privy Purse Expenses of Henry VIII* (1827).
Nichols, J. G., *The Literary Remains of King Edward VI* (Roxburgh Club, 1857).
Nichols, J. G., *The Chronicle of Queen Jane* (Camden Society, 48, 1850).
Nichols, J. G., *The Diary of Henry Machyn* (Camden Society, 42, 1848).
Strype, J., *Ecclesiastical Memorials* (1721).
Strype, J., *Annals of the Reformation* (1725).
The State Papers of King Henry VIII (11 volumes, 1830–1852).
Tres Cartas de lo succedido en la viaje de su Alteza in Inglaterra (1877).
Vertot, R. A. de, *Les Ambassades de Mss. De Noailles* (1743).
Wilkins, D., *Concilia Magnae Brittaniae et Hiberniae* (1737).

PUBLISHED SECONDARY WORK
Anglo, S., *Spectacle, Pageantry and Early Tudor Policy* (1969).

Archer, Ian, et al., *Religion, Politics and Society in Sixteenth Century England* (Camden Society, 5th Series, 22, 2003).

Bernard, G. W., *War, Taxation and rebellion in Early Tudor England* (1986).

Bernard, G. W., 'The downfall of Sir Thomas Seymour', in Bernard, ed., *The Tudor Nobility* (1992).

Bernard, G. W., *The King's Reformation* (2005).

Boynton, L. O., *The Elizabethan Militia, 1558–1638* (1967).

Braddock, R. C., 'The Rewards of Office Holding in Tudor England', *Journal of British Studies*, 14, 1975.

Brigden, Susan, *New World, Lost Worlds* (2000).

Burnet, Gilbert, *The History of the Reformation of the Church of England* (1679).

Bush, M. L., *The Government Policy of Protector Somerset* (1975).

Chastel, A. (trs. Beth Archer), *The Sack of Rome, 1527* (1983).

Collier, J., *An Ecclesiastical History of Great Britain* (1714).

Dowling, Maria, *Humanism in the Reign of Henry VIII* (1987).

Duffy, E., *The Stripping of the Altars* (1992).

Duffy, E., and David Loades, *The Church of Mary Tudor* (2006).

Duffy, E., *The Fires of Faith* (2009).

Edwards, J., and R. Truman, *Reforming Catholicism in the England of Mary Tudor; the Achievement of Fray Bartolome Carranza* (2005).

Elton, G. R., *Policy and Police* (1972).

Fenlon, D., *Heresy and Obedience in Tridentine Italy* (1972).

Fisher, F. J., 'Influenza and Inflation in Tudor England', *Economic History Review*, 18, 1965.

Frede, Carlo de, *La Restaurazione Cattolica in Inghilterra sotto Maria Tudor* (1971).

Gasten, Andrea C., 'The Kingship of Philip and Mary', in Wim de Groot (ed.) *The Seventh Window* (2005).

Glasgow, T., 'The navy in the French Wars of Mary and Elizabeth 1557–1559', *Mariners Mirror*, 53, 1967, 54, 1968.

Gunn, S. J., *Early Tudor Government., 1485–1558* (1995).

Gwynn, Peter, *The King's Cardinal; the Rise and Fall of Thomas Wolsey* (1990).

Harbison, E. H., *Rival Ambassadors at the Court of Queen Mary* (1940).

Haugaard, W. P., 'Elizabeth Tudor's Book of Devotions; a neglected clue to the Queen's life and character', *Sixteenth Century Journal*, 12, 1981.

Hillgarth, J. H., *The Spanish Kingdoms, 1250–1516* (2 vols., 1978).

Hoak, D. E., *The King's Council in the Reign of Edward VI* (1976).

Hoak, D. E., 'Two Revolutions in Tudor Government; the formation and organisation of Mary I's Privy Council', in C. Coleman and D. Starkey, *Revolution Reassessed* (1987).

Hoak, D. E., 'The Coronations of Edward VI, Mary I and Elizabeth I, and the transformation of Tudor Monarchy', in Knighton, C. S., and Richard Mortimer, *Westminster Abbey Reformed* (2003).

Hoyle, R. W., *The Pilgrimage of Grace and the Politics of the 1530s* (2001).

Ives, E. W., 'Henry VIII's will: a forensic conundrum', *Historical Journal*. 35, 1992.

Ives, E. W., *The Life and Death of Anne Boleyn* (2004).

Ives, E. W., *Lady Jane Grey; a Tudor Mystery* (2009).

Jordan, W. K., *Edward VI: the Young King* (1968).

Jordan, W. K., *Edward VI: the Threshold of Power* (1970).

Knowles, M. C., *The Religious Orders in England*, III; *the Tudor Age* (1959).

Loach, Jennifer, *Parliament and the Crown in the Reign of Mary Tudor* (1986).

Loach, Jennifer, *Edward VI* (1999).

Loades, David, *Two Tudor Conspiracies* (1965).

Loades, David, *The Tudor Court* (1986).

Loades, David, *Mary Tudor, A Life* (1989).

Loades, David, *The Reign of Mary Tudor* (1991).

Loades, David, *John Dudley, Duke of Northumberland* (1996).

Loades, David, *Intrigue and Treason; the Tudor Court 1547–1558* (2004).

Loades, David, *Elizabeth I* (2003).

Loades, David, *The Six Wives of Henry VIII* (2010).

Loades, David, *The Religious Culture of Marian England* (2010).

MacCaffrey, W., *The Shaping of the Elizabethan Regime, 1558–1572* (1968).

MacCulloch, D., *Thomas Cranmer* (1996).

Marcus, L. S., J. Mueller, and M. B. Rose, *Elizabeth I: Collected Works* (2000).

Mattingly, Garrett, *Catherine of Aragon* (1942).

Mayer, T. F., *Reginald Pole, Prince and Prophet* (2000).

Murphy, Beverley, *The Bastard Prince; Henry VIII's Lost Son* (2001).

Pierce, Hazel, *Margaret Pole, Countess of Salisbury* (2003).

Potter, David, 'The Duc de Guise and the Fall of Calais', *English Historical Review*, 98, 1983.

Redworth, G., *In Defence of the Church Catholic; a Life of Stephen Gardiner* (1990).

Redworth, G., '"Matter Impertinent to Women"; male and female monarchy under Philip and Mary', *English Historical Review*, 112, 1997.

Richards, Judith M., 'Mary Tudor as "Sole Quene"; Gendering Tudor Monarchy', *Historical Journal*, 40, 1997.

Richards, Judith M., *Mary Tudor* (2008).

Robinson, W. R. B., 'Princess Mary's Itinerary in the Marches of Wales, 1525–1527; a provisional record', *Historical Research*. 71, 1998.

Rodriguez-Salgado, M-J., *The Changing Face of Empire; Charles V. Philip II and Habsburg Authority, 1551–1559* (1988).

Russell, Elizabeth, 'Mary Tudor and Mr. Jorkins', *Historical Research*, 63, 1990.

Scarisbrick. J. J., 'The Pardon of the Clergy, 1531', *Cambridge Historical Journal*, 12, 1956.

Scarisbrick, J. J., *Henry VIII* (1968).

Shagan, Ethan, 'Protector Somerset and the 1549 Rebellions; New Sources and New Perspectives' *English Historical Review*, 114, 1999.

Shagan, Ethan, *Popular Politics and the English Reformation* (2003).

Slavin, A. J., 'The Fall of lord Chancellor Wriothesley; a study on the politics of conspiracy', *Albion*, 7, 1975.

Southworth, J., *Fools and Jesters at the English Court* (1998).

Thorp, M. R., 'Religion and the Rebellion of Sir Thomas Wyatt', *Church History*, 47, 1978.

Tittler, R., and S. L. Battey, 'The Local Community and the Crown in 1553; the Accession of Mary Tudor Revisited', *Bulletin of the Institute of Historical Research*, 36, 1984.

Warnicke, Retha, *The Rise and Fall of Anne Boleyn* (1989).

Warnicke, Retha, *The Marrying of Anne of Cleves* (2000).

Weikle, A., 'The Marian Council Revisited', in J. Loach and R. Tittler, eds., *The Mid-Tudor Polity, 1540–1560* (1980).

Wizeman, W., *The Spirituality of Mary Tudor's Church* (2006).

UNPUBLISHED THESES

Boscher, P. S., 'Politics, Administration and Diplomacy: the Anglo-Scottish Borders 1550-1560' (Durham Ph.D., 1985).

Morgan, P., 'The Government of Calais, 1485–1558' (Oxford D.Phil., 1967).

Rowley Williams, J., 'Image and Reality: the Lives of Aristocratic Women in Early Tudor England' (Wales Ph.D., 1998).

LIST OF ILLUSTRATIONS

1. Mary from a group portrait of Henry VIII and his family, painted in about 1545. The female figure in the background is supposed to be her jester, Jane the Fool. © Jonathan Reeve JR997b66fp40 15001550.
2. Princess Elizabeth from the same family group. The figure in the background is supposed to be Henry's jester, Will Somers. © Jonathan Reeve JR997b66fp40b 15001530.
3. Princess Elizabeth at about the time of her father's death, aged twelve. By an unknown artist, in the Royal Collection. © Jonathan Reeve JR998b66fp56 15001600.
4. Edward VI from the same family group as illustrations 1 and 2. © Jonathan Reeve JR997b66fp40 15001550.
5. Holbein's design for a jewelled pendant for Mary, probably executed during his first visit to England in 1527–8, when Mary was still the king's heir. © Elizabeth Norton & The Amberley Archive.
6. Margaret Tudor, Mary's aunt. She married James IV of Scotland, and after his death at Flodden in 1513, remarried Archibald, Earl of Angus. She was the grandmother of Mary, Queen of Scots. From a drawing by an unknown artist. © Jonathan Reeve JR982b20p837 15001600.
7. Lady Jane Dudley (Grey). Put up by Edward as an alternative to Mary for the succession, she was defeated in July 1553, and executed after the Wyatt rising in February 1554, at the age of seventeen. © Jonathan Reeve JR1002b66fp107 15001600.
8. Edward's 'Device' for the succession, naming Jane Grey as his heir. The document is in the king's hand throughout, except for the amendments, which make all the difference to its meaning. © Jonathan Reeve JRCD2b20p987 15001550.
9. A page from Edward VI's journal, for 18 March 1551, in which he refers to Mary and his dispute with her over the mass. © Jonathan Reeve JR2288b7p233 15501600.
10. A later pastiche of Henry VIII and Mary, based on portraits by Holbein and Hans Eworth. The figure in the background is again Will Somers. © Jonathan Reeve JR1019b66fp8 15001600.
11. Thomas Cranmer, Archbishop of Canterbury, in 1546. A painting by Gerhard Flicke in the National Portrait Gallery. © Elizabeth Norton & The Amberley Archive.
12. Mary at the age of twenty-eight (in 1543), by the sergeant painter known as 'Master John'. In the National Portrait Gallery. © Elizabeth Norton & The Amberley Archive.
13. Thomas Wolsey, Cardinal Archbishop of York and lord chancellor. A drawing by Jacques le Boucq in the Bibilotheque d'Arras. © Jonathan Reeve JR1169b2p7 15001550.
14. Stephen Gardiner, Bishop of Winchester and Mary's lord chancellor, by an unknown artist. © Jonathan Reeve JR1001b66fp100.
15. John Fisher, Bishop of Rochester, by Hans Holbein. A fierce defender of Catherine's marriage and of Mary's legitimacy, he was executed by the king for treason in 1535. © Jonathan Reeve JR2299b4p681 15001600.
16. A cartoon of Thomas More and his family, executed in 1527–8. A painting based on this cartoon, was made by Rowland Lockey in 1593, and is now in the National Portrait Gallery. © Jonathan Reeve JR2295b2p137 15001600.
17. An allegorical representation of the betrothal of Mary to the Duke of Orléans, the second son of Francis I of France in 1527. © Jonathan Reeve JR2298b4p645T 15001600.
18. Third Succession Act (35 Henry VIII, *c*. 1), 1544. This was the act which designated Mary and Elizabeth to follow Edward if he should die without heirs, and broke new ground in that it authorised the succession of illegitimate children. © Jonathan Reeve JR1185b20p920 15001550.
19. A nineteenth-century representation of Mary entering London on 3 August 1553, having successfully overcome the challenge of Jane Grey. The kneeling figures are Thomas Howard, Duke of Norfolk and Stephen Gardiner, Bishop of Winchester. The third figure, concealed by Norfolk, is Edward Courtenay, the son of the Marquis of Exeter, who was released on the same day. © Jonathan Reeve JR2292b61p731 15501600.
20. A plan of Charing Cross from the 'Ralph Agas' map. After a brief skirmish at the Cross on 7 February 1554, Wyatt led his force down the Strand and Fleet Street, only to find the gate of the City held against him. © Jonathan Reeve JRCD3 893.
21. Mary's instructions to John Russell, Earl of Bedford, sent to Spain in June 1555 to escort Prince Philip to England for his wedding. He is to brief Philip about the affairs of the kingdom. © Jonathan Reeve JRCD3 998.
22. Philip II as King of Spain, from a contemporary miniature. © Jonathan Reeve JR188b4p823 15501600.
23. The reverse of the Great Seal of Philip and Mary, used for the authentication of important documents in both their names. © Jonathan Reeve JR2300b4p721 15501600.
24. An equestrian portrait of Philip II. © Jonathan Reeve JR1051b66fp72 15001600.
25. Obverse side of the Great Seal.© Jonathan Reeve JR2301b20p996 15501600.
26. Passport for Richard Shelley to go into Spain, signed by both Philip and Mary. Shelley's mission was to have been to announce the safe arrival of Queen Mary's son, so the passport remained unused. © Jonathan Reeve JRCD3b20p999.
27. The charter of Philip and Mary confirming the foundation of Trinity College, Oxford, by Sir Thomas Pope, dated 28 March 1555. The ornate capital shows both sovereigns enthroned. © Jonathan Reeve JR2302b20p1001 15501600.
28. The title page of John Foxe's *Ecclesiastical History*, better known as the *Acts and Monuments of the English Martyrs*. This was a revised and expanded version of the work originally published by John Day in 1563. © Jonathan Reeve JR985b20p1003 15001600.

List of Illustrations

29. The burning of Thomas Tompkyns, from the 1570 edition of the *Acts and Monuments*. The same woodcut was used for a number of victims. © Amberley Archive.

30. The burning of John Hooper at Gloucester on 9 February 1555. Hooper, who was former Bishop of Gloucester, was burned on a slow fire. He was one of the first victims to suffer. © Jonathan Reeve JRCD2b20p1004.

31. 'The cruel burning of George Marsh'. Marsh was supposed to have been soaked in tar to make him burn more fiercely. From the 1570 *A & M.* © Amberley Archive.

32. The burning of Ridley and Latimer at Oxford on 16 October 1555. The sermon was preached by Richard Smith, who had been driven from his Regius Chair in Edward's time for his Catholic beliefs. © Jonathan Reeve JRCD2b20p1005.

33. The burning of John Rogers on 4 February 1555. Rogers was the first Protestant to be burned, and the example of his courage inspired many to follow him. From the 1570 edition of the *A & M.* © Amberley Archive.

34. The burning of Margery Polley. A number of Foxe's martyrs were women, and he emphasises how the Holy Spirit helped them to overcome their natural 'imbecility'. © Amberley Archive.

35. The burning of Rowland Taylor. Taylor was taken down to Hadley to suffer where he had ministered, with the intention of making an example of him. The evidence suggests that this did not work. © Amberley Archive.

36. The burning of Margaret Thurston and Agnes Bongeor at Colchester. Essex was a strong centre of Protestantism in Mary's reign, and a number of men and women deliberately provoked the authorities to act against them. © Amberley Archive.

37. The racking of Cuthbert Simpson. The use of torture on the victims was unusual, but Simpson was the deacon of the London congregation, and he was racked (unsuccessfully) to make him reveal their names. © Amberley Archive.

38. 'Strait handling' was more common, as this reconstruction of the ordeal of prisoners in the Lollards' Tower at Lambeth makes plain. © Amberley Archive.

39. An account of the disputation held at Oxford in April 1554. This extract is from the exchanges between Hugh Latimer and Richard Smith, with Dr Weston as Prolocutor. It was from this manuscript that Foxe printed his version. © Jonathan Reeve JR2289b7p277 15501600.

40. A lively depiction of the burning of Thomas Haukes in June 1555. Haukes was one of the few gentlemen to suffer during the persecution. Most protestants of that status fled abroad. © Amberley Archive.

41. One of the most appalling atrocities of the persecution was the burning of a pregnant Margaret Cauches on Guernsey. The hapless woman gave birth in the flames, and her infant perished as well. An enquiry was launched under Elizabeth, from which most of our knowledge of the incident is derived. © Amberley Archive.

42. The burning of Thomas Tompkyns' hand by Bishop Bonner. This example of Bonner's alleged cruelty was a part of Foxe's campaign against the Bishop. Whether the incident actually occurred is uncertain. © Jonathan Reeve JR239b7p321 15501600.

43. Richmond Palace. © Jonathan Reeve JR2297b2p233T 15001600.

44. Calais and its harbour, from a sixteenth-century drawing. It was the loss of Rysbank (the tower in the middle of the picture) which sealed the fate of Calais during its capture by the French in January 1558. © Jonathan Reeve JR1186b20p1009 15001550.

45. Hampton Court, acquired by Henry in 1525, and subsequently much rebuilt. Edward VI was born there in September 1537. © Jonathan Reeve JR2296b2p232 15001600.

46. Henry VII, Mary's grandfather, from the cartoon by Holbein in the National Portrait Gallery. © Elizabeth Norton & The Amberley Archive.

47. Henry VIII. A statue in the great gate at Trinity College, Cambridge (a royal foundation), showing a mature Henry. About 1541. © Elizabeth Norton & The Amberley Archive.

48. Catherine of Aragon, Mary's mother, showing her as a mature woman, about 1520. By an unknown artist. © Ripon Cathedral.

49. Anne Boleyn, Henry's second wife and Mary's *bête noire*. She was reckoned to be 'no great beauty'. By an unknown artist. © Ripon Cathedral.

50. Jane Seymour, Henry's third wife and the mother of his son, Edward. Painted in 1537 by an unknown artist. © Ripon Cathedral.

51. Funeral effigy of Elizabeth Blount, Lady Tailboys, Henry's mistress and the mother of his son Henry Fitzroy. © Elizabeth Norton & The Amberley Archive.

52. A lady, supposed to be Mary at the age of about seventeen. By Hans Holbein, in the Royal Collection. © Elizabeth Norton & The Amberley Archive.

53. Henry VIII's will, dated 30 December 1546. It was signed with stamp rather than the sign manual, which was to cause problems in the future. © Jonathan Reeve JRCD2b20p961 15501600.

54. Lady Anne Shelton, Anne Boleyn's aunt, and the governess of the household for the two princesses in 1533-4. From a stained glass window in Shelton church. © Elizabeth Norton & The Amberley Archive.

55. Mary Stuart, Queen of Scots. Mary came to the throne of Scotland at just over a week old, in December 1542. Her claim to the English succession was ignored in Henry VIII's final Succession Act of 1544. © Jonathan Reeve JR996b66fp68 15001600.

56. Edward VI as a child, playing with a pet monkey. A painting by Holbein in the Kunstmuseum at Basle. © Elizabeth Norton & The Amberley Archive.

57. Wolsey dismissed by Henry VIII. An imaginative Victorian reconstruction. © Jonathan Reeve JR1092b20fp896 15001550.

58. A view of Greenwich Palace, from a drawing by Anthony van Wyngaerde, (c.1550) in the Ashmolean Museum at Oxford. © Jonathan Reeve JR944b46fp180 14501500.

59. A page from a book of hours (prayer book) once owned by Mary. © Jonathan Reeve JR2143b97plate6 13001350.

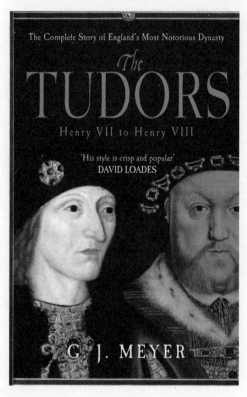

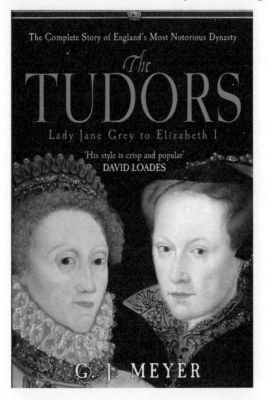

Also available from Amberley Publishing

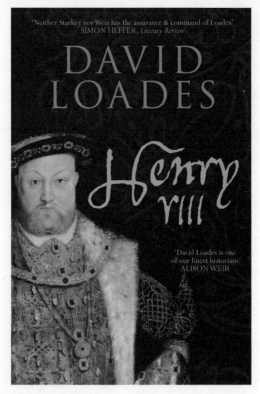

A major new biography of the most infamous king of England

'A triumph' THE SPECTATOR

'The best place to send anyone seriously wanting to get to grips with alternative understandings of England's most mesmerising monarch... copious illustrations, imaginatively chosen' BBC HISTORY MAGAZINE

'David Loades Tudor biographies are both highly enjoyable and instructive, the perfect combination' ANTONIA FRASER

Professor David Loades has spent most of his life investigating the remains, literary, archival and archaeological, of Henry VIII, and this monumental new biography book is the result. As a youth, he was a magnificent specimen of manhood, and in age a gargantuan wreck, but even in his prime he was never the 'ladies man' which legend, and his own imagination, created. Sexual insecurity undermined him, and gave his will that irascible edge which proved fatal to Anne Boleyn and Thomas Cromwell alike.

£25 Hardback
113 illustrations (49 colour)
512 pages
978-1-84868-532-1

Available from all good bookshops or to order direct
Please call **01453-847-800**
www.amberleybooks.com

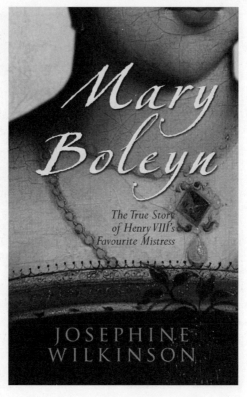

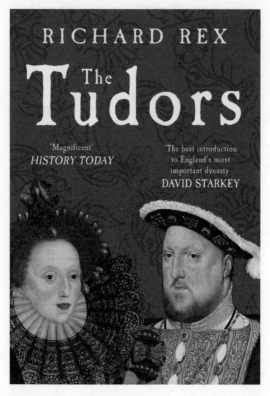

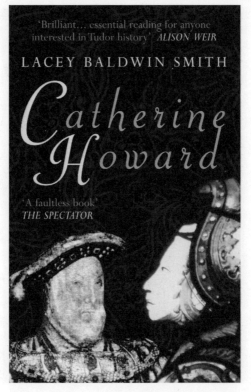

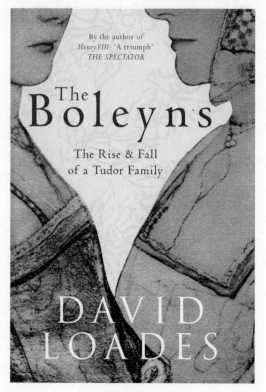

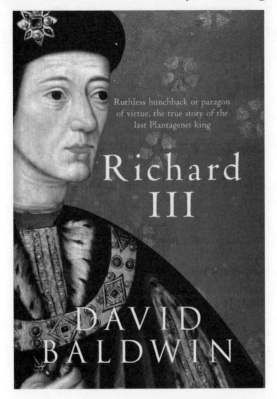

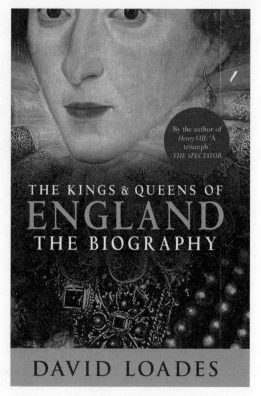

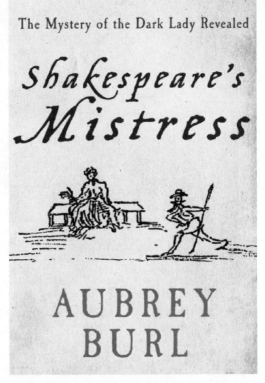

The Mystery of the Dark Lady Revealed

Shakespeare's Mistress

AUBREY BURL

The mystery woman in Shakespeare's love life revealed

She was musical, alluring, married and faithless. Shakespeare never identified her. Scholars have – but for different women. She was well-born, or a slut, or a housewife, even a phantom of Shakespeare's poetical mind. She was an anchor and agony to him. His sonnets sang of her loveliness and cursed her for her infidelity.

Aubrey Burl's challenge also is to find her. But there is no deception. The 'Dark Lady' can be found in Shakespeare's unshuffled sonnets.

£20 Hardback
40 illustrations (8 colour)
288 pages
978-1-4456-0217-2

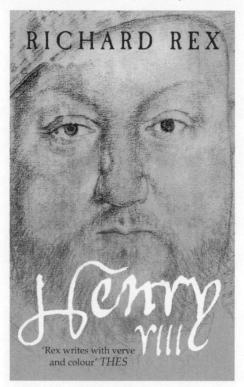

Also available from Amberley Publishing

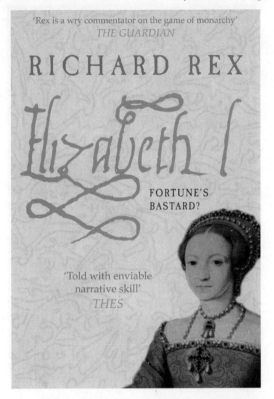

'Rex is a wry commentator on the game of monarchy'
THE GUARDIAN

RICHARD REX

Elizabeth I

FORTUNE'S
BASTARD?

'Told with enviable
narrative skill'
THES

An accessible biography of Elizabeth I by a leading Tudor expert

Richard Rex highlights the vivid and contrary personality of a Queen who could both baffle and bedazzle her subjects, her courtiers, and her rivals: at one moment flirting outrageously with a favourite or courting some foreign prince, and at another vowing perpetual virginity; at one time agonising over the execution of her cousin, Mary Queen of Scots, then ordering the slaughter of hundreds of poor men after a half-cock rebellion. Too many biographies of Elizabeth merely perpetuate the flattery she enjoyed from her courtiers, this biography also reflects more critical voices, such as those of the Irish, the Catholics and those who lived on the wrong side of the emerging North/South divide. To them she showed a different face.

£9.99 Paperback
75 illustrations
192 pages
978-1-84868-423-2

Available from all good bookshops or to order direct
Please call **01453-847-800**
www.amberleybooks.com

Also available from Amberley Publishing

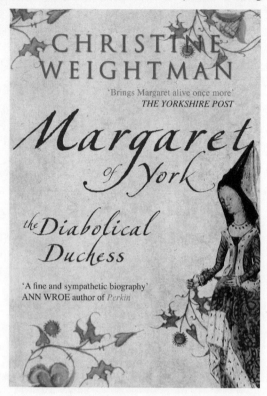

Also available from Amberley Publishing

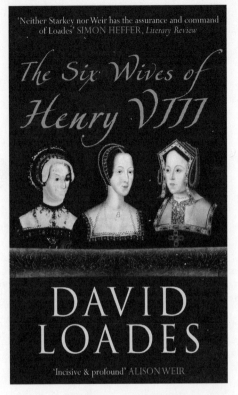

The marital ups and downs of England's most infamous king

'Neither Starkey nor Weir has the assurance and command of Loades'
SIMON HEFFER, LITERARY REVIEW

'Incisive and profound... I warmly recommend this book' ALISON WEIR

The story of Henry VIII and his six wives has passed from history into legend – taught in the cradle as a cautionary tale and remembered in adulthood as an object lesson in the dangers of marrying into royalty. The true story behind the legend, however, remains obscure to most people, whoe knowledge of the affair begins and ends with the aide memoire 'Divorced, executed, died, divorce, executed, survived'.

£9.99 Paperback
55 illustrations (31 colour)
224 pages
978-1-4456-004-9

Available from all good bookshops or to order direct
Please call **01453-847-800**
www.amberleybooks.com

INDEX

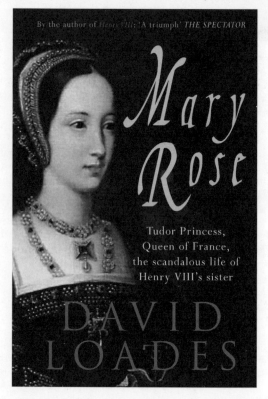